The Conflict and Communication Activity Book

The Conflict and Communication Activity Book

30 High-Impact Training Exercises for Adult Learners

Bill Withers & **Keami D. Lewis**

AMACOM AMERICAN MANAGEMENT ASSOCIATION
New York I Atlanta I Brussels I Buenos Aires I Chicago I London I Mexico City
San Francisco I Shanghai I Tokyo I Toronto I Washington, D.C.

Special discounts on bulk quantities of AMACOM books are available to corporations, professional associations, and other organizations. For details, contact Special Sales Department, AMACOM, a division of American Management Association, 1601 Broadway, New York, NY 10019.
Tel.: 212-903-8316. Fax: 212-903-8083.
Web site: www. amacombooks.org

This publication is designed to provide accurate and authoritative information in regard to the subject matter covered. It is sold with the understanding that the publisher is not engaged in rendering legal, accounting, or other professional service. If legal advice or other expert assistance is required, the services of a competent professional person should be sought.

PERMISSION: *Culture-Centered Counseling and Interviewing Skills: A Practical Guide* by Paul B. Pedersen and Allen Ivey. Copyright © 1993 by Paul B. Pedersen and Allen Ivey. Reproduced with permission of Greenwood Publishing Group, Inc., Westport, CT.

Library of Congress Cataloging-in-Publication Data

Withers, Bill.
The conflict and communication activity book : 30 high-impact training
exercises for adult learners / Bill Withers and Keami Lewis.
  p. cm.
Includes index.
ISBN 0-8144-7167-6
    1. Conflict management—Problems, exercises, etc.   2. Communication in
    organizations—Problems, exercises, etc.   3. Interpersonal
    communication—Problems, exercises, etc.   4. Conflict management—Study
    and teaching—Activity programs.   5. Communication in
    organizations—Study and teaching—Activity programs.   6. Interpersonal
    communication—Study and teaching—Activity programs.   I. Lewis, Keami.
    II. Title.
HD42.W578 2003
658.4'053—dc21   2003000648

Printing number
10 9 8 7 6 5 4 3 2 1

Dedication

We gratefully dedicate this book to our families.

Keami would like to thank her husband, Ralph Lewis II and her children, Ralph III and Bianca Rae, for their love and kind support while writing this book, and her mother, Dorothy Pitts Jones, and her parents-in-law, Joyce Lewis and Ralph Lewis Sr., for the many lifelong lessons they have shared.

Bill is grateful for the love, support, and patient interest of his family—Julia Hawrylo and Michael Withers and his parents, Charles and Jeanne Withers.

Contents

TEACHING ABOUT CONFLICT AND COMMUNICATION WITH GAMES AND EXERCISES

CONFLICT AND COMMUNICATION EXERCISES

MY WORKSHOP STARTS IN FIVE MINUTES

Preface

This book will help you to zero in on conflict and communication issues in your company, school, organization, or community. Teachers, trainers, facilitators, and students can follow the step-by-step directions in this book to guide adult learners through these creative, highly interactive activities.

We asked trainers around the country, "What would make a book of communication and conflict exercises more helpful to you?"

The responses included requests to:

- ➤ Provide easily understood theoretical or background information on the topic, not just exercises.
- ➤ Categorize the exercises based on how much prep time may be needed.
- ➤ Make it easy to look up exercises by learning objective.
- ➤ Include options to adapt the exercises to different sized groups, where possible.
- ➤ Incorporate detailed instructions for each exercise—everything from setup to debrief.
- ➤ Note the usual responses participants have to the exercises or discussion questions, including any potential surprises and how to handle them.
- ➤ Dig deeply by focusing on one topic area—such as the learning environment.

Conflict and Communication covers all of these bases. It features the top thirty proven activities selected from the authors' "tried-and-true" lists collected from trainers and teachers working in Europe, Asia, and the Americas.

Use this book for everything from quick exercises you can do "on the run" to a step-by-step guide to daylong workshops that highlight key communication and conflict areas. You can easily copy any of the handouts, overheads, and flipcharts by turning to the Toolbox section in the back of the book.

Acknowledgments

People who write books of training exercises must acknowledge the trainers they have never met. Training exercises are a part of our oral tradition—trainers make up an exercise, show it to someone else, other people adapt it, and the exercise takes on a life of its own. Whenever someone has directly given us an exercise or idea for this book, we have made sure to give proper credit.

The generous teachers, trainers, and consultants who sent us exercises and spent time with us getting things just right—Jenny Beer, Cass Bing, Linda Booth-Sweeney, Sarita Chawla, Zachary Green, Kathy Hale, Frank Hoffmann, Angelo Lewis, John McGlaughlin, Dennis Meadows, Paul Pedersen, Jay Rothman, and Chris Thorsen—made the most immediate contribution. There is more information about these wonderful people and their work alongside their exercises and in the Toolbox section.

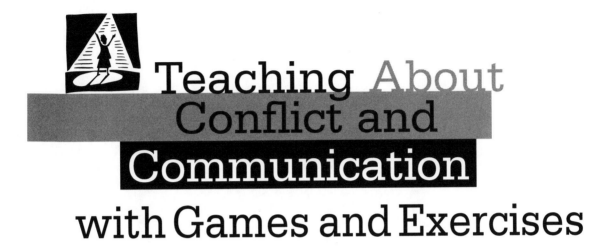

Teaching About Conflict and Communication

with Games and Exercises

Why Playing Games
in the Classroom
Is Serious Business

Think of the best seminar that you have ever attended. What made it so good? Was it fun, interesting, and interactive? Did you remember most of the things presented? What did the instructor do that made you enjoy the experience? How did you participate or not participate? What did you see, hear, or feel? To whom did you talk or not talk? How long or short was the session?

Now think of the worst seminar you have ever attended. Was it easier for you to think of a "worst seminar" example than it was to think of a "best seminar" example? Why? What happened at that seminar? Who or what made the session bad? How would you have changed it? What did you decide that you would never, ever, ever do when facilitating a seminar because of this class? How did the instructor, location, format, or content shape your feelings about this class?

Many things contribute to how participants react to a workshop and the material presented. Sometimes the reaction can begin even before the seminar does. For example, if the boss sends a participant to the training, he or she can feel resentful. This person may ignore or criticize the workshop or the instructor, be unreceptive, or even disruptive. On the other hand, a participant who is excited about attending training, and who is thinking of how he or she will apply what is learned, can really add to the class experience for both themselves and others.

SUCCESS FACTORS

Success factors for workshop design fall into five categories: 1) Preparation, 2) Content, 3) Presentation, 4) Applicability, and 5) Follow-through. Simply stated, these categories include the following:

1. Preparation How prepared is the instructor to teach the material? Is he or she familiar with the topic and able to present relevant examples and answer questions? Are the materials of good quality? Will the room setup help people to learn and share ideas?

How prepared are the participants? Are there other things they feel they need to be doing instead? Do they feel a need to learn the things being presented? Did they do the pre-work assignment?

2. Content The actual knowledge, skills, experience, or information the course aspires to teach. Considerations for the facilitator:

> ➤ Which information or topics to include and how much
> ➤ How long to cover a particular topic or segment during the session

These decisions should be based on the skill and knowledge level of the participants. If during the class the content seems too simple or too difficult, the instructor may need to change the content on the spot. Preparing by having a depth of knowledge about the topic allows the facilitator to make changes as the workshop unfolds.

3. Presentation How the information is presented. This area includes course format, a/v devices used, handouts, prework, activities, lecture, discussion, etc. It also includes the instructor's personal style, language, appearance, vocal quality, personality, etc., and the instructor's ability to alter exercises and/or course content in real time, if an activity or topic is not working as planned.

4. Applicability How applicable the material presented is to the real-life world in which participants operate. In other words, when participants leave, what will they change about how they are doing something because of what they learned in the course? Do they see the connection? Do they want to apply what was learned? Will what was presented realistically help them in their daily functions and activities? Do they want to try it out and see?

5. Follow-through This includes measuring course goals and promises against what actually happened, participant action planning, and checking back after the course is over to see how effectively lessons were retained, applied, and results realized.

More than likely, the reasons you liked or disliked the courses you thought about in the beginning of this chapter could fall into one of the five categories listed. The instructor has a lot of control over the course and the success factors.

Creating a Successful Learning Environment

This brief essay will show you how to create a successful learning environment using Accelerated Learning Techniques. You will get a good overview of some thinking on this topic, along with actual accelerated learning tactics to increase the effectiveness of all five of the success factors.

The first part of the chapter defines Accelerated Learning, including Right/Left Brain Thinking and Learning Style Theories. It then moves into how to apply these theories to an actual workshop or other learning environment. You will get tried-and-true examples and techniques for accelerating your workshop. These will include how and when to reenergize your class, how and why to use a/v, and some tips for creating flipcharts, overheads, and handouts.

ACCELERATED LEARNING TECHNIQUES

Accelerated Learning Techniques (ALT) reduce training time because the time spent is more effective for learners. When you apply ALT, participants learn more, quicker. New information is more readily recognized, retained, and recalled, and everyone has more fun doing it.

Here is our working definition for accelerated learning:

> Accelerated Learning stimulates the learner's senses, while targeting his/her preferred learning style during the lesson. This result is a more highly effective learning event. The learner is drawn into the learning process as an active, interested partner by using music, pictures, colors, hands-on activities, role plays, outdoor experiences, group discussions, lectures, and other methods that fulfill individual learning needs.

Learners are more likely to apply what was taught when using ALT because each participant learns more quickly and easily and is able to remember the information when he/she returns to work.

Creating an Accelerated Learning Environment

To really learn, people need a stimulating environment free from fear. Think back to preschool and kindergarten. Remember all the fun and colors and friends and finger paint? All the nurturing, exploring, naps, cookies, and juice? All the 'at-a-boy, 'at-a-girl, daydreams, green elephants, and imaginary friends? This is what people need in order to learn: fun, freedom, excitement, and caring feedback.

Continue thinking about those first years of learning. Children are involved at that age, because the teacher has little or no choice. Using play to learn is one of the most effective methods of learning. Besides, what is not actively taught will be found out through trial, error, and exploration. Accelerated Learning is like that. It places the responsibility for learning on the learner, and encourages him or her to participate in it by creating opportunities to try it, do it, see it, read it, hear it, etc. Workshops that use Accelerated Learning Techniques are filled with activities, hands-on practice, discussions, dialogue, and other interactive processes that help learning happen.

Learning is much more effective when the learner feels that everyone in the class is in it together. Participants exchange ideas while they discover the key points of the class. Accelerated Learning encourages sharing and collaboration rather than rewarding competition.

When you include many different approaches during the session, you stimulate the different senses for the learner, thereby increasing the success of the learning event. What you get is a learner-centered experience that is driven by results.

The age-old "WIIFM" concept also needs to be played out in the classroom. Learners participate in your class continuously thinking, "What's in it for me?" and "How can I apply this?" Tie your information to real-life situations that the learner is experiencing. Of course, this also implies that the learning does not just take place in the classroom. It needs to extend to the workplace before and after the session for true success to occur.

LEARNING THEORIES

ALT incorporates several common theories about learning. The most significant are Left Brain/Right Brain Thinking, The Triune Brain Theory, and Multiple Intelligences/Learning Style Theories. It is important to understand each of these concepts when including ALT in your program design and delivery.

Left Brain/Right Brain Thinking

Although new research has shown us that the brain is more complicated than the simple "left brain/right brain" model, it is still a useful metaphor to use when thinking about learning. The idea is that the brain has two distinct functioning halves. The left side focuses on language, reading and writing, mathematics, and linear processes. The right side houses imagination, art, colors, movement, music appreciation, dancing, storytelling, and other creative and artistic activities. The more we stimulate both sides of the brain during the learning event, the better we are able to learn what is being presented.

So as a facilitator, including activities that help people use both their left brain and right brain increases the likelihood that learners will absorb and retain the information presented. When designing your course, create a good balance between linear, processing-type activities, and visual, creative-type activities.

Another important element to remember when teaching is that the brain triggers responses in people. For example, when participants feel threatened or unsafe, or feel they need to compete with other participants, the instructor, or their boss, they are operating from the reptilian, or oldest, most primal part of their brains. This part of the brain focuses on safety and self-preservation.

The emotional, or limbic, area of the brain causes us to have emotional responses and make connections and associations between things. Trainers can tap into this area by stimulating an emotion or using music, poetry, rhymes, etc. during the workshop.

And of course, without the neocortex, the thinking part of the brain, participants would be unable to process what is said, read, or otherwise presented. Targeting each section of the brain during a session helps make the learning stick.

LEARNING-STYLES SURVEYS AND TOOLS

There are several popular learning-styles surveys that you may wish to use during the training session in order to help participants recognize and understand their individual learning style. Sometimes, doing a learning-styles inventory before presenting course materials helps people better understand why the material is being presented the way it is. It also involves the learner in the learning process, because he or she will know exactly which sections were included just for their style!

The main thing to remember about learning styles is that people learn by doing, seeing, hearing, or feeling. If you include activities that engage each of these actions, you will appeal to everyone in the class at some point during the training. For example, lectures, discussions, and audiotapes appeal to those who learn by hearing. Role-plays, practice exercises, and group activities appeal to those that learn by doing. Visual aids—flipcharts, videotapes, etc.—appeal to those who interact visually with material. People who learn by feeling can be engaged through storytelling, by relating the lessons to their own experience, and by being actively involved in the success of the workshop. Your workshop should also provide some "downtime," allowing people a chance to think about what is being learned so that they can incorporate it through quiet reflection.

When ALT are used correctly, each learner, as well as the facilitator, has fun and feels a sense of purpose and accomplishment. To summarize the many theories and principles introduced in this section:

Accelerated Learning takes into account every person's need to feel safe and secure while learning. It includes many types of activities and methods to stimulate major senses and learning styles, and creates an atmosphere of camaraderie, feedback, and fun among learners and the facilitator.

ACCELERATED LEARNING TIPS & TACTICS:
HOW TO APPLY THE THEORY

Flexibility

Always prepare, or have in mind, several ways to present ideas during a seminar. For example, be prepared to conduct a role-play using all participants in the class, as well as being able to conduct it with two people in the front of the room with everyone else watching.

Another example would be the ability to increase or decrease the pace of the class or level of material presented if you find that your participants need to go faster or slower.

Always be willing to change your course design and level of content to fit the learning needs of your participants.

Create a Safe Learning Environment

This can be accomplished in several ways. If you are able, you can begin by ensuring that participants are at the same learning or organizational level prior to conducting the class. For example, you can consider the following:

Participants:

> ➤ Title or job grade
> ➤ Job function or position
> ➤ Educational level

Class setup:

> ➤ The location of the training class
> ➤ The number of people attending
> ➤ What topics are covered

Here are tactics for use during the workshop:

> ➤ Stating that all questions are good and welcomed: "There are no 'dumb' questions"
>
> ➤ Placing a "parking lot" sheet at the back of the room where participants can express questions during break without asking them aloud
>
> ➤ Telling the class that your room is a safe place to learn; that they are all learners, all in this together today (including you as the facilitator)
>
> ➤ Creating and posting ground rules with the class that include a rule about not making disparaging remarks or making fun of anyone
>
> ➤ Personally relating to each question that is asked and rewarding participants for asking them. For example, making comments like, "I am sure there are others that wanted to know that also. Thank you for asking that question." Or, "I used to wonder the same thing; let me tell you how that works." Or, "You know, people ask that all the time when I teach this. . . ."
>
> ➤ Watch participant behavior and reaction to your exercises and activities. If the participants seem to be threatened or feel uncomfortable with the level of interaction you have chosen, then change your approach.

Comfort Level

Comfort level refers to how quickly or slowly you move the class into highly interactive activities. For the most part, we should raise the bar slowly. For example, we usually start with an icebreaker to get everyone acquainted, then move into discussions and less active exercises until people are comfortable with the topic and with one another. You wouldn't begin a seminar with role-playing because such activities usually make people nervous.

Here are a few things to remember about your participants' comfort level.

➤ Start the class with techniques that require less activity and input from participants. Open with discussions, demonstrations, videos, observing others, etc.

➤ Gradually increase the level of activity, movement, interaction, and input among participants throughout the session. The pace will vary from session to session. As a rule, "safer" activities include lecture, discussions, group activities at the table, one-on-one or paired activities, reading, and some brainstorming. Once people have shown that they are comfortable with one another, you can move to such "riskier" activities as role-plays, moving around the room, touching other people in some way, physical activities, sharing personal feelings or opinions, simulated activities, debates, competitive games, and presentations.

➤ If participants seem unwilling or very uncomfortable with high energy or interactive activities—for example, if they are very quiet; rarely or never volunteer information or answer questions you ask; look scared; don't maintain eye contact; complain about moving around or participating—you need to move to less threatening activity.

➤ One the other hand, if participants look bored, are leaning on their elbows, doodling, talking among themselves, making jokes, or otherwise being disruptive, then they need more activity.

Using Music

Good times to use music:

➤ at the beginning of class
➤ during breaks
➤ during quiet or individual activities
➤ during group activities
➤ with simulations or role-playing sometimes

Using Pictures & Artwork

Pictures can be incorporated on flipcharts, overheads, handouts, and other materials. You can also decorate your training room with motivational sayings, banners, and other artwork that help participants learn and remember. A very common tactic is to hang workshop flipcharts around the room once the point has been made. They add pictures and artwork, and you can also refer back to them during the class.

Flipcharts, Handouts & Notebooks

Because some people learn by reading, seeing, and through independent study, it is very important to provide some form of handouts or notebooks. This allows these participants their preferred learning style, reading, while you talk during the class—and also allows them to read the material later as a learning tool or for independent study.

Flipcharts and overheads also offer the opportunity for this learning style—to read or look at pictures—while you speak. Many people are visual learners and need to see more than an instructor during class.

Some Good Questions about Conflict

If conflict is so much a part of our lives, then why aren't we more comfortable with it? This is a good question to ask as we start to think about conflict training. Some other thoughts to sort through are:

> Why should we have workshops about conflict?

> Can conflict really be that good for us?

> What are some of the things that can get in the way of having a successful workshop about conflict?

> What is the best reason for people to come to a conflict workshop?

Let's take a look at these questions one at a time.

Q: Since conflict is so much a part of our lives, why aren't we more comfortable with it?

A: It hurts.

Conflicts happen when what we want is different from what we can have. The conflict will go away only if we change either what we want or what we can have. This almost never happens all the way, so conflict almost never goes all the way away.

To make matters worse, very often the thing that keeps us from getting what we want is that someone else either wants the same thing or wants something that may keep us from getting what we want. When this happens, we tend to focus on that other person instead of the conflict. So instead of working to change either what we want or what we can have, we work against the other person's getting what they want. It usually seems like a good idea at the time—if what they want is keeping us from getting what we want, then we can get what we want if we make sure they don't get what they want.

We know we are not really supposed to act that way, so we have to figure out reasons why it is okay in this particular case. Maybe the other person is evil or greedy or stupid or less deserving. Maybe there is some rule, such as "I saw it first," or "They are not being fair," or "I am stronger," or "I am weaker," that can help us to justify keeping them from what they want.

The more we work on these reasons, the more the prize becomes keeping them away from what they want. After all, if they can't get what they want, then we can get what we want.

Many times the other people are working on good reasons to support their own fight to keep us from getting what we want. By the time we are all convinced of the reasons we have created to keep the other side from getting what it wants, we are emotionally invested and it is very difficult to disengage.

Q: Why should we have workshops about conflict?

A: It does not have to hurt—at least not as much.

Of course there is another way to respond when we do not get what we want. Instead of focusing on those other people whose wants are getting in the way of our wants, we can put our minds to work on what it is about one another's wants that seem to be getting in the way. In other words, we can look at the conflict as a puzzle to solve. What if one side goes first? What if we both get only a little of what we want? What if you get what you want this time and I get what I want next time? What if we flip a coin? There are many more possible approaches to solving the puzzle than there are approaches to defeating the other side.

When people come together for a workshop about conflict, they can practice lots of ways to solve problems. There is, of course, a problem that is built into all of these good problem-solving approaches—they still hurt at least a little. After all, either one side gets what it wants and the other does not, or each side gets less than everything it wants.

A successful conflict workshop should help people think about all of the problem-solving approaches, because sometimes we can stand a little pain in return for a partial or later gain. We should also look at a third, more inventive approach. Instead of seeing conflict as a problem to solve, we can actually approach it as an opportunity to see ourselves, the other people, and even the world in a whole new way. In order to do this, we need to relax long enough to remember that we (or someone who came before us) made up the reasons that justify our getting what we want at the expense of somebody else. Imagine what we can learn about ourselves as we examine the origins of our strongest wants and opinions.

We can also look to try to understand the origins of the other people's wants and opinions. Imagine our surprise as we learn how often the other side's wants, needs, and logic is the same or runs parallel to our own.

Conflict also gives us the chance to see how our point of view and its origins, the other people's point of view and its origins, and everything else comes together. Imagine the power we have over our futures and ourselves as we learn more about how society works and how we work in society. We will gain an increased ability to work with people while we get better at figuring out what is most important to us and knowing how we can get closer to having it while helping other people to get closer to having what is most important to them.

Q: What are some of the things that can get in the way of having a successful workshop about conflict?

A: The trainer and the participants.

We have all been working on the reasons to turn conflict into a contest to be won for a lot longer than we have been thinking about conflict as an opportunity to learn. The need to fight it out may actually be somewhere in our DNA. It is certainly in the maps of the world that we carry in our minds and hearts. Giving them up is not easy. The first step is that we as trainers and teachers must challenge our own maps—try to remember where they came from, test some new ones, and see what happens. Next we need to build workshops that allow people safely to explore the origins of their own maps.

Even if we trainers and teachers have spiffy new maps of our own, we will not help much if we try to teach our maps to the people in our workshops. We need to build an environment and an experience that allow them to redraw their own maps for themselves. The exercises in this book help us to do just that.

Q: What is the best reason for people to come to a conflict workshop?

A: It depends.

Conflict and Communication EXERCISES

My Workshop Starts in Five Minutes

This first section has twelve tried-and-true conflict and communication exercises that you can use on the run. We all have workshops that we need to design on the plane or just before we are charging down the hall on the way to class. We sometimes need to add an exercise in the middle of a workshop to change direction or emphasize a specific point. Once you understand the exercises in this section, you will be able to pull them out of your hip pocket and lead them successfully on a moment's notice. They are simple, yet help people to learn key points about communication and conflict.

Three Similarities and One Difference

TYPE	Communication Skills, Diversity Awareness, Teamwork
PURPOSE	Participants identify and talk about the many differences there are among people that can lead to conflict, and the similarities that can help us build relationships.
EQUIPMENT NEEDED	None
PREP	None
TIME NEEDED	20–30 minutes

EXERCISE OUTLINE

INTRODUCTION	Break the workshop group into small teams with from three to five people each.
THE ACTIVITY	Subgroup members find three similarities and one difference among them.
INSIGHTS	Participants talk about the effect similarities and differences have on relationships, communication, and resolving differences.

CONDUCTING THE EXERCISE:
THREE SIMILARITIES AND ONE DIFFERENCE

INTRODUCTION	Introduce the exercise by talking about how we all have differences and similarities that can sometimes help and sometimes get in the way of effective communication.

SAY
We human beings organize our world by comparing one thing with another. This includes categorizing people. We notice differences and similarities among both objects and individuals.

We call something "large" because it is not as small as something else. We call something "near" because it is not as far as something else is. We call something "new" because it is not as old as something else is. We call something "dangerous" because it is not as safe as something else is. I call you "you" because you are not "I."

Our minds make these yes/no, up/down, and me/you decisions constantly and automatically. It helps us to keep track of everything that is going on in the world.

We run into problems when we start to think that old/new, large/small, here/there, and me/you are values—when we start to think of all of these as good/bad. If we fall into the habit of assigning values to things about people—especially things they have no control over—we really can get into trouble.

Relationships can be put at risk because of the differences and similarities that we all have. Because differences can lead to conflict, we have a taboo in our society about talking about them. Trouble is, if we never get a chance to talk to people about what we see as differences, we never get a chance to question some of the assumptions we make about people who may be different from us.

Explain that it can be helpful to be able to talk about the many differences that make each of us unique. By talking about differences and similarities, we can begin to understand them and how they affect how we communicate and interact with others. We can also become more comfortable talking openly about differences with people who are different from us.

 SAY
It is very important to be able to talk about these things freely so that we can all learn and grow, and maintain healthy relationships and effective interactions with others.

Just being able to say to someone, "I think we are having trouble talking about this topic because we are different," can move the conversation forward. Statements like this create starting points for understanding and mutual respect.

For example, compare the last statement—"I think we are having trouble talking about this topic because we are different."—to "I can't talk to you people!" In the first example, I did not judge the other person; I just acknowledged that we are different. I also sent the message that we are both in this together, and that I am comfortable enough with our differences that we can work things out.

When I said, "I can't talk to you people!" I shut down the conversation by being negative and by lumping the other person and her or his whole group together.

Tell participants that this exercise will help them to get used to talking openly and more comfortably about what makes each of us different and all of us the same.

 SAY

Now you will have a chance to identify similarities and differences that exist among the members in your group. You'll get to talk about them a little and then tell the rest of us what you found.

Break the class into teams of from three to five people each.

THE ACTIVITY

Have the subgroups sit together. Tell them that you would like them to find three similarities and one difference among the people in their group. The similarities and difference have to be consistent among the group.

Here are some examples of group similarities and differences that you can use to be sure that your instructions are clear:

SIMILARITIES
- ➤ All of the people in our group work for the same company.
- ➤ All of us have brown hair.
- ➤ All of us were born in the United States.
- ➤ All are married or have children.
- ➤ All like the same kind of music.
- ➤ All of the people in the group are managers.

DIFFERENCES
- ➤ Each of us has a different number of siblings.
- ➤ Two of us went to college and two did not.
- ➤ One is married and four are not.
- ➤ Three of us have blue eyes, one has brown eyes, and one has green eyes.
- ➤ There are two women in the group and three men.

 SAY

Some other examples include hair color, skin color, or some other physical trait. Marital status, parental status, where you went to school or grew up, the car you drive or neighborhood you live in, where you are from or where you grew up—anything can work.

You will have about five minutes to come up with your list. When everyone is finished, each group will share their list with the rest of us.

Does everyone understand what you are doing? Are there any questions?

After about five minutes, ask each group to tell you the similarities and differences that they came up with. List their answers on a flipchart.

INSIGHTS   Point out to participants that although the some of the groups were made up of people who appeared to be all the same, that each group was able to come up with at least one difference. Point out that many groups came up with several differences.

ASK   Which were more difficult to find—differences or similarities? What did you find out about your team members?

Here you are looking for how they decided what to ask about. Have them tell you their process for finding their answers.

ASK   Why do you think it is important to note similarities as well as differences?

You can expect answers such as:

➤ Similarities give us something to talk about together.

➤ It is easier to make friends with people when you have something in common.

➤ Having something in common can make it easier to get through disagreements or other rough times.

➤ Knowing some similarities helps us to break the ice.

Some groups talk more than do others. Some just seem to "get it" right away. If you have a group that seems uncomfortable with the topic, these questions can help:

ASK   ➤ What happens to you if you or your group are not valued or treated fairly because of differences?

➤ What are some other differences we could have listed on our flipchart?

➤ How can these things affect people? Processes? Performance? Energy? Teams? Relationships? Communication? Conflict? Problem-solving?

These questions can help the people in your group to understand why being comfortable talking about differences and similarities is important:

➤ How does being comfortable with discussing differences and similarities help with problem-solving and conflict resolution?

These last two questions can also be used for action planning:

ASK

> ➤ Do you have more communication problems with people that are similar to you or different from you?

> ➤ How can you use similarities to help resolve some of those problems?

Sometimes people will say that they have more problems with people who are similar to them. It may be because they both want to dominate the conversation, or they both want to be right, or they both get angry fast or give in too quickly.

Conflicts happen between people who are different, and with people who are very much the same. You want to help participants realize that they can use the similarities they share with the other person in both cases to improve the relationship and the communication process.

You want participants to be comfortable with putting the difference on the table and talking about it. The similarity opens the door to the relationship. The relationship makes it easier for people to talk about their differences.

SAY

One of the reasons this activity is so important is that some people do not value differences. For example, here we found that everyone at the table has a degree. Some people do not value the opinions of those who do not have degrees. Others do not value the opinions of people who do. These attitudes can affect how people react to people with or without degrees.

As a matter of fact, everyone in this room knows firsthand how it feels to be undervalued because of something, or how it feels to undervalue someone else because of some trait. At the same time, we may also know what it is like to automatically be accepted or included because of some characteristic.

Basically, because we as people judge others based on different traits, our conversations and interactions with other people are affected. This is why it is so important to be able to recognize how we feel about different characteristics and why.

Learning to do this, and becoming comfortable with talking about the differences and similarities will open the door to understanding, appreciation, and, ultimately, more effective, productive conversations and relationships with others.

A New Leaf

TYPE   Teamwork, Worldview

PURPOSE   To help the group get in the habit of checking the origins of their points of view

EQUIPMENT NEEDED   Handout 1: A *New Leaf* (page 205)
An overhead projector and slide of Handout 1: A *New Leaf* (Optional)

PREP   Make one copy of Handout 1: A *New Leaf* for each participant

TIME NEEDED   30 minutes

EXERCISE OUTLINE

INTRODUCTION   Break into groups with four or five people in each.

THE ACTIVITY   Pass out the handout, A *New Leaf*; each group decides how to classify the plants.

INSIGHTS   Participants discuss their findings and examine their "mental models."

CONDUCTING THE EXERCISE: A NEW LEAF

BREAK INTO GROUPS   Divide your workshop group into smaller groups with about four or five people each. There are some good ideas for breaking into groups on page 268.

This simple exercise can really get people thinking. It was created by Dr. Kathy Hale, chair of the graduate program in conflict resolution at The McGregor School of Antioch University. In her work as a mediator and educator, Kathy stresses a systems approach to communication and conflict. She encourages people to examine the source of their "mental models" of the world around them—those personal internal maps of reality that we all have—as a tool for questioning their own conclusions. The point of this exercise, she says, "is to help people take greater responsibility for their own choices in defining the situation in which they must act, in defining the people with whom they must work, and in assessing the data relevant to the issue." Use this exercise when teaching conflict resolution, diversity, or performance assessment. It will also work well for continuous improvement teams (TQM, Six Sigma, etc.) as they learn to interpret data, or to help people with any other task that requires them to make decisions based on how they prioritize their experience.

DISTRIBUTE THE HANDOUT

Pass out copies of the handout A *New Leaf* (page 205). Tell the group that they are now scientists who have discovered several new types of plants. Their assignment is to classify the plants by placing the plants into classifications with others that are similar. Each group will decide on its classifications, then report back and compare notes.

INSIGHTS

Allow about ten minutes for them to complete the assignment, then ask each group to report in.

On a board or flip chart, write down each group's solution. For example:

GROUP 1	GROUP 2	GROUP 3
1,3,8,9	1,2,4,7	2,6
2,6,7	3,5,6	1,3,8
4,5	8,9	4,9
		5,7

You may want to project a copy of the handout on a screen and point out the groupings as you list them.

When you have listed each group's solution on the flip chart, ask them:

ASK

How did you come up with your classifications?

People usually classify the leaves according to their appearance. Some will sort them by number of petals, some by how smooth or jagged they are, some by stem type, etc. While it is important for the group to hear the rationale behind each of the other group's classifications, it is important for you as facilitator to remember that there is no one right way to sort the plants. Ask the group:

ASK **?** Which group did the best or most correct job of sorting the plants?
What can we learn from this exercise?

The group will make many points about how we come to conclusions. Some individual members may say that they differed with their particular group about how to classify the plants. Some key points for the group to discover include:

➤ The decisions each group made regarding how to sort the plants required them to focus on one part of each plant and ignore some other part. The way we see the world is based as much on what we choose to ignore as it is on what we choose to give importance.

➤ The only way to agree on the "best" job of sorting is to agree on what is important to notice and what can be ignored.

➤ Many times we will fight to defend a point of view because we have either forgotten or never knew that it started as a set of decisions about what to ignore and what to emphasize.

➤ It is good to check our "mental models"—the personal maps we draw in our heads to define "reality"—from time to time. The way to do this is to look back at the decisions we made about what to keep in and what to leave out of our process.

Right Listening

TYPE   Centering, Communication Skills, Conflict Skills, Teamwork

PURPOSE   Participants practice a listening skill beyond the typical advice to focus and rephrase. The focus is on sympathy—understanding the speakers' emotion without necessarily having to feel the same way.

EQUIPMENT NEEDED   Flipchart and markers

PREP   Prepare enough handout sheets for each participant.
Handouts:
2. *Right Listening* (page 206)
3. *Emptiness* (page 207)
4. *Right Listening Observer Checklist* (page 208)

We learned this listening technique in 1996 at a National Multicultural Institute conference workshop in Washington, DC. The workshop was entitled *Dialogue and Identity*. Drs. *Angelo John Lewis and Zachary Gabriel Green led a Method for Creating Multicultural Conversation.* We have been teaching it ever since in seminars that focus on effective communication, conflict resolution, team building, and valuing diversity.

Prepare flipcharts and post them around the room.
Flipcharts:
1. *Statistics* (page 238)
2. *Active Listening* (page 239)
3. *Right Listening* (page 240)
4. *Activity* (page 241)

TIME NEEDED   30–40 minutes

EXERCISE OUTLINE

INTRODUCTION   Ask participants to describe effective listening. Introduce "right listening" concepts.

THE ACTIVITY   Participants practice right listening, and give each other feedback.

INSIGHTS   Participants use the workshop materials to help them talk about what they are learning.

CONDUCTING THE EXERCISE: ACTIVE LISTENING

INTRODUCTION   Review the *Statistics* flipchart. Get the participants' reactions to the statistics and find out what courses they may have taken or what experience they have with communication skills.

    To help the conversation along, ask the group:

ASK

➤ What do you think of these statistics?

➤ What do these statistics say about our ability to listen, understand, and remember what we hear?

➤ Do any of these statements ring true especially for you?

Most participants will identify with the different items presented on the flipchart. Point out the final bullet in particular.

SAY

We spend most of our time listening, don't we? Yet when we think of communication courses, they often focus on speaking, not listening. How many of you have taken a course or courses on these topics? Raise your hand if you have attended workshops on:

➤ Public Speaking

➤ Communication Skills

➤ Writing: Business, Creative, Marketing, etc.

➤ Presentation Skills

➤ Communicating Nondefensively

➤ Communicating Assertively

➤ Communicating Professionally

➤ Communicating for the Masses

➤ Etc. etc.—The list goes on and on, doesn't it? What other courses have you taken?

Now, how many of you have taken courses on listening? At best, there may be one or two of these available.

Get their responses. Typically, people have taken more courses on spoken or written communication than on listening.

 ASK   Isn't it interesting that we spend more time and effort learning how to express ourselves than we do learning how to listen to others?

Ask participants what they think of as good listening skills, and list their responses on a flipchart. You can expect answers such as:

➤ Make eye contact
➤ Ask questions
➤ Remove distractions
➤ Avoid interrupting the speaker
➤ Take notes

Tell participants that they have come up with a good list.

 ASK   What are some things that hurt the listening process?

You can expect answers such as:

➤ interrupting
➤ not looking at the person who is talking
➤ trying to solve the problem instead of listening
➤ offering opposing points of view
➤ thinking about other things instead of focusing on the speaker
➤ doing other things while the person is talking

Post the two flipcharts side by side.

Now tell participants that you are going to introduce a listening technique called "Right Listening." Give out the three handout sheets to participants. Tell them that this technique takes "Active Listening" a step further. Compare the *Right Listening* flipchart with the good listening techniques you have just listed on the flipchart. There will usually be some parallels.

 SAY   Active Listening is a skill that more and more people are learning, and is a very helpful tool to improve communication. Today we are going to move to another level of listening: Right Listening.

Go over the *Right Listening* flipchart with the group:

➤ Release tension and assume a posture that allows for listening without resistance.

SAY   This means making yourself comfortable. It means getting into a position that allows you to stay pretty still, one that makes you very relaxed and comfortable, without making you drowsy or putting you to sleep. You want to be comfortable, but not cozy. In other words, you may want to sit back in your chair or on a soft couch, but not lay your head down or put your feet up.

➤ Perceive the speaker's feelings; step into their thoughts.

SAY Try to understand what the speaker was going through—what he or she is feeling about what he or she is describing to you. You need to understand why they are angry, or how what happened made them feel sad. You need to notice that they are frustrated, happy, or some other emotion to help you understand, remember what is being said, and continue listening effectively.

➤ Silence your own sympathy and antipathy.

SAY Once you have identified what the speaker is feeling, you have to avoid feeling the same emotion, sympathy, or antipathy for what he or she is saying. Right Listening involves a certain level of objectivity. You try not to become emotionally charged. Even though you note what the speaker is feeling, you remain neutral. This way, your own feelings don't cloud or influence what the speaker is saying to you. When we add our own spin on the story, we tend to add things to the story or take things away from the story that the speaker wants to be there.

For example, in one workshop a woman told another woman a story about going to a country music festival. They ate hush puppies [fried corn bread] and crowded into a hot tent so they could sit on benches and hear the music. The woman telling the story had a wonderful time at the concert. The woman listening to the story thought she had just heard about a vacation disaster: bad food, bad music, and uncomfortable seats. Even if we agree with what the person is saying, or support them, it is best to try to remain neutral in order to hear them. We all know how difficult that can be. It takes practice.

➤ Feel the other person cognitively, not emotionally.

SAY The goal is to be analytical about the speaker's emotion without passing judgments about the speaker while he or she is talking. For example, if a woman is upset about something that happened between her and a male coworker, the listener has to avoid making judgments such as: "Women are always getting upset over nothing," or "Men are always pushing women around!" Another example would be to avoid letting past history with the speaker influence your reaction to what is being said.

➤ Check to make sure you understand the speaker and hear the details.

SAY This just means checking with the speaker to make sure you are getting the details. You can ask questions to make sure you understand the details or the point of the story.

When you feel that everyone understands the basic concepts behind right listening put the participants into groups of three each. (See page 268, *Fun Ways to Break into Groups.*) Ask participants to read the *Right Listening* handout in their groups and talk about it.

THE ACTIVITY

Ask participants to determine who in each group will be the listener, the speaker, and the observer for the first round of the role-play.

Have the speakers think of an interesting topic to tell their listeners about.

Now we are going to practice Right Listening. Each of you will get a chance to talk, listen, and observe. First, take a moment to decide who will speak, who will listen, and who will observe for the first round.

 SAY Pause a moment to let them figure it out.

Now think of a topic that you can talk about for two or three minutes. The listener is going to have to figure out what your emotion is or was, so be sure to pick a topic that you have an opinion on or some feeling about.

You may need to recommend a few topics for the activity. Here are some that work well:

➤ My Best Vacation Ever
➤ A Project I/My Team Completed Successfully
➤ A Favorite TV Show or Movie
➤ Something I Have Improved Upon
➤ Our Last Office Party or Meeting
➤ A Current Project: Goals and Status
➤ Why I Chose My Current Job/Profession
➤ A Significant Accomplishment in My Life
➤ Why I Signed up for this Class
➤ What I Hope to Learn Here Today and Why

Show the group the *Activity* flip chart. Tell the trios that each round will last five or six minutes, and will be broken down as follows:

➤ 2 minutes—Speaker tells story/Listener practices right listening
➤ 1–2 minutes—Listener "tells back" speaker what was told to him/her
➤ 1 minute—Speaker gives listener feedback; makes corrections
➤ 1 minute—Observer gives listener feedback

Be sure that everyone has a copy of the *Observer Checklist* handout and that they understand the assignment.

SAY

Let me explain how each round will go. The speaker will tell her or his story and the listener will listen using the right listening technique. Observers should use the Observer Checklist. As you observe, you can check off the boxes for each listener behavior as you see it. For example, if the listener asks a few questions, you would check box number three. If the listener checks for understanding, check number six.

On the other hand, if the listener starts trying to solve the problem or disputes what is being said, then you would not check box number five.

At the bottom of the sheet, you can make general comments or write notes about why you checked or did not check certain boxes. After the role-play, you'll use the sheet to share your observations with the listener. Does everyone understand the instructions? Great, let's get started.

You will tell participants when to start, stop, and switch roles. Begin the activity, keeping time for each round. Make sure you tell participants when to stop talking and start feedback sessions with the speakers and observers.

After everyone has had a turn to be the speaker, listener, and observer, bring everyone back to the large group for the debriefing.

INSIGHTS

Start the conversation by asking the listeners how they felt using the new technique. Then ask the speakers what they thought about the listener's ability to effectively listen this way. Ask observers what they heard and saw during the conversation.

ASK

What do you think are some benefits of being able to realize "cognitively" the speaker's emotion without sympathizing or showing antipathy toward him or her?

You can expect responses such as:

➤ My own ideas don't get in the way.

➤ I can be sure to hear the whole story before jumping to a conclusion.

Another way of looking at listening beyond the emotion of the moment while still taking that emotion into account is what Jay Rothman calls "analytic empathy." Jay is the author who shared some of his ideas on conflict resolution with us for the *Write Your Own Case Study* section. He suggests that we learn to listen to an adversary in such a way that we can understand that the source of this other person's emotion has its own logic. In fact, the emotion and its logic may be very similar to our own. For more on Jay Rothman's work, see the *Toolbox* at the end of the book.

You may also want to look at *The Conflict Management Skills Workshop* (Withers, AMACOM, 2002) for more information and exercises about listening and how to begin disciplining yourself to serve others as a neutral party.

➤ I can notice some things that the speaker may leave unsaid about how she or he feels about whatever we are talking about.

➤ I don't start planning an argument in my head before the other person is finished.

➤ I can stay calm even if I disagree with the other person.

Ask the group to talk about the difference between the active listening stance and the "relaxed, attentive posture" required for right listening.

Finally, ask what they learned from the exercise. Talk about how this technique can be used to reduce conflict and resolve differences.

Building Bridges

TYPE Communication Skills, Diversity Awareness, Teamwork

PURPOSE Gives participants the opportunity to experience the value of finding common ground with someone who is different.

EQUIPMENT NEEDED Flipchart Paper
Markers

PREP Handout 5: *Building Bridges* Action Plan (page 209)
Flipchart 5: *Building Bridges* (page 242)

TIME NEEDED 30 minutes

EXERCISE OUTLINE

INTRODUCTION Each participant chooses a partner who they think is different from him or herself.

THE ACTIVITY Partners brainstorm a list of things they have in common.

INSIGHTS The partners bring what they are learning back to the group.

OPTIONAL ACTION PLANNING STEP Participants commit to build some new bridges in the workplace.

CONDUCTING THE EXERCISE

INTRODUCTION   Ask the people in the group to each find a partner for the exercise. Their partners should be someone with whom they think they will have the least in common.

Explain that sometimes it can be difficult to communicate with someone who seems to be very different from us.

SAY It can sometimes be difficult to talk or interact with people who are different from us. The more different they seem to be, the harder it gets. One way to try to break the ice is to build "bridges" with the person. This means finding things you both have in common. Finding these "bridges" helps you to begin to talk. It can also help when two people are having problems because of a difference between them.

Sometimes the only bridge you can find is that you both work for the same company, or that you both want to resolve a difference. If that is all there is, then work with it. Any bridge can help to open communication to other things.

You are going to have a chance to build some bridges today. I would like you to find things in common with your partner. I have written some sample "bridges" here on this flipchart that you can use if you cannot think of anything.

Show participants the prepared *Building Bridges* flipchart. Ask them if there are other "bridges" they would add to the list. As the group comes up with other ideas for bridges, write them on the flipchart.

> To lead this exercise without the prepared *Building Bridges* flipchart, have the participants brainstorm a list of possible bridges.

THE ACTIVITY

SAY You and your partner will have fifteen minutes to talk with one another and build as many bridges as you can. Remember, bridges are areas that you have in common that will help you develop greater appreciation or understanding of one another.

As you work together, write a list of your "bridges." Try to talk with your partner a little bit about each thing you come up with. Get to know one another some. You will report back to the group in about fifteen minutes.

INSIGHTS When time is up, help the group to talk about what they are learning by asking questions such as:

ASK

➤ What were some of the bridges you and your partner were able to build?
➤ Were you surprised to find how much you have in common?
➤ How or why did you select your partner in the first place?
➤ What made you think that your partner would be different from you?
➤ Do you still feel that way?
➤ What does that tell us about our perceptions and assumptions?

To sum up, say:

SAY One of the best ways to create understanding, appreciation, and open dialogue with those different from us is to try to find common ground. This doesn't mean that we ignore our differences or the issues that might divide us. Building bridges gives us a starting point to get the conversation flowing so that we can move forward.

Focusing on similarities can help us realize that the person who seems so different is still a valuable person. We may find out that he or she may also share some of the same experiences, values, and beliefs that we do. We may be able to learn something about ourselves as we learn about people who are different from us. You may even end up making a friend.

Explain that this activity helps us to face the discomfort of interacting with someone different or who has very different views. They had a chance to practice finding common ground—a necessary skill in resolving differences, communication, and valuing diversity.

OPTIONAL ACTION PLANNING STEP As an Action Planning step, you may want to have participants think about and write down the names of up to three people at work with whom they need to build a bridge. You can use the *Building Bridges Action Plan* handout for this.

After they write the name, have them jot down five potential bridges (things they may have in common) they can try to build with this person. Then have them set a date by which they will contact each one. Invite them to follow up with you via E-mail to share how it went.

Climbing Life's Ladders

TYPE   Diversity Awareness, Worldview

PURPOSE   Shows how different factors can impact how much we value others

EQUIPMENT NEEDED   Handout 6: *Climbing Life's Ladders* facilitator's sheet (page 210)
Large area in which participants can form a line
Masking tape (optional)

PREP   Mark a straight line down the center of the training room floor with the masking tape (optional)

TIME NEEDED   20–30 minutes

EXERCISE OUTLINE

INTRODUCTION   Ask participants to line up shoulder to shoulder, on the masking tape line. Tell them you are going to read several statements. After each statement, you will tell them to take steps forward or backward.

THE ACTIVITY   Read each statement and tell participants to step forward or backward according to the sheet. Participants should only move if the statement pertains to them.

> This activity examines different factors that can contribute to how much a person is valued. It also provides some insight into how others in the world might be experiencing life in society as a whole and in the company in which they work.
>
> Because this activity asks people to disclose information about themselves in a public arena, you must take careful steps to make them feel safe and comfortable. This is not one that you will do early in the session.

INSIGHTS Talk about where participants ended up in relation to the line and to each other. Discuss their positions in real life, taking into account the different value statements that were read.

Explain that these statements were based on mainstream U.S. culture. Ask participants to name other success factors that can matter in our culture.

> You will need enough room for participants to be able to take several steps in front of, and behind, the taped line. At least 5 large steps either way. When I conduct this activity, I often do it outside of the training room in a large hallway or break out area.

CONDUCTING THE EXERCISE: CLIMBING LIFE'S LADDERS

INTRODUCTION Have participants follow you to the "value line." Ask them to stand shoulder to shoulder on the line.

Now tell participants:

There are many factors that cause us to value or not value a person. Because of shared values in a culture, many of these factors will determine how successful that person is in life.

What do you think some of those factors or characteristics may be? Can you think of some things in our society that would make someone more successful or more valued than not?

Get some answers from the group. If they are a bit quiet, you can offer your own suggestions to get the conversation going. Some answers you can expect are:

➤ whether someone is male or female
➤ education levels
➤ social or economic status
➤ how one speaks
➤ appearance
➤ etc.

Explain that these factors can impact how well we do in life and how others interact with us.

SAY These factors can help or hurt our relationships with others, our chances for getting a job, being asked to join a social club, and other things in life that may be important to us.

We are going to measure some of those value points now. The value statements that I am going to read will be based on mainstream U.S. culture. Remember, there are always exceptions.

I will read a statement and tell you whether to step forward or backward. I only want you to move if the statement pertains to you. It's like the childhood game, "Mother, May I" or "Red Light, Green Light." If the statement is not true for you, then stay where you are. At the end, we'll see where everyone ends up in relation to everyone else.

Are there any questions? Okay, let's try it!

THE ACTIVITY

Read each statement from the *Climbing Life's Ladders* facilitator's sheet and tell participants how many steps to take forward or backward. Be sure that they know that if they do not want to react to a particular statement, they can stay in place. Read the first few statements in order. Then you can read them in any order that you like. You can also add statements that you think are important to the people in the workshop.

INSIGHTS   Ask participants how they felt during the activity. People who took the most steps backward or forward may say they felt embarrassed or uncomfortable.

Have participants talk about where they are standing at the end of the exercise. Some questions that you can ask to help the conversation are:

ASK

> ➤ Are the higher level leaders in the corporation the farthest ahead?
> ➤ Are there concentrations of certain types of people in the front or back?
> ➤ How accurately are the value statements illustrated by participants' real life status?
> ➤ What other values can affect how far we get in life?
> ➤ How can we overcome some of these things?

Ask participants what they think the activity shows. Then ask what they have learned from it. Ask them to think about who they may have trouble talking to. Could this be because of some difference? Use the sheet of value statements to give them hints and help them discuss this question.

Be aware that some people may be mildly offended or upset by what the activity shows and may have difficulty talking about it. Some may be more offended or even in denial about it. Still allow them to express their opinions as long as they are not being hostile or overtly offensive to anyone.

SAY

I am going to ask some questions for you to think about. It is okay if you want to answer out loud or talk about these questions. It is also okay if you want to just think quietly about how you might answer.

Now ask the following questions, pausing between each one so that people have time to think or speak up. Ask the group:

ASK

➤ Are there types of people with whom you find it difficult to interact?

➤ For example, do any of you have trouble communicating with high-level leaders?

➤ Or with line workers?

➤ What about with people that are financially well off?

➤ Those who come from poorer neighborhoods?

➤ Those with disabilities?

➤ Those that are a different color or who belong to a different ethnic group?

➤ Those with a different sexual orientation or gender?

Continue the discussion with questions like:

➤ How might these different backgrounds affect workplace relationships or interactions?

➤ Do we judge people based on some of these things?

➤ How do you think those judgments affect people?

➤ How do they affect us?

Explain to participants that the first step in improving your communication and relationships with those different from yourself is to realize how you feel about the difference.

ASK

➤ What kinds of things can we do to reduce problems caused by differences and improve the relationship and/or communication process?

➤ How do you think our company can benefit from having different types of people working here?

➤ What do you think this organization needs to do to ensure the relationships and communication processes are effective between these groups?

> I have used this activity in many diversity classes to show how who they are and how others see them affect people's lives. Be sure to explain that there are exceptions, and that people (1) do overcome some of the obstacles; and (2) not everyone perceived as has advantages in fact does. Lots of factors go into a person's successes and downfalls. But some things make it easier or harder for particular groups of people.—Keami

End the activity by letting participants know that activities like this one are designed to raise awareness. From awareness we build skills and then take action on what needs to be done.

From this particular activity, the main thing to remember is that not everyone is experiencing the world in the same way. Some of us do have advantages and are valued above others because of the group to which people feel we belong. Others suffer disadvantages and negative consequences for the same reason.

In trying to manage differences, communicate effectively, and just go through life, it is important to understand our personal feelings about different groups of people so that we can make an effort to engage in positive behaviors instead of negative ones.

Draw a House

TYPE   Communication Skills, Conflict Skills, Teamwork

PURPOSE   Demonstrate the different ways people respond to conflict. Recognize the importance of good communication when dealing with others. Help participants see their own reaction to conflict.

EQUIPMENT NEEDED   Blank sheets of paper
Pens, pencils, crayons, or markers
Flipchart and markers

PREP   Place blank sheets of paper, pens, pencils, crayons, or markers on tables

TIME NEEDED   20 minutes

EXERCISE OUTLINE

INTRODUCTION   Participants will work in pairs. Have each pair choose a pen/pencil/marker and a sheet of paper.

> This is one of my favorite exercises. I have used it in diversity classes, team-building workshops, and different types of communication seminars. The exercise is fun, easy to lead, and it provides valuable insight for learners. It drives home the importance of effective communication, and reveals how each participant responds to conflict. Participants are usually eager to show their drawings and share what happened in their group. This makes having a conversation that much easier. *Draw a House* works best right after a break—it works well right after lunch as a recap of what was covered in the morning or as a preview of what is coming up next.—Keami

THE ACTIVITY Have the people in each pair hold the one pen/pencil/marker they selected so that both of them can write on the paper together. Have them draw a house without talking to one another.

INSIGHTS Talk about everyone's pictures and how the activity went.

VARIATION Facilitating the exercise for a large group

CONDUCTING THE EXERCISE: DRAW A HOUSE

INTRODUCTION Tell the participants to each find a partner, or use one of the activities on page 268 to get them to pair off. Once everyone has a partner, ask them to choose just one sheet of paper and just one pen/pencil/marker per pair.

THE ACTIVITY

Tell the pairs to hold their one pen/pencil/marker so that each of them can write on the paper. Both people will be holding one pen/pencil/marker. It is important to let them figure out how. Avoid telling them which hand to use or where to place their hands on the pen. Once each pair is holding one pen/pencil/marker, tell them to draw a picture of a house without talking. Remind them that the goal is for them to work on the picture together.

SAY   I want each team to hold your maker and prepare to write on the paper. Both of you should have your hand on the marker. (*Wait.*) Okay, without speaking to one another, please draw a house on the paper. Don't worry. Nobody is expecting a great work of art. Just do your best to draw a simple picture without talking to each other. You have about two minutes to finish your picture. Ready? Go!

Watch the pairs as they draw their houses, and jot down some notes for you to bring up during the discussion part of the exercise. Here are some things you can look for:

➤ Which partner takes control?

➤ Does one person dominate, or do they take turns?

➤ How are the pairs making decisions without talking to each other?

➤ What gestures, faces, eye contact, postures, and sounds are they making at one another?

➤ How do they "correct" problems with the drawing?

➤ Make note of people that begin with one demeanor and end with another. Do they start seriously and then loosen up? Is it a game at first and then becomes competitive? Does one partner give up or check out?

➤ Notice what people do when they get frustrated. Do they push or pull on the pen? Do they stop from time to time?

➤ If they stop drawing for a while, who starts again?

After about two minutes, or when everyone has a picture that looks something like a house, ask them to put their pens down. Expect immediate talking and laughing. Walk around the room and listen. Join in the conversations with different pairs as you look at their pictures.

INSIGHTS   Ask the participants to hold up their pictures and to talk about what they did. You can ask them some of these questions if they need help getting started:

ASK

➤ Is this the picture you had in mind when you started drawing? If not, how did it end up the way that it did?

➤ How did you decide what to draw?

➤ Who was in control of the pen?

➤ Was it easy working with your partner?

➤ How did you start drawing?

➤ What did you do when one person wanted to go one way and the other person wanted to go in a different direction?

➤ How did you communicate without talking?

Although this is a "harmless" exercise, there are plenty of people who get very uncomfortable when you ask them to draw. Be sure that you are careful and constructive when you share your observations. It helps for you to remind your participants (and yourself!) that the exercise isn't about drawing, but about what goes on when people with different approaches have to work together. As with most of the exercises in this book, there is not a "right" way or "right" answer. We just want to get people thinking and talking.—Keami

➤ Is there anyone who just softly held the marker and let his or her partner make all of the decisions? Why did you do that?

Now talk a little about what people learned from the exercise.

SAY This activity caused a little conflict between you and your partner—some teams more than others. [*You can share one or two specific observations here.*] What were some of the causes for this conflict?

List their responses on the flip chart. You can expect comments like:

➤ couldn't talk with each other

➤ no time to plan

➤ did not know what the other person wanted

➤ could not tell the other person what I wanted

➤ I was worried I would come off as too pushy or offend my partner in some way

SAY Many of the things you mentioned cause conflict in everyday situations, don't they? Did you notice any similarities between how you handled the conflict in this activity and how you handle it in real life?

List their responses on the flipchart.

Here are some questions and comments you can use to sum up the exercise:

ASK ➤ What did you hear that has helped you see different ways of handling conflict?

➤ Did you notice anyone in this class that approaches conflict in a way that is similar to someone you know in real life?

➤ How did you and your partner finally finish your house?

➤ What were some ways you resolved your conflicts?

➤ What are some things we could have done that would have reduced the amount of conflict in the exercise?

List their responses on the flipchart.

If you want, participants can hang their pictures on the wall as reminders during the rest of the workshop. Congratulate them on a job well done. Use the comments that you have been writing on the flipchart to review quickly some of their insights about what leads to conflict. You will probably have a list that looks something like this:

➤ poor communication

➤ unclear goals

➤ being convinced that there is only one way to draw a house

➤ assuming you know the other person's point of view

➤ unequal ability or participation in resolving the issue

➤ communication style

➤ personality traits

Now ask the group for their ideas about how to keep conflicts from getting out of hand. Write their comments on the flipchart. You can expect such ideas as:

- ➤ set goals together before starting
- ➤ maintain two-way communication
- ➤ recognize differences in style
- ➤ listen to and acknowledge the other person's ideas
- ➤ recognize your own strengths and weaknesses
- ➤ try to see the other person's point of view

VARIATION   Facilitating the Exercise for a Large Group
It is easy to adapt this exercise for large groups, even for groups of more than one hundred. Simply make the following changes:

1. Allow for at least 40 minutes for the exercise.

2. Break a large group of 50 or more into smaller groups of 15 to 20 people.

3. Give each group a flipchart and markers.

4. Project the Draw a House discussion questions on an overhead, and pass them out as handouts.

5. Have each group discuss the activity and report key findings to the larger group.

Energy Jump

TYPE	Centering, Conflict Skills
PURPOSE	To help people talk about how their bodies tell them it is time for "fight or flight."
EQUIPMENT NEEDED	None
PREP	None
TIME NEEDED	5 to 10 minutes

EXERCISE OUTLINE

INTRODUCTION	Tell the group that you want them to jump up out of their chairs every time you clap your hands.
ENERGY JUMP	Surprise the group by clapping your hands when they don't expect it. Surprise the group by not clapping your hands when they do.
INSIGHTS	Help the group talk about how it feels to be ready for something that does not happen the way one expects.

CONDUCTING THE EXERCISE: ENERGY JUMP

INTRODUCTION   Tell the group that it is time to wake them up and test their reactions. Explain that while you are talking, you will clap your hands from time to time—sometimes when they least expect it. Whenever you clap your hands, they should all jump up from their chairs.

Tell them to get ready, and clap your hands once so they can practice.

THE ACTIVITY

Now that the group has the idea, begin talking about something else—the next thing you will cover in your workshop, questions about what you have just covered, etc. Surprise them by clapping your hands and see how many people jump. Once they have settled in their chairs, clap again. Be playful with this, and let them enjoy the game with you.

The group will be ready for you now. Continue talking for a minute or so, and then move your hands together as if you are going to clap. Stop just short of clapping, and see what the group does. Some of the group will either get set, start to get up, or even jump up. Everybody will have some reaction—even if they have not moved.

INSIGHTS   Ask the group why they think you did what you did. You can expect answers like:

➤ to trick us
➤ to see if we were paying attention
➤ to keep us on our toes
➤ to be sure we are awake

Tell them that the real reason is that you wanted to give them a chance to feel what it is like for your body to be ready. Ask them:

ASK

➤ What did it feel like to be ready?
➤ What was happening in your body?
➤ What was happening in your head?

Of course, since they are telling you about their experience, there are no wrong answers to these questions. You can expect to hear answers such as:

➤ I was tense.
➤ I wanted to get it right.
➤ My muscles were ready to go.
➤ I leaned forward.
➤ My toes curled.
➤ My heart beat a little faster.
➤ I tuned in to what you were doing.

Explain that when we want to be ready for something, our bodies get a rush of energy. If we are paying attention to our bodies, we can feel this energy rush. What we are feeling is the "fight or flight" response. (For more on fight or flight, see *Staying Cool in a Conflict* on page 77.) It is a normal reaction to any challenge, and our bodies will react that way even if the challenge is not a physical one.

To let the group shed the energy they have built up from your "almost clap," tell them you are going to have them jump one more time. Tell them that if they want to shout or yell when they jump this time, it is okay.

Organizational consultant and Aikido master Chris Thorsen taught this exercise to us. For more about Chris and his work, please turn to the Toolbox section.

SAY Whatever you do, make this jump a big one. Yell or scream if you want. This one is a chance to let off steam. I'm going to count to three and then clap my hands, and I want you to jump as high as you can.

Count to three and clap your hands.

SAY Feel better? It's good to remember that our bodies want to move when we are challenged in any way. In a conflict, we sometimes react to what we think is going to happen instead of what is really happening—just like jumping out of your chair when you think I am going to clap. When we know what our bodies feel like when they want to move, we can take that energy and direct it toward what we want instead of reacting without thinking.

Meet the Press

TYPE Communication Skills, Conflict Skills, Diversity Awareness, Worldview

PURPOSE To help participants understand that the meaning that one culture assigns to another culture's behaviors and words can be inaccurate.

EQUIPMENT NEEDED Reporters "props":
Pens and pads
Press hats or badges

PREP Flipchart 6: *Meet the Press* (page 243)

TIME NEEDED 20–30 minutes

> I use this little icebreaker for any course that examines differences or communication styles. It's a great way to prepare participants for the Synthetic Cultures Lab on page 168. It's quick, fun, and gets people ready for role-playing. It is also a good introduction to any communication course, especially those in which participants diagnose and correct communication problems.—Keami

> It is a good idea to use props for this activity. Props help participants to relax and take on the roles they are supposed to be playing. The more real you can make a role-play seem, the better the results will be.

EXERCISE OUTLINE

INTRODUCTION Some members of the group volunteer to be "reporters." The rest will belong to a "country" with specific cultural rules.

ACTIVITY The reporters visit the country and find out as much as they can about it by talking to the people.

INSIGHTS Participants talk about where and why the process broke down, how each group felt, and what they could have done about it if it were a real assignment. They compare the activity with real-life situations.

The more creative you can be with setting up this activity, the more fun and effective it will be. I don't always use the reporter role. Sometimes I try to draw a parallel between the activity and a real request that might be made by real people in the organization instead.

For example, I was working in a company that was planning on expanding and told the "reporter" group that our CEO needed some information on a country in which we were going to expand. I told them to imagine that he had asked them to go over to this country and find out as much as they could about the people, traditions, business, etc. He wanted them to come back prepared to give him a full report about the culture and make a recommendation as to whether or not we should open a business there.

When you make the situation real like this, it adds an even greater element of realism to the role-play. People can better imagine the importance of the task and the outcome it will have.—Keami

CONDUCTING THE EXERCISE: MEET THE PRESS

INTRODUCTION   Start by asking for volunteers. You will need the number of volunteers to equal about one fourth of the entire workshop group. Make sure that your volunteer group and the remaining group have both men and women in them.

You can either let the volunteers know ahead of time what their assignment will be, or you can get the volunteers first, and then tell them. It works well either way.

Once you have your volunteers, ask them to step outside of the room. Tell the larger group that you will be right back. Go out with the volunteers to tell them their assignment.

SAY   You are going to play the role of reporters that have been asked to visit another culture in another country. Your assignment is to find out as much as they can about this new culture.

You are working for *60 Minutes* [or *Good Morning America* or some other popular news show] and will be preparing a report for the nation.

You will need to find out things like:

➤ what language they speak
➤ their customs
➤ celebrations
➤ food they like to eat

➤ the role of men and women
➤ what kind of jobs and companies they have there
➤ what kind of government
➤ the climate
➤ anything that they feel would be good for people to know

Now distribute the reporter props and ask the volunteers to wait outside of the room while you talk to the larger group about their role. Tell them you will call them when everyone is ready.

While the reporters are out of the room, explain to the rest of the group the rules of their simulated culture.

SAY I am going to explain your culture to you. It is very important that you follow all the rules of your culture. No matter what happens or who tries to talk to you, you cannot break the rules of your culture.

This is just like real life. We all have cultural norms that we follow. We may not think about them every minute of the day because they become second nature after a while, but they do exist. For example, we value honesty and other moral behaviors in this country, right? What happens when people do not fit the mold? They go to jail, they are ostracized, talked about, etc.

So everyone here has to follow the rules of this little culture just as you would in real life, okay?

Good. You may write these rules down on a piece of paper so that you don't forget them, but be sure that you don't let the other group see them.

Uncover the *Meet the Press* flipchart and go over it with the group.

➤ In this culture, it is rude for men to speak to women they don't know. If a woman that a man does not know approaches him and starts talking to him, it is best to ignore her to save her the embarrassment she is causing herself.

➤ If someone that is talking to you smiles, they want you to give a positive answer, so you say "yes" to whatever they are asking you. It doesn't matter what the question is, you say, "Yes."

➤ If someone that is talking to you does not smile, they are very serious and want a stern "no" for an answer. They want you think more about it, so you must say, "No."

SAY The group outside are reporters who are coming to your country to ask you questions. Remember that what you do and say is based on what the reporters do. The only things you can say to them are "yes," or "no." There are no other answers that you can give. It doesn't matter what the question is. Take particular care to follow the rule about men and women. You are a very caring society and you don't want to offend others. You only try to give them what they want from you. You are answering the way you are because you care and because you only want what is best for the visiting reporters.

When you are sure that everyone understands the cultural rules, cover up the *Meet the Press* flipchart and call the reporter group into the room.

Tell the reporters to take good notes and to talk to as many people as possible. Tell them that at the end of the interview process, they will stand in front of the room and tell everyone what they found out. Encourage them to split up and roam around the room.

THE ACTIVITY

Give the reporters five or ten minutes to ask their questions.

If some people in the culture group forget their rules, remind them of the rules without letting on what the rules are in front of the reporters.

Some of the reporters may get discouraged and stop trying to interview people and complain that no one will talk to them, that all the people say is "yes" and "no." You will need to gently tell them to keep trying.

SAY

Come on, people are counting on you. If you don't get this information, we won't know what to do. You have to try to find out something. Try talking to someone else—maybe that will help.

Did you try to talk to this person over here? What about this group?

Remember to encourage the reporters to sit down with the different people in the group. Tell them to spread out; not to all move around together, but rather move about alone gathering information.

Near the end of the session, many of your reporters may be complaining to one another and may be getting a little hostile. They may already be making generalizations about the culture and voicing recommendations not to go there—ever!

If there is a reporter that has been more successful (for example, a woman reporter that spoke only to women versus a male reporter that kept trying to talk to women but kept getting ignored) than another, you may even see (and hear) a little jealousy.

After five or ten minutes, you can ask the reporters to come to the front of the room and tell us what they found out. Expect laughter, jeers, complaints from both groups—all in fun, of course.

INSIGHTS   The reporters will typically report some variation of these conclusions:

➤ They will have no real substance to report but will offer many assumptions about the culture and ultimately recommend that no one go to this country. Most of the assumptions will be negative—some extremely so.

➤ They will have a report full of inaccuracies based on what happened during the interviews.

➤ They will guess what the cultural rules are.

➤ They will say that they need more information in order to report anything.

After the reporters share their reports, ask someone in the group to let them know about the cultural rules. At this point, you can show your flipchart. Get reactions from the reporters.

   Ask them what tactics they used to get information. Ask how they felt, what worked, and what didn't.

   Now ask the culture group how they felt during the activity. The reporters will be very surprised to learn how frustrated the culture group was; how much they wanted to help, but couldn't. Talk a little about how it felt to have to follow cultural rules even when it didn't feel good to do so.

How does this play out in real life?

Do any of you have examples of real situations that are similar to this activity?

What did you learn from this activity?

Brainstorm ways we can try to communicate more effectively when cultural differences are very great. Some answers may be:

➤ Read about the culture ahead of time.

➤ Keep trying to find someone with whom you can relate.

➤ Ask others in your own culture how they handled communication.

➤ Spend some time just watching and learning.

➤ Suspend your own beliefs, values, and assumptions.

➤ Avoid making snap decisions, judgments, and comments.

➤ Change your own approach first.

➤ Try many ways to make contact.

➤ Don't give up!

> If your workshop does not have enough men or women in it, then change the culture rules. Instead of using the rule of men not talking to women, have blondes unable to speak to brunettes. Other alternatives are: eye color, age, hair color, and wedding bands—marriage. Make sure that the difference you choose is visible and unchangeable.

End the activity by telling everyone they did very well. Thank them for their great acting ability and efforts.

Not "I"

TYPE	Communication Skills, Diversity Awareness, Worldview
PURPOSE	Helps participants realize the importance of balancing and talking about the interests of both self and others
EQUIPMENT NEEDED	Flipchart and markers (optional)
PREP	None
TIME NEEDED	30 minutes

EXERCISE OUTLINE

INTRODUCTION	Participants talk about how to change the focus of their conversations.
THE ACTIVITY	Each participant tells a detailed story about a personal experience to a partner without using the words "I" or "my."
VARIATION	*Not He, Not She*
INSIGHTS	Participants talk about what they are learning.

If you conduct the activity with two people in a group, each will take a turn talking and listening. If you conduct it with three people in a group, each will take a turn talking, listening, and observing. If you decide to use this exercise in a large group setting, one or two volunteers will talk and the rest of the group will observe. All three approaches work well.

CONDUCTING THE EXERCISE: NOT "I"

INTRODUCTION Introduce the activity by explaining to participants that it can be very hard for many of us to focus on others' points of view. We naturally tend to go through life acting and speaking from our own experiences and values. This behavior can add to or even create difficulties in communication and managing differences.

 SAY Sometimes, one of the hardest things for us to do during a conversation is to remove the focus from ourselves. We often express our opinions, offer recommendations, lobby for our wants, and so on instead of really listening to and understanding the needs or wants of others.

Just think of small children and babies. We come into the world thinking that it revolves around us, don't we? We gradually learn that there are other people and other responsibilities that we have to tend to. It can be a hard lesson. The "terrible twos" and the teenage years offer strong testimonies to that.

Even as adults, it can be hard to listen to ideas, values, approaches, and practices that are different from our own.

Ask them what they think of this idea—find out whether they agree or disagree and why.

Continue the introduction by asking participants if there are benefits to focusing on one's self. Ask them what they are. You may wish to list these on flipchart.

 ASK
➤ There are benefits to focusing mostly on ourselves, aren't there?

➤ What do you think some of the benefits are?

People often feel that it may not be "correct" to talk about the benefits of self-centeredness in a conflict and communication workshop. You may have to offer a few suggestions of benefits to get them started.

Some of the benefits you can expect people to mention are:

➤ We get what we want.

➤ If everyone does what we want, people will think we are smart or important.

➤ It feels good when people listen to us.

➤ We like to be seen as "in charge."

➤ People that get heard, get respect, are promoted, etc.

➤ It is easier than trying to please everyone.

➤ People need someone to follow; some people are leaders, some are followers; the leaders get heard.

➤ If you don't speak up or make a decision or set a course of action, sometimes no one will.

The goal is not to analyze these answers, but just to bring them to light and write them down.

If someone says something that could be perceived as offensive, try to have him or her rephrase it in more generic, appropriate terms, if possible.

For example, you might want to rephrase a comment such as, "I talk from my perspective because I'm a man, and men are smarter than women, especially certain men. We deserve to be heard over others." You might say, "So what you are saying is, 'Some people feel that their ideas and practices are better than others, based on who they are, or to what group they were born.' Okay, let's put that up there."

In the rare case when the answer is so offensive that it cannot go on the board, just handle it by saying, "I don't think that is quite what we're looking for here." Explain the activity again, and quickly move on to the next person.

Now find out if participants think there are downfalls to focusing mostly on one's self. Ask what some of those may be and list them on flipchart. Some of the answers you may get are:

➤ You don't get as many perspectives.

➤ You don't learn from people around you.

➤ You may not make as many friends.

Because this activity focuses on a diversity issue, it is okay that you list things that are mildly egocentric. These are real reasons why people think, speak, and act from their own perspectives. When you get a strongly self-centered response like the one in our example, be encouraged, and stay focused. Try not to let someone's point of view offend you. Having someone in your session who is willing to offer this type of statement means he or she knowingly communicates this way. This is good, because awareness is the first step to changing behavior.

It is always better to have a workshop full of people that know they do something and why, than a classful that deny what they are doing, or do not realize they are doing it.

➤ People won't like talking to you.

➤ You may not have the best idea or all of the information.

➤ It's rude.

➤ You may not make the best decision.

➤ You can sound as if you don't know what you are talking about.

➤ You will not make the best decisions or plans.

➤ People won't want to do what you want because they are not included in making the decision.

➤ You won't get the buy-in from others on decisions and implementing plans.

It is okay to have more downfalls than benefits. The point of the session is that it is better to communicate in a more inclusive way.

THE ACTIVITY

Ask participants to think of a favorite vacation, personal accomplishment, the best job they had, a favorite city that they lived in, or some other interesting subject of a story. Encourage participants to think of something that excited them. Explain that they are going to tell this story to a partner in a few minutes. While telling the story, each team member will try to communicate how and why the story is significant or interesting.

SAY I'd like you think of a good story about your life—something that excites you or makes you feel proud, happy, or important. It could be a favorite vacation that you took with your family. It could be a great accomplishment that you or your team realized. It could be the best job you ever had or the best place you have ever lived.

Pause while they think, then continue.

It could be the birth of your first child, a trophy you won, the time the president of the company asked your opinion on something—anything that is important to you and that would make a good story.

Have each participant choose a partner. Tell them that they will each have two minutes in which to tell their story to their partner. Let them know that you will keep time, informing them of when to start, stop, and switch.

Inform participants that while telling one another their story, they are not to use the words "I" or "my." Tell them, however, that they need to explain why they chose this story, why it is interesting or important, and other significant details. Participants will need to find a way to communicate the information to their partner without breaking the rule.

SAY

There is one thing I did not tell you about this activity. One important rule that you must obey while telling your story: You will not be able to use the words "I" or "my."

This means you will have to find a different way to tell your story. I still want you to try to tell the story as passionately as you always do! Your partner should be thinking "Wow" while you are talking. Does everyone understand? Great! Let's get started!

Look at your watch to set the start time. Tell the first person in the teams to begin telling their story without using the words "I" or "my." After two minutes, tell participants to stop talking. Give them a couple of minutes to react or "vent" before going on to the next person.

People will typically laugh and/or complain a little, and start to discuss the activity immediately following the first story. Many will begin processing how they felt, how hard it was, etc. Give them a little time to do this. Then tell the second person to start talking, and begin timing.

If you are doing this with small groups or in trios, make sure the second and third speakers are identified at the beginning so the groups do not spend time figuring out who will go next.

INSIGHTS

When everyone has told his or her story, acknowledge how difficult it can be to completely change one's communication pattern, especially when there is important information to get across. Randomly ask people how the activity went, how they felt, what they observed in themselves and their partners, etc.

Start with the speakers.

ASK

When you were the speaker, were you able to complete the exercise without making a mistake? Was it difficult? Why? Why not?

Were you able to get all of the points across that you wanted to? Why not?

If you were, how did you do it?

How uncomfortable was it for you not to say directly what you felt or thought about something?

Did you bring out different points and highlight other things and other people since you couldn't directly focus on yourself?

What were you able to say instead?

What was your focus?

Now, address the listeners, and ask:

When you were listening, what did you notice about the speaker and his or her story?

Now move the discussion toward closure and insights.

ASK Could changing our perspective and way of speaking during a conflict change the outcome of the conversation? How?

What must one do in order to focus on something other than one's own perspective during a conversation?

What tactics could he/she use to accomplish this?

It was hard to do this today, but if you were to practice speaking this way more often, would it become easier for you?

End the debrief by telling participants that it takes thought, preparation, and practice to shift the focus from one's self to another person during a conversation. Explain to them that making this shift in communication style could help make their conversations more effective, especially when communicating across differences.

SAY Shifting the focus to another person is hard to do at first. It can feel uncomfortable. You may feel that you can't really say what you are thinking. However, shifting the focus allows you to look at the topic through "new lenses." It allows you to see other points of view that could be valuable to the outcome.

This style of communication also allows others to be included. The outcomes are generally more effective because of all the different types of input. No matter how wonderful we are, no one can think of everything! Sharing the conversation takes the pressure off and allows others to fill in the gaps. Everyone participates, everyone learns, and everyone helps create the solutions or outcome—even if the topic is just "where to go for dinner."

Further explain, that win–win outcomes are more likely in discussions where both parties try to see each others' perspective. Seeing another point of view is the first step to resolving differences.

Continue by explaining the importance of expressing one's own needs and wants.

ASK How happy do you think you will be with a conversation if you only focus on the other person's point of view? How frustrated?

I am not suggesting that you ignore your own feelings, thoughts, or ideas. Each person should contribute without having one person dominant.

VARIATION   *Not He, Not She*

This is an ideal variation of *Not I*, for use in diversity awareness workshops. Having people tell a story without referring to gender is a powerful demonstration of how difficult it can be for someone whose ideas or other diversity are not accepted. It can also demonstrate something of how it feels to try to fit in with the dominant group. The premise of telling a story to a partner is the same. The restriction is just a little different.

When using this or any exercise in a diversity session, plan for an extra ten to fifteen minutes for the debriefing. You will find that people will either have a lot to say (some things that could be perceived as negative) or very little to say. In the latter case, you'll want to make sure you highlight the main points yourself, and gently draw participants into the conversation.

People react differently based on how they feel about valuing diversity, and/or how experienced they are with the topic, awareness activities, behaviors, and people different from themselves.

THE ACTIVITY: NOT HE, NOT SHE

Ask participants to tell their partners a story without indicating the gender of anyone in the story. This means the speaker cannot say:

➤ He, she
➤ Her, his
➤ Wait**er**, wait**ress**
➤ Mail**man**, milk**man**
➤ Wife, daughter, mother, grandmother, niece
➤ Husband, son, father, grandfather, nephew
➤ Etc.

When pairing participants for this variation, it is best to pair people that know one another's style of communication. It can take place early in the session if participants know each other well. Otherwise, it is best to use the exercise later in the session after people have begun interacting. This way, new participants have a chance to gauge how others typically speak and interact.

INSIGHTS   Highlight how differently the person communicates when following the rule of not using gender. Storytellers are usually less animated, less descriptive, more serious, and are generally "not themselves" when telling this story. It is visually obvious that they are concentrating and thinking very hard in order to follow the rules of not using gender. Sometimes they appear frustrated or even give up.

In both versions of this exercise, the speakers will find it hard to tell their stories; however, removing gender seems to be an even more difficult challenge because so many of our words naturally comprise gender in their meaning.

SAY What does this tell us about our culture? Gender is important in our culture. There are roles, responsibilities and expectations attached to each gender. We have masculine and feminine words because of this.

You can partner this activity with Exercise 25: *What's in a Word?*

Key discussion points for this variation will focus on the listener and the speaker. In addition to some of the questions listed in *Not I*, be sure to ask these as well:

Ask the listener:

ASK
➤ What did you notice about the speaker's communication?
➤ Did the story make sense? Do you feel you know what happened?
➤ How was the telling of this story different from others this speaker has told you?
➤ Was the story interesting?
➤ How did you feel when you were listening to this story?

Ask the speaker:

ASK
➤ Did you get all the main points across?
➤ What did you leave out?
➤ How did you get around the rules?
➤ How did you feel when you were telling the story?
➤ Do you think the listener really grasped the significance of it?

End the discussion by telling participants that it can be very stressful when someone has to hide the personal point of view, some idea, or something personal that is not valued by others. This means that more effort typically goes into trying to be accepted, saying the "right" thing, or in not having their differences stand out than goes into adequately expressing themselves.

Sentence Relay

TYPE   Teamwork

PURPOSE   Participants practice using a shared goal to overcome obstacles.

EQUIPMENT   Flipchart paper and markers
NEEDED   Masking tape

PREP   Determine how many teams you will create. Plan on one flipchart per five to ten people.

Tape one sheet of flipchart paper to the wall for each team.

TIME NEEDED   15–30 minutes

EXERCISE OUTLINE

INTRODUCTION   Break the workshop group into teams with between five and ten people each.

THE ACTIVITY   Without talking to each other, the team members in turn write a sentence one word at a time.

INSIGHTS   The participants compare sentences and talk about what they are learning.

VARIATION 1   *Assigned Topic:* The facilitator assigns a specific topic for the sentences.

VARIATION 2   *Paragraph Relay:* Teams add sentences to other teams' sentences to create paragraphs.

CONDUCTING THE EXERCISE: SENTENCE RELAY

INTRODUCTION Introduce the activity by explaining that sometimes the most important thing people can share is a common goal, especially during times of difficulty.

SAY

We are now going to focus on the importance of shared goals and objectives—particularly when trying to resolve differences. Sometimes, the only thing two or more people can agree on is what they want to accomplish. Even when their approach differs or they don't see eye to eye on *how* to achieve their objective, just having a common idea of what needs to be done may help them be successful.

This can be especially true during times of conflict or when communication is strained. For example, if both parties simply decide that their goal is to speak to one another with respect, a lot more can be accomplished.

Now create teams of five to ten people. Have each team line up in front of a blank flipchart that has been taped to the wall. Give the first person in each line a marker.

Explain to the teams that they are to write a sentence on their flipchart by having each person on the team write one word. Tell them that they are not allowed to speak to one another during the activity.

Review the following rules. If you'd like, you can write them on a flipchart, whiteboard, or in participant handbooks.

➤ Each person in line must write one word in the sentence and pass the marker to next person behind them.

➤ Team members are not permitted to speak with one another during the activity.

➤ Each person on the team is to write only one word. The first person in the line writes the first word. The last person in the line writes the last word and punctuation mark.

➤ Sentences can be in any form: question, statement, or exclamation.

SAY

What I'd like you to do is write a sentence on the flipchart as a team. Each person on the team will contribute one word.

The first person will write one word and pass the marker to the person behind him or her. Then, that person will write one word and pass the

> Sometimes, you may want to specify a topic or theme for this activity. If you know that the team is dealing with a particular issue, or if you are going to be introducing a topic, or would like to review a topic, you can assign the subject matter. This helps to create an additional discussion point later. For example, you may ask them to write a sentence about teamwork, or communication, or resolving differences.
>
> If the activity is an icebreaker or mental break, I sometimes give them lighter topics to write about, such as a cartoon character or type of food or vacation spot.—Keami

marker to the person behind him or her, and so forth until each person on the team has written a word in the sentence. The last person on the team will write the last word and punctuate the sentence.

The most important rule for this activity is that you are not allowed to speak to or communicate with your team members in any way while you are writing the sentence. Just write your word and quickly pass the marker along.

The challenge is that the team must create a sentence that makes sense.

Ask participants if they have any questions before beginning the exercise. Answer their questions according the rules stated above.

THE ACTIVITY: SENTENCE RELAY

Once the teams are in place and you have answered their questions, ask the participants to write their sentences. If they finish quickly, you can have them create another sentence pertaining to the previous sentence. Watch them to make sure they are following the rules and having fun.

INSIGHTS Ask the participants to read their sentences and find out how they think it went. Start the conversation by asking:

ASK   Read your flipchart to us. What do you think of your sentence or paragraph?

Ask the first person in each line:

How did you decide what word to write first?

Then ask others in the room the same question:

How did you decide what word to write?

People near the front of the line will typically say that they were trying to write words that would allow the people behind them something to go on or write further about. The people near end of the line will say they were trying to start bringing the sentence to an end.

Continue the conversation using some of these questions:

ASK

➤ How did you decide how or when to end the sentence?
➤ Was this easy or difficult to do? Ask them to explain.
➤ How did you communicate without talking? Or did you communicate?
➤ Was anyone amazed that you achieved the goal?
➤ Was it difficult to add to other teams' sentences?

Now talk a little about key things people are learning from the exercise.

ASK

What were some of the obstacles you had to overcome in order to achieve the goal?

List their responses on the flip chart. You can expect comments like:

➤ couldn't talk with each other

➤ no time to plan

➤ didn't know what to write about or how to start

➤ did not know what others wanted to write about

➤ could not tell the others what I wanted to write about

➤ was worried that I wouldn't write a "good word" and that the next person wouldn't be able to add anything

SAY

Many of the fears and obstacles you listed also happen in everyday situations. Sometimes we have a common goal but cannot agree on how to achieve that goal. Sometimes we run into obstacles along the way. What are some real-life situations?

What this activity shows us is that when we find a way to focus on a common objective, we can overcome many of the challenges we are facing. Even if the outcome is not perfect—like the grammar in some of these sentences—we can still achieve some success by establishing an objective.

This is particularly true when communicating with someone with whom you are having a strong difference of opinion, or other really difficult challenge. Taking the time to set a communication goal that both of you can agree with, can help you overcome the conflict you are experiencing. The goal can be as simple as, "We'll talk about this for ten minutes, then take a break." Or "When we talk, we won't call each other names or throw things." Or it could be more tactical such as, "During this conversation, we'll identify all the things we agree on and all the things we disagree on. We won't talk about them, just list them."

Now ask the group for their ideas about the types of goals they can set with someone with whom they are having a hard time communicating. Write their comments on the flip chart. You can expect ideas such as:

➤ agree on an amount of time to spend talking
➤ maintain constructive communication
➤ respect differences in style and opinion
➤ listen to and acknowledge the other person's ideas
➤ agree to disagree
➤ find areas on which both people agree
➤ try to see the other person's point of view
➤ agree to treat one another with respect
➤ etc.

End the activity by telling everyone they did a nice job on their sentences. Let them know that they can practice setting little communication goals throughout the day so they can see just how effective goal setting is.

VARIATION 1   *Assigned Topic*
The main benefit of assigning a topic is to find out what people are thinking about that topic or idea, or to get them to think about the topic or idea. It will be a little harder for them to write the sentences because people in line will have different ideas about the topic, but will still be struggling to write a sentence that makes sense. This point will come up during the debriefing, and you will have a chance to address everyone's ideas and thoughts.

If you do not assign a topic, the activity works just as well. As a matter of fact, the sentences and paragraphs tend to be very funny and light because they can be about anything under the sun. This is a good approach if one of your goals during the session is to help people bond or feel more comfortable with one another; particularly people who work on the same team or for the same company which is trying to work out team issues.

VARIATION 2   *Paragraph Relay*
Once each team has written a sentence, and read it aloud, have the teams move to another team's flipchart and write another sentence that pertains to the previous team's topic. They must still follow the same rules. Then have them move again and write another sentence pertaining to the topic on that flipchart. Continue this until each flipchart has three or four sentences on it about a particular topic. This way, each person in the workshop will get a chance to add something to each flipchart.

Participants are usually able to create complete paragraphs about distinct topics, with each person in the room contributing, yet with no one speaking or planning what was to be written. The more sentences they are able to write, the more the group has to talk about.

The Squares Game

TYPE	Teamwork
PURPOSE	Shows how sharing points of view can sometimes generate a new way of seeing things
EQUIPMENT NEEDED	Flipchart and markers Markers, pens, or pencils for each table
PREP	Make a copy of Handout 7: *The Squares Game* (page 211) for each participant Draw the squares on a flipchart or overhead Place markers at each table
TIME NEEDED	20 minutes

EXERCISE OUTLINE

INTRODUCTION	Participants find as many squares as they can in *The Squares Game* handouts.
TEAM ACTIVITY	Participants compare what they found and find new solutions with partners and in teams.
INSIGHTS	Teams compare results with other teams and the facilitator and talk about what they are learning.

CONDUCTING THE EXERCISE: THE SQUARES GAME

INTRODUCTION	Distribute the handouts to each participant. Ask them to find as many squares as they can alone, without working with the people around them.

Tell them to use the markers in the center of the table to mark off the squares they find.

SAY Please take a look at the handout I just passed out to you. What I'd like you to do is count the squares you see on the page, and write that number at the bottom of the worksheet.

At this point, I don't want you to work with anyone, please work alone. Let's see who can find them all.

TEAM ACTIVITY Once everyone has found as many squares as they can, go around the room and ask participants how many they found. You will get many different answers. The most common answers:

> When I introduce the activity, I usually imply that this is a competition. Sometimes I even tell them that whoever finds the most will win some sort of prize. Doing this ensures that people will work independently at first and not speak with one another.—Keami

➤ 16

➤ 21

➤ 23

➤ 26

Once everyone has given an answer—and if no one has said "30"—tell them that they did very well, but there are more squares to find. If someone does say "30," continue with the exercise without yet giving away that 30 is correct. The puzzle solution is in Sample Chart 1. Have fun with it.

At this point, participants may start to catch on. The ones that found fewer than others know they are missing some. Whoever found the most will look particularly pleased with him- or herself. You can even be a little bit of an instigator here.

Say things like:

SAY What's going on here? Did I give out the same handout? Everyone hold up your sheet.

Wait until they all hold them up and look around.

John, how many did you get—24? Tracy, how many did you count—17? But you both have the same sheet.

Well, you've all done very well, but it looks like we can do better. There are obviously more squares than some of us thought. Let's try it again in teams.

Now, pair participants up with someone that has found a different number of squares. Try to remember the number that people found so that they can be paired accordingly.

SAY John, you said there are 24 squares. Tracy, you said you found 17. I'd like you two to work together now as a team.

Pair everyone up and wait until they are sitting together before you continue.

Okay partners, I want you to come to agreement about how many squares there *really* are on the sheet. Take a few moments to see which of you was right.

The partners start having even more fun now. The person who found the least in the pairs might even say something like, "Well, I think we know who is right in this group."

Typically, when participants are paired, they find even more squares. If John originally saw 24 and Tracy saw 17, when you ask them again, they may have found 26 or 28. This happens because they often are not counting the same squares when they started out alone. So when the first partner shows the second a group of squares, it gives the second partner more ideas about where there are more squares. Then they both start to see squares that neither of them saw before.

This does not always happen, so do not be discouraged if when you bring the groups back, they merely report the answer from the partner who originally had found the higher number of squares. If that happens, at least you have more people who are closer to the right answer.

Go around the room and ask each pair for their new answer. Again, have fun with it. Challenge the different answers; ask them all to hold up their sheets again.

SAY Hey! John, I thought you said there were 24. Tracy, what happened to 17? Now you both tell me there are 26?

Do not allow participants to tell you where the newfound squares are just yet.

Now have the participants form into groups of four or five people each and do the activity again. Check to see what progress they are making, then have them form two evenly sized groups (half the workshop group in each). They will continue to work together to find the most number of squares.

Finally, have someone from the group that has found the most squares come to the front of the room to demonstrate where the squares are on the model flipchart.

If neither group has found 30 squares, ask the person to show as many as they have found. Then ask the other group if there are any that they found that the first group did not. Have someone from that group come up and illustrate.

When both groups are finished, use *The Squares Game Answer Sheets* to show them where all the squares are on the model.

INSIGHTS Thank the participants for their work, and start a conversation about the exercise so far. Some questions to help get people talking include:

ASK

> ➤ How did you feel when you first found out that you did not find all the squares? How did you feel when you found out that others had found more than you did?
>
> ➤ How many of you were pretty sure you had found them all the first time I asked you to do this activity?
>
> ➤ How did you feel when you discovered that you had found the most or the least?

Now move on to how the teams worked together:

ASK

> ➤ Many of you were able to do much better with a partner. What methods did you use to come to consensus when you were working in pairs and groups?
>
> ➤ How did working with others help the process?
>
> ➤ How did it feel to have to listen to someone tell you the solution?
>
> ➤ How did it feel to offer the solutions you found?
>
> ➤ Were you open to what your partner or group was saying to you?

Comment on the different methods they used to communicate with one another while in pairs and in groups. You can also share things that you saw them doing or heard them saying during the activity that you thought were helpful.

Next, move the conversation to key learning points by asking some of the following:

ASK

What does this say about different perspectives?

Are there any benefits of having different points of view?

Do you think you would have been able to find all the squares if you had continued to work alone?

How did it feel at the end when I told you that you still had not found all the squares?

Are there times that we don't have all the information?

What are some things we can do to make sure we get the full picture when we are trying to resolve a difference?

End the discussion by reviewing some of the ways the pairs and groups worked together. Some common methods teams use in this exercise include:

DEMONSTRATION

➤ teams/groups counted the squares together
➤ traced the squares in colored markers
➤ showed each other their handouts to point out the different squares
➤ drew the squares on blank sheets of paper to show one another

COOPERATION

➤ one person spoke and then the next person spoke
➤ took turns telling each other what they found
➤ ignored their own sheets and started all over finding the squares
➤ copied from another group that was close to them
➤ just listened to what their partners/everyone else said

CHALLENGE

➤ questioned partner/team on what they found
➤ questioned whether the squares could be of different sizes, 2x2, 3x3, etc.
➤ asked others about their sheets

End the discussion by telling participants that we all have different perspectives and views of the world.

SAY During the activity, we had a goal of finding the most squares. We questioned one another, we demonstrated our findings on the model, and we did many things to help others see what we saw. Sometimes, we are not as patient in real life. We forget that not everyone thinks exactly the way we do, or sees a situation the same as we do.

It's important to remember during communication, and when differences of opinion arise, to do all you can to remain patient and explain to the other person what you are seeing or feeling. Most importantly, though, you must be ready to listen to the other person to hear what they see as well. If you both have the goal of finding the best solution, the exchange can be more successful.

Sometimes, the first thing you want to do is state and agree on the goal—just as we did with *The Squares Game*.

The more different viewpoints are available to you, the more options you will have. Our unique points of view help us to create new and wonderful approaches to all sorts of things—including problem-solving.

These differences can also cause a great deal of stress and conflict. Embracing this diversity takes practice.

Even though sometimes it is hard to see another's point of view at first, if you keep trying, a light bulb will eventually click and will often lead to more ideas and better approaches. When we remember to remain open to others' perspectives, we can learn things that will help us to find good solutions.

What You See
Is What You Get

TYPE   Conflict Skills, Diversity Awareness

PURPOSE   Participants learn about the impact our individual points of view can have on how we think and feel about other people's behavior.

EQUIPMENT NEEDED   Flipchart and markers

TIME NEEDED   30–45 minutes

EXERCISE OUTLINE

INTRODUCTION   Participants are told that the exercise will test their abilities as unbiased observers.

OBSERVATION   Participants watch two volunteers act out a conflict and watch carefully for specific actions.

REPORT   The facilitator writes the participant reports on a flipchart.

REFLECTION   The facilitator helps the group decide which of its observations are evaluations and which are observations.

INSIGHTS   The group talks about how easy it is for us to attach our own meanings to what we see around us.

> This exercise comes to us from Dr. Jennifer E. Beer, the author with Eileen Stief of The Mediator's Handbook (New Society Publishers, 1997). Turn to the Toolbox section to find out more about Jenny's work.

CONDUCTING THE EXERCISE: WHAT YOU SEE IS WHAT YOU GET

INTRODUCTION   Tell the group that this activity is a chance for them to test their listening and observation skills. Let them know that they will be watching as two volunteers act out a dramatic and noisy conflict for them.

Ask for two volunteers and help them to pick something to "fight" about in the role-playing. They can create their own scenario, but it is usually quicker if you help them by suggesting some topics they can choose from. Some scenarios that work well to get the role-play started are:

➤ Roommate A left a twenty-dollar bill on the kitchen table and now it is gone. Roommate A accuses roommate B, who says, "I didn't take your money. Leaving your money lying around shows how stupid you are."

➤ A teenager wants to borrow the family car and go on a weekend camping trip. The parent refuses, citing bad grades, missed curfews, and irresponsible friends. The teenager says, "You have ruined my life. I hate you."

➤ Neighbor A has asked neighbor B three times to turn down the music. B tells A, "Go away and mind your own business." A tells B, "I wouldn't mind so much if you listened to something decent for a change."

Talk privately with the volunteers for a few minutes. Tell them that you want them to take the argument to extremes: yell, stomp around, pound the table, and call names (within the bounds of the place you are conducting the workshop). Give them a minute or two to talk about some details between themselves while you explain their assignment to the group.

OBSERVATION   While the two volunteers are getting organized, tell everyone else that they are about to see a dramatization of a conflict. You want them to be unbiased observers.

 SAY   A lot can happen very quickly during a conflict. As you watch this demonstration, take notes about what you see and hear. Your notes should be clear enough so that we can reconstruct what you have seen. Be as specific as possible. Be as fair and nonjudgmental as possible. Whatever you see the actors do, write it in your notes.

Now let the volunteers act out their conflict. Encourage them to have fun misbehaving and to be as nasty as they can. People usually enjoy acting out this oway. If your volunteers seem hesitant, let them start again.

THE REPORT   Thank the volunteers for their courage, and have them take their seats. Ask the people in the workshop what they saw. Write their comments on the flipchart. You can expect comments such as:

➤ Devi raised his voice.
➤ Molly stomped out of the room.
➤ Molly slammed the door.
➤ Devi was being a jerk.
➤ Molly was being unreasonable.
➤ Devi was angry.
➤ Molly made a face.
➤ etc.

REFLECTION   Read the list on the flip chart to the group. Ask the participants if they think it is a list of observations, or a list of evaluations.

Allow some comment, then say:

SAY   It looks to me like we have a list that includes both observation and evaluation. What I mean is that an observation is "just the facts." An evaluation interprets the facts. It can be very difficult for us to observe without evaluation.

For example, a comment such as "Devi raised his voice," seems like a pretty straightforward observation. But it may be an evaluation if the observer has an opinion about "raised voices." A less evaluative observation might be, "Devi's voice was sometimes louder than it was at other times." In this case you could talk with the group about the point that while we can be fairly sure that Devi's voice was louder from time to time, we don't know why. He may have been angry, he may have a hearing impairment, or maybe Devi has a habit of talking louder from time to time.

As you read through the flipchart list again, ask the group about each item. Is it an observation, or is it an evaluation? Use a different color to mark an E next to evaluations and an O next to observations.

Comments such as "Devi was being a jerk" will be easy to see as evaluations. The group will have to practice for a while before it can identify comments such as "Molly made a face" as evaluative. A more accurate observation may be, "Molly's eyes opened wider as she pursed her lips," or "Molly's facial expression changed." For this example you could talk about how "making a face," is usually seen as a way to send a message. All we know is that we saw Molly's expression change. We may know what we mean when our face looks the way Molly's did, but we cannot be sure that we know what Molly meant. Molly may have been unaware of her change of expression. Maybe Molly is nearsighted and changes her face to see better, or maybe her face looks that way when she is thinking, or maybe she means exactly the same thing that we do when our face is that way.

INSIGHTS   When you have finished marking the list with Es and Os, you will usually have found that most of the comments have at least some evaluation built into them.

Ask the group how what they are learning from this exercise might help them with communication and conflict.

You can expect answers such as:

➤ We can catch ourselves when we are judging other people.

➤ We can see how what we assume about another's actions can color our reaction to that person.

➤ It shows us how misunderstandings arise.

➤ It makes me think about how easy it is to jump to conclusions.

Explain that some actions mean different things in different cultures. For example, several harmless hand gestures used in the United States, such as "thumbs up," "V for Victory," and "Okay," are actually considered offensive in other cultures.

Ask the participants:

ASK   If someone from the United States used those gestures while in one of those other countries, do you think people would make an observation or an evaluation of what they saw?

Another example:

ASK   Men in many cultures are comfortable walking hand in hand. What evaluation might people in a U.S. city make about two men holding hands in public?

It can also happen that a behavior that one person thinks of as extreme is thought of as minor by somebody else. Explain that in different countries and even within the same countries, different groups have different customs about eating, talking, touching, respect, etc.

If you have time, ask for some examples from the group's own experience of harmless actions that can be evaluated as wrong, strange, or even aggressive by people.

Exercises to Prepare
in Advance

The exercises in this section require more preparation than the quick idea generators in Section One. Some need handouts, overheads, flipcharts, or mailings to be finished ahead of time. All require that you have carefully thought through your objectives and have a clear understanding of the material.

Before you conduct the centering exercises in this section, you will want to read the next section, *Staying Cool in a Conflict*. Your preparation will pay off with exciting interaction and real learning for you and the other people in your workshop.

STAYING COOL IN A CONFLICT

"By the time I thought of what I should have said, I was at home, had dinner, and was lying in bed looking at the ceiling."

Some people seem to be better than others are when it comes to knowing what to say and do under pressure. They come across to us as unflappable, in control, maybe even wise. How do they do it?

There are many things that may help people stay unruffled in a conflict. One is that they have a lot of practice being in conflict situations. Another is that they feel reasonably sure that things will work out the way they want. A third way is that they are not upset because they have decided not to be upset.

[handwritten: MINDSETS FOR STAYING COOL.]

Practice counts for a lot. Exercises like the ones in this book, in *The Conflict Management Skills Workshop*, and others can help even very inexperienced people to invent new ways for themselves to respond to conflict. The more practice we have—in workshops and in real life—the more nimble we are when a conflict seems to be about to boil over.

A great exercise to give people a chance to practice staying calm in response to "in your face" conflict is *Hold Please* on page 163. This exercise was adapted from psychologist Paul Pedersen's triad training model. When Pedersen and others have used this model with counselors-in-training, they have found that the students become more able to get through to people who are aggressively resisting their help. In *Hold Please*, your group participants will get a chance to work calmly to get through to a resistant, emotional person whom they are trying to help.

STAYING "CENTERED"

People sometimes can stay calm in conflict when it is pretty clear that things will turn out okay. They may be confident in the outcome because of a powerful position they have. Sometimes a person feels that he or she is holding a trump card. This person may recognize this particular type of conflict or pattern and know that it is survivable and that all will be well in the end. What we will look at in many of the exercises in this section is how to stay "centered"— calm and relaxed while being able to make extremely rapid choices about what you will say and do.

Practice and experience are important and helpful when dealing with conflict, but they can come together to help you the most when—in the thick of things—you can calmly make effective choices about what to do.

Beyond the help that practiced strategies, experience, attitude, or even being powerful can give us is the ability to exercise what might be called "controlled relaxation." Martial artists, yoga practitioners, and others refer to this ability to relax mind and body together deliberately at a moment's notice and without thought as "centering." In order to facilitate the exercises in this section, you will need to be able to practice and demonstrate simple centering techniques.

If you are already familiar with a simple centering technique from martial arts, yoga, dance class, or some other source, then skip right to the exercises. If you need to learn or review some basics, read on. . . . You may be surprised at what you already know.

If you paint or draw, play a musical instrument, ski, golf, or play any sport, you probably already have been centering yourself from time to time. If you can tell a joke well without effort, or dance, or just automatically seem to know what piece to move on a checkerboard, you have probably been centering.

HOW CENTERING HELPS YOU IN A CONFLICT SITUATION

Centering is better than strategizing when you are in a conflict situation. With a strategy, you plan to do or say something based on your expectation of the other person's action—"I'll say 'A,' and he'll say, 'B.' Then I'll say 'Z,' and that'll get him!" Of course, your carefully planned strategy goes right out the window if the other guy says "Z" (or something unexpected, like "LMNOP") before you do.

Centering is a technique that leads to the abandonment of strategy in favor of allowing the appropriate choice of action or relationship with the other person to emerge.

Sound strange?

You have probably heard or read something about "fight or flight." The idea is that our brains tend to react in one of two ways when we are under stress. For example, if we are in a conflict we can either confront the other person (fight) or walk away and hope nothing else happens (flight). This may have worked pretty well for our ancestors. If you were confronted with a saber-toothed cat, for example, you would quickly either run away or hit it with something, depending upon your preferences. Nowadays, when we are faced with a conflict, we can often sense our body getting ready for fight or flight—our muscles tense, our heart pumps a little harder, we get an adrenaline rush, etc.

This physical fight or flight reaction still happens when we are centered. The difference is that when we are centered, we are able to send this energy toward a third choice. Think about it: One choice is to fight; the other choice is to flee. Both can make things worse than they already are. When you are centered, you can calmly apply what you have practiced and make split-second adjustments depending on what will work best for you and the other person.

A SIMPLE CENTERING EXERCISE

Here is how you do it:

You can find your physical center about three inches below your navel. Stand comfortably with your feet about shoulder width apart, take a deep breath in, pulling your shoulders up toward your ears as you do so. Let the breath out and let your shoulders fall as you breathe out. Imagine any muscular tension running like water from every part of your body, down your legs, and out through the soles of your feet into the floor.

> Chris Thorsen, who supplied many of the exercises in this section, describes the power of combining physical practice with centering in his section of the book *The Dance of Change* (Doubleday, 1999). He also has some tips for staying centered when you get off track. You may want to pick up a tape to help you relax and get centered. There are several. One that I use is *Aiki Mastery*, by Richard Moon. For ordering information, please look in The Toolbox section.—Bill

Smile a little smile as you relax. Breathe normally and enjoy the image of stress flowing into the floor through the soles of your feet. For example, if you have some tension in your neck, keep smiling and imagine the tension starting as a slow trickle that runs through your body and out through the soles of your feet and into the floor. Picture it in your mind.

For a more detailed relaxation and centering exercise, please see page 154 in *The Conflict Management Skills Workshop*.

When you feel ready, take the fingertips of one hand and lightly touch your center point— two or three inches below your navel. Breathe in and out: Let your belly go in and out like a lung as you breathe. This will help you to feel where your center point is and remember it.

Relax and smile as you continue to breathe. It's funny, but when you pay attention to yourself breathing, it can sometimes be difficult to not "make" yourself breathe. As you focus on your center, let yourself breathe easily—as naturally as if you were not paying attention to it. Stay focused on your center point—you can keep your hand there if you want—and notice each one of

> "So how long do I have to keep breathing before I get it?" Remember when you do this that you are learning, and that your mind will wander. His students once asked Morihei Ueshiba O Sensei, the martial artist who founded Aikido, how he managed to be so centered all the time. O Sensei answered that he was not more centered, just centered more often.

your natural breaths. Each time you breathe in, say quietly to yourself, "Breathe in." As you breathe out, say, "Breathe out."

You won't be perfect as you do this, but enjoy it, continue to breathe, smile, and say, "Breathe in . . . breathe out," with each breath.

Once you get the hang of it pretty well, you are ready to practice the centering exercises in this section. They are very straightforward, and once you run through them a few times, you will be able to lead them in a workshop. Find a friend to play with and have fun.

Four Roads to Resolution

TYPE Communication Skills, Conflict Skills, Teamwork

PURPOSE Participants test four roads to resolution: debate, withdrawal, paraphrase, and itemized response

EQUIPMENT NEEDED Three flipcharts on easels, with markers
Enough poker chips, matchsticks, paper clips, or some other token so that each participant will have two

PREP Prepare Flipcharts:
10: *Debate Schedule* (page 247)
11: *Paraphrase* (page 248)
13: *Recap* (page 250)

TIME NEEDED 4.5 hours, including a break

EXERCISE OUTLINE

INTRODUCTION Participants randomly select a point of view that they will argue for and defend.

PREPARATION Participants meet in separate groups to organize their thinking and prepare to support their points of view in a debate.

DEBATE Participants follow a structured debate format as they try to influence others' points of view.

BUY A POINT The facilitator leads a discussion of the various points of view, but limits participation by requiring participants to "purchase" the right to make a point.

PARAPHRASE   Participants talk over their differing points of view again. This time they must paraphrase what the other person has said before they can make a point.

ITEMIZED RESPONSE   Participants must now paraphrase and find one point of common agreement before they can make a point.

INSIGHTS   Participants talk about what they are learning.

APPLICATION   The group applies what they are learning to a specific difference.

CONDUCTING THE EXERCISE: FOUR ROADS TO RESOLUTION

INTRODUCTION   Tell the group that they are going to get a chance to look at several ways to approach a difference. In order to do this, you will assign them sides in an argument. The argument topics should be "hot" enough so that people are truly engaged, but not so controversial as to shift the focus from learning to the actual debate. Some topics that will work for this exercise include:

➤ Should the government subsidize airlines?

➤ Are consultants a good investment for our company?

➤ Is growing a company always a good idea?

➤ What is most important to look for when hiring a new manager—people skills or business knowledge?

Divide your group into two teams and tell them their topic and which team will take which side. There are some creative ways to split your workshop into smaller groups on page 268 of the Toolbox section.

PREPARATION   Ask each group to sit near one of the blank flipcharts. Have them turn the flipchart away from the other group, so they can secretly prepare for the next part of the exercise.

SAY   You will now have fifteen minutes to prepare for a debate with the other team. Use the flipchart to organize

Organizational psychologist John McGlaughlin came up with this exercise as a way to help a stalled group work through an argument they were having. John called time out, had them test various ways to talk about a difference, then had them apply what they had learned to their original problem. For more about John and his work, see the Toolbox section.

your main argument points and the logic to back them up. You may want to turn the flipchart around so the other side can't see your notes as you work.

Show the two groups Flipchart 10: *Debate Schedule*, and say:

SAY As you work, keep this debate schedule in mind. Each side will make an opening statement, and each side will have a turn for a rebuttal. Finally, we will open things up for questions. At that time, anyone from either side may ask questions of the other group.

Keep time for the groups as they prepare. Let them know when there are only five minutes left. When fifteen minutes have passed, check to see if they need more time to wrap things up.

DEBATE When the two groups are ready, set up the debate. Show the participants the *Debate Schedule* flipchart again, then let them begin their turn-taking. Your job during the debate is to keep track of time and to stay on schedule. You should not try to play peacemaker at this time. The debate usually becomes an argument by the time the groups reach the Q&A section. This is all right for now—you will work with them on more effective approaches later on.

BUY A POINT Interrupt the argument and quiet everybody down. Tell the two groups that they will continue to support the point of view you assigned to them for the rest of the exercise. Explain that they will now be able to talk in support of their topic for fifteen minutes without the structure of the debate.

For this discussion, they will need to make careful choices about what to say and when to say it.

Give two paper clips, poker chips, or other tokens to each participant.

SAY Now you will support the point of view I assigned to you in a general discussion. I have given you each two tokens that you can spend to make a point. As the discussion goes forward, you will need to choose the points you want to make very carefully. Each time you make a point, you will need to give me one of your tokens.

Be sure that everyone understands the rule, then start the discussion. As people speak up to make a point, collect a token from them. If someone spends both of their tokens, they will no longer be able to make a point in the discussion. You may have to stop the discussion at some point to re-explain the rules.

Stop the discussion after fifteen minutes. Ask people to hold up either one or two fingers to show how many tokens they have left. You will generally find that most people have kept at least one token.

Tell the group that you will all talk about what happened in the debate and in the "buy a point" conversation later.

SAY We have been through a lot in the last hour or so. You have debated and been in a conversation that required you to choose what to say and whether to speak up. We will talk about this later on. First, we will try a couple of other approaches.

BREAK At this point, your workshop group has been arguing, debating, and discussing for over an hour. Take a ten-minute break to allow them to clear their heads.

PARAPHRASE Now the group will have a fifteen-minute conversation with a new twist. They must listen carefully to what the other person has said, and paraphrase what they have heard before responding.

Show the group Flipchart 11: *Paraphrase*, and explain the steps.

SAY **1. LISTEN** You will be repeating back what you are hearing the other person say, so it is very important that you listen well. Try to notice their key points, and also how he or she feels about them.

> *Right Listening* on page 26 is a good followup or companion to this exercise.

2. PARAPHRASE When the other person has finished, you will paraphrase what you have just heard. You won't be reciting it back word for word. You will cover key points and give your impression about how the other person is feeling as well.

For example, if you were talking about airline subsidies, one person might say, "Subsidies are stupid. I can't understand why we have to keep bailing these guys out. If I go broke, I'm stuck with it!" A paraphrase might sound like, "You seem frustrated about airline subsidies. You question the need for them and see them as a double standard."

When you are sure that the group understands how to paraphrase, continue to explain the steps on the flipchart.

3. CHECK IN When you have finished your paraphrase, you will check in with the other person to be sure you were accurate. This is as simple as asking, "Did I get it right?" If they correct your paraphrase, redo those parts, and check in again.

4. MAKE YOUR POINT Now—after listening, paraphrasing, and checking in—you finally get to make your point.

5. LISTEN The last step is for you to listen again. This time you need to listen well while the other person paraphrases your point. Pay attention, because he or she will be checking in to be sure that the paraphrase is correct.

Check to be sure that everyone understands what to do, and then begin the conversation. You may need to prompt someone to get it started.

Liam, you had a strong point to make in our last discussion. Please get us started by making it again. All of you on the other side will need to listen carefully to what Liam is saying so that you can paraphrase and check in before making your point.

As the conversation goes forward, be sure that people are following the steps on the *Paraphrase* flipchart. Things may move slowly at first until people become comfortable with the steps. Let the group practice for at least thirty minutes.

ITEMIZED RESPONSE After about thirty minutes, stop the conversation. People will have noticed a difference in the quality of the communication. Congratulate the participants on how well they did, and ask them to hold onto their comments while you try one more approach.

 SAY What an amazing difference there is between this last conversation and our first debate. A lot was going on, and I am sure that you want to talk about it, but let's try one more wrinkle first.

Go to the *Paraphrase* flipchart and write "1 point of agreement" after "Check in" and before "Make your point." Your flipchart will now look something like Flipchart 12: *Itemized Response* (page 249).

 SAY What we will do this time around is to add this step—"1 point of agreement." This means that after you listen, paraphrase, and check in, you will need to find some common ground to agree on before you make your point.

Remember my example from before? The first person said, "Subsidies are stupid. I can't understand why we have to keep bailing these guys out. If I go broke, I'm stuck with it!"

After paraphrasing and before making a point, I will need to find one point of agreement. I may not agree with the other person's points, but I could say something like, "I agree that this is a frustrating and confusing topic." I could also find all or part of one of the other points toon which to agree.

Obviously, if there is no common ground that you can think of, then wait and let someone else on your side begin.

Now begin the conversation again. Remind people to follow each step.

INSIGHTS   Allow the conversation to continue for thirty minutes or so, then stop it and tell the people in your workshop that now it is time for them to talk about what they are learning. Show them Flipchart 13: *Recap*.

ASK ?   We have tried four different approaches to this topic. We debated, we limited people's ability to speak up, we paraphrased, and we found common ground. What did you notice that was different among these different approaches?

As the people talk about what they are learning, set an example by paraphrasing key points. Encourage others to do the same. If there are disagreements about key points, remind the participants to use what they are learning.

Some other questions that can help with this conversation are:

What is it about the debate format that makes it difficult for people to come to an agreement?

It is designed as a contest, not a collaboration.
It does not give an opportunity for finding common ground.

What happened when you had to pay to make a point?

I held back.
I was not sure if I should speak up or not.

Are there other times when you feel hesitant to speak up? What does that do to a conversation?

All ideas are not heard.
I may end up getting something I do not want.

What happens when you have to listen carefully enough to be able to paraphrase and check in?

You really have to think before you speak.
You may begin to understand the other person.
If you are missing the other person's point, you know right away.

What happens when you are forced to find common ground?

It is difficult.
You have to adjust your message.
People start looking for ways to cooperate.

APPLICATION   When the group is ready, ask them how they can apply what they are learning to work situations. If you are working with a team that works together all the time, ask if there are any differences inside the group or with other groups or departments that cause them to get stuck.

List these differences on a flipchart, and then ask the group to practice scripting what they might say in order to find common ground.

If you have time, members of the group can say some of the points the other side may usually make. The group would then practice responses—listening, paraphrasing, checking in, and finding common ground.

A Time You Felt Different

RIGHT LISTENING

*HW PREVIOUS NIGHT →
THINK OF A TIME YOU
FELT DIFFERENT.*

TYPE	Diversity Awareness, Worldview
PURPOSE	Participants learn about difference by telling and listening to stories from their own experience
EQUIPMENT NEEDED	Flipchart paper and markers
PREP	Prepare Flipchart 3: *Right Listening* (page 240) Have a copy of Handout 2: *Right Listening* (page 206) for each participant
TIME NEEDED	30–40 minutes

EXERCISE OUTLINE

INTRODUCTION   The group reviews listening skills.

ACTIVITY   Each participant tells a partner about a time when he or she felt different.

INSIGHTS   Participants talk about what they are learning and how they can use it to improve working relationships.

CONDUCTING THE EXERCISE:
A TIME YOU FELT DIFFERENT

INTRODUCTION   Take your time as you introduce this activity. You are going to ask people to tell a story about a time when they were uncomfortable or upset. Remember that your main function during the introduction is to help people feel comfortable enough to talk about themselves.

SAY   In this activity, we are going to look at how differences can affect relationships, inclusion, communication, and many other aspects of our lives. As human beings, we tend to categorize our world. This includes people. We notice differences in others—both physical traits and other characteristics, like education level or economic status. We also tend to place values and judgments on those characteristics.

Whether we do it consciously or not, people tend to react to the differences we represent. Those reactions shape how we see the world, how we treat others, and, ultimately, what we experience.

Pass out the *Right Listening* handout and show the group Flipchart 3: *Right Listening*.

To help with this, I am going to review a technique called Right Listening.

Go over the *Right Listening* flipchart with the group:

➤ Release tension and assume a posture that allows for listening without resistance

SAY   This means making yourself comfortable. It means getting into a position that allows you to stay pretty still, one that makes you very relaxed and comfortable, without making you drowsy or putting you to sleep. You want to be comfortable, but not cozy. In other words, you may want to sit back in your chair or on a soft couch, but not lay your head down or put your feet up.

➤ Perceive the speaker's feelings; step into his or her thoughts

SAY   Try to understand what the speaker was going through—what he or she is feeling about what he or she is describing to you. You need to understand why he or she is angry, or how what happened made him or her feel sad. You need to notice that they are frustrated, happy, or have some other emotion to help you understand, remember what is being said, and continue listening effectively.

➤ Silence your own sympathy and antipathy

SAY   Once you have identified what the speaker is feeling, you have to avoid feeling the same emotion, sympathy, or antipathy for what they are saying.

Right Listening involves a certain level of objectivity. You try not to become emotionally charged. Even though you note what the speaker is feeling, you remain neutral. This way, your own feelings don't cloud or influence what the speaker is saying to you. When we add our own spin to the story, we tend to add things to the story or take things away from the story that the speaker wants to be there.

For example, in one workshop a woman told another woman a story about going to a country music festival. They ate hush puppies (fried corn bread) and crowded into a hot tent so they could sit on benches and hear the music. The woman telling the story had a wonderful time at the concert. The woman listening to the story thought she had just heard about a vacation disaster: bad food, bad music, and uncomfortable seats.

Even if we agree with what the person is saying, or support them, it is best to try to remain neutral in order to hear them. We all know how difficult that can be. It takes practice.

➤ Feel the other person cognitively, not emotionally.

 SAY The goal is to be analytical about the speaker's emotion without passing judgments about the speaker while he or she is talking. For example, if a woman is upset about something that happened between her and a male co-worker, the listener has to avoid making judgments like: "Women are always getting upset over nothing" or "Men are always pushing women around!" Another example would be to avoid letting past history with the speaker influence your reaction to what he or she is saying.

➤ Check to make sure you understand the speaker and hear the details.

 SAY This just means checking with the speaker to make sure you are getting the details. You can ask questions to make sure you understand the details or the point of the story.

THE ACTIVITY

When you feel that the group has a good grasp of right listening, ask everyone to choose a partner. Have the pairs sit with one another. Ask the participants to think of a time when they felt different. Let them know that they will be talking about this time with their partners, and then sharing it with the group at the end of the activity.

 SAY I would like you to think of a time when you felt different. It can be when you were little, or an adult—a personal experience or a work experience.

The difference may be related to work, a childhood experience, or something else.

Give the group some examples. You can list them on flipchart or create handout if so desired. Or you can just mention a few of them as an example.

SAY Perhaps it was the first time you started school, or when you moved to a new neighborhood. Or maybe it was when you wanted to play football and the boys wouldn't let you because you were a girl; or maybe it was when you first started with this company or were promoted into your new position. All of these are valid answers.

Here are some examples you can use:

➤ when you first started high school, junior high, or college

➤ moved to a new city or neighborhood

➤ attended a meeting with people two or three titles above yours (VPs, Board Meetings, etc.)

➤ attended a meeting in place of your boss to take notes (i.e., secretary attending meeting with other managers, directors, etc.)

➤ traveled to another country

➤ the new person in a department or on a new project team

➤ arrived at a party where everyone was dressed more formally/casually than you were

➤ a card game/ball game/etc. starts up and you're the only who doesn't know how to play

➤ shopping with friends when you have the least amount of money (especially if it's a significant amount)

➤ test scores came back, and you had one of the lowest scores

➤ visited a neighborhood very different from your own; especially at night

➤ when you weren't allowed on the local sports team because you were a girl; and they didn't have a girl's team

➤ you were allowed on the team and were the only girl

➤ you joined an activity and were the only boy

➤ other boys were good at a particular sport, and you couldn't play well— and didn't really want to, anyway

➤ you spoke with a different accent than others

➤ you held a different point of view during an important vote or meeting

➤ as a leader, you had to explain a new, unpopular policy to your people

➤ you were the tallest/shortest/fattest/skinniest person in the main group

➤ you were the only one without/or with a college degree/diploma, etc.

Take your time to explain this. While you are talking, people will be thinking about the difference they feel comfortable sharing with others in the room. Give them time to think about it while you are talking by explaining the exercise slowly.

Continue by saying:

 SAY

Both you and your partner will each have five minutes to tell your stories to one another. I will keep time for you, telling you when to start and stop. While one person is talking, the other should be listening intently and commenting, when appropriate.

When telling your story, try to explain to your partner things such as how you felt, why it was difficult, how you handled the situation, whether or not it was resolved, how it was resolved, who helped you, and other key points.

Tell participants to decide who will speak first and second. Let them know that you will tell them when to switch. Ask them to start.

Keep track of the time and allow five minutes for each partner to speak. When the first five minutes is up, ask them to switch. When the second partner's five minutes are up, ask everyone to rejoin the workshop group.

INSIGHTS   Ask the different pairs what kinds of things the groups talked about. Record differences that were discussed on a flipchart in front of the room.

Some people may have told a story to their partner that they do not feel comfortable telling to the whole group. If this happens, respect their privacy and ask for volunteers to tell what they talked about. As people tell their stories about a difference, others will usually add to the conversation—especially if they experienced something similar.

As each person tells his or her story, encourage the group to talk about it. Some questions that will help the conversation along are:

 ASK

Has anyone else experienced something like that?
Was the experience the same for you?
How did you handle it?
What helped you?

You can also add your own story if you have experienced it. If it is something that is still going on, find out if others have any ideas on how to make it better.

Some of the key insights are as follows:

On what was the difference based?

When you ask this question, you are looking for a general trait, characteristic, or theme. For one of the items in the sample topic list, *"Only one without/ with a college degree,"* the difference is *education*. For *"You were allowed on the team, but were the only girl,"* the difference was *gender*. List the traits on the flipchart, not the entire situation. After listing the ones participants tell you, you can also ask for other differences that might matter, and list those as well.

 ASK How did you deal/or are you dealing with the situation?

Here you are moving into problem-solving mode. Some people will have anecdotes for how they solved the problem, some will not. For those that do not, ask:

What would have helped the situation?
What could someone else have done to make it better?

You can also get recommendations from others in the room.

In most cases where the situations were resolved or improved, there is usually someone that helped the person. This is important to point out as people are telling their stories. This will help move the discussion to problem solving and to proactive measures that help to reduce and remove conflict.

 SAY Have you noticed that in most cases where the situation was resolved that someone helped? What do you think this means?

The answer you are looking for here is that we cannot stand idly by and allow others to exclude some people. When we do this, we hurt others.

SAY All of us have the power to help a situation, ignore it, or perpetuate it ourselves. We can choose what action to take. What we are hearing is, when others get involved, situations improve.

Think of your example of when you felt different. Think of how nice it would have been to have someone support you, and help you, to be on your side. We can all relate to the feelings and frustrations that come with being alone—even though the situations might be different.

In order to experience good communication, build effective relationships and promote positive work and personal environments, we actively have to avoid leaving people out and making them feel different.

Now move the conversation to action planning.

 SAY One of the main goals of this activity is to help you identify with those who may be excluded, and to come up with some ways to keep it from happening or to fix it when it does.

This activity has shown that we can all feel different or left out some-times—often about some of the same sorts of things. In other words, we as people tend to be alike in many ways. The similarities between us can be key in resolving whatever differences we may be experiencing. Even if the similarity is simply knowing what it is like to be left out. The similarities help us build bridges and open communication.

Ask participants if they have ever been involved in a conflict with, or had trouble communicating with, someone who was different from themselves. Tell them the difference might have just been a strong difference of opinion. Ask how this situation is similar to the activity we just did.

ASK How might the feelings and solutions be the same?

Have you ever considered that the person with whom you are having the problem might be feeling very hurt or embarrassed or uncomfortable—similar to how you all said you felt during "a time you felt different"?

Get some responses. And watch the light bulbs come on as people start to connect and empathize with what their "foes" may be feeling.

To finish, ask the participants to brainstorm some things they can do to help remove, or at least reduce, the problems that can exist between two or more people that are different. Write these on a flipchart labeled *Resolutions.* Hang the *Resolutions* flipchart next to the *Differences* flipchart.

ALTERNATIVE DISCUSSION POINT   This exercise can also be used to begin a discussion around which differences are valued, and which are not by different groups of people. See the discussion in Exercise 1: *Three Similarities and One Difference.*

Centering
under Pressure

TYPE Centering, Diversity Awareness

PURPOSE Give people a chance to practice staying calm under the pressure of confrontation.

EQUIPMENT NEEDED None

Centering under Pressure works well by itself or in combination with I *Lean*. These exercises come to us from organizational consultant and Aikido master Chris Thorsen. For more about Chris and his work, please turn to the Toolbox section.

PREP You need to be able to explain and demonstrate a simple centering technique. For help with this, see *Staying Cool in a Conflict* on page 77

You may also want to prepare Flipchart 7: *Centering under Pressure Practice Steps* (page 244) as a flipchart or overhead in advance.

TIME NEEDED One hour

EXERCISE OUTLINE

CENTERING EXERCISE Make sure that everyone understands the basic concept.

DEMONSTRA-TION AND INTRODUCTION Work with a volunteer while explaining the exercise.

PRACTICE Participants work with a partner to practice staying centered under pressure.

INSIGHTS Everyone reflects on the exercise and talks about lessons learned with the group.

ACTION PLAN   The facilitator checks for ideas about how to apply what was learned to the workplace.

CONDUCTING THE EXERCISE: CENTERING UNDER PRESSURE

CENTERING EXERCISE   Tell the group that you are going to work together on being centered and see what it feels like to keep your center when distracted by a confrontation. If you have not done centering exercises with this group before, ask for someone to explain what centering means for them. You may get responses from people with experiences in workshops like yours, or from people who have learned about centering through meditation, yoga, martial arts, or some other activity.

Explain that one way to look at centering is as a tool that actually helps you to stay calm enough to approach conflict the way you would like. When you are centered, you can calmly make split-second assessments and adjustments to what you are saying and doing in order to help you and the other person get through the conflict all in one piece. Practicing good technique along with centering can help you act honestly without hurting others or yourself.

Now lead the group through the simple centering exercise from *Staying Cool in a Conflict* on page 77. If you have already done centering exercises with this group, you can skip directly to the next step—Demonstration and Introduction.

DEMONSTRA-TION AND INTRODUCTION   Ask for a volunteer who doesn't mind being touched lightly on his or her chest. Have the volunteer join you in front of the group. You and your volunteer will demonstrate the exercise while you explain it.

Ask the volunteer to stand with her or his feet shoulder-width apart, to relax, and to get centered. When the volunteer is ready, explain that you are going to push against his or her chest.

Say to the volunteer:

SAY   I'm going to stand next to you and gently push you on your chest with my fingers. Your job is to prevent me from pushing you backwards without using your hands or moving your feet.

Ready?

Check to be sure your volunteer understands, then quickly move your hand up to the volunteer's chest as if you are going to push. Instead of pushing, stop about an inch away from the volunteer's chest. Most people will stumble forward a little, because they have anticipated your push. Others may flinch back. This can get a laugh from the group, so enjoy it, but be sure not to embarrass your volunteer. Thank them for helping you out, and explain that almost everyone would have a similar reaction. Leaning into the expected push is the fight reaction in "fight or flight." Flinching is the flight reaction. (For more on "fight or flight," see *Staying Cool in a Conflict* on page 77.)

Tell your volunteer:

 SAY I won't move that quickly again. Now we will work together so that you can stay centered while being distracted by a confrontation. The confrontation will be me pushing you while you want to stay put. If you push against me, that is the fight reaction. If you duck or back away, that is the flight reaction. Your third choice is to be centered. Let's see what happens when you are centered and I push gently and steadily against your chest.

Ready?

When your volunteer is centered and says "ready," place your fingertips on her or his chest—on the breastbone an inch or two below their throat.

 ASK Still centered?

If the volunteer says yes, then start a firm but gentle push on her or his chest. If the volunteer is centered, you will be able to gradually increase pressure without moving her or him backward. This may take a few tries. If the volunteer is having a little trouble, do some coaching. The volunteer can focus on breathing or shift her or his upper body forward a bit. Talk the volunteer through it until you can push without moving her or him. Tell the group:

 SAY Now that my volunteer is centered, I can push pretty hard. This is the same kind of coaching and practice I want you to do with one another in a little while.

Stop pushing and let your volunteer relax. Ask her or him for comment. Congratulate the volunteer and ask for some applause—your volunteer is becoming quite good at this. Tell the volunteer you are going to demonstrate one more time. When he or she is ready, start your gentle push again.

Now—still gently pushing—say quickly to your volunteer:

SAY What did you have for breakfast yesterday?

This small distraction will usually throw your volunteer off center, causing her or him to stumble back a little. Stop pushing, and say:

SAY My volunteer has done a great job. See how easy it is to be pulled back off center? These exercises come to us from a martial art called Aikido (*eye-key-dough*). The founder of Aikido, called O Sensei, knew that even the best of us lose center from time to time. When his students asked him how he could be so centered, he said, "To you it looks as though I don't lose my center. This is not so. . . . I simply notice it sooner and return more quickly."

Now it is time for all of us to practice.

> It is important for you to stay centered during this exercise so that you do not lose sight of what you are trying to show. Be sure that you speak gently to your volunteer and partner with her or him so that you both are centered together. The object is not to trick the volunteer, but to show the group a typical reaction.

PRACTICE Ask the participants to each find one partner to work with. Tell them that they each should get a chance to push and to be pushed. Before they begin, remind them of the steps. You may use the overhead *Practice Points*, or simply list them on a flipchart:

➤ Ask permission to touch.
➤ Both get centered.
➤ Ask if your partner is ready.
➤ Push while your partner remains centered.
➤ Ask your partner a question to distract them from center.
➤ Trade places and do it again.

Walk quietly around the room while the pairs are practicing. Offer coaching here and there if it is needed. Be sure that people are being gentle with one another.

Let the exercise go until everyone has a turn. You will know the group is finished when you hear them talking about other things. Stop the exercise by thanking the group and asking them to return to their seats.

INSIGHTS Once everyone has settled down, ask them how it went and what they noticed or learned during the practice. Here are some questions you can ask if the group needs some prompting:

ASK ➤ What more have you learned about centering? Any new insights?
➤ How is centering different when you are under pressure?

> One of the first times I saw Chris Thorsen and his partner Richard Moon lead these centering exercises, it was with a group of about thirty customer service representatives and their managers. Their volunteer was a woman who weighed about 120 pounds. It was quite impressive to see this physically powerful black belt push on this small woman and not budge her. The point was well taken: centering isn't about physical strength or about beating somebody at a game. It is about focusing and relaxing. As Chris and Jeff Dooley write in an article in the systems thinking book *The Dance of Change* (Doubleday, 1999). "You are your personal terra firma."—Bill

➤ Did anyone have any trouble?

➤ Was your coach able to help you?

(If someone had a lot of difficulty, you can work with them on the spot or during a break.)

ACTION PLANNING Centering can be a foreign concept for some people. They may have some difficulty figuring out how to apply this and other centering exercises to business. This is understandable. It is a good idea to bring the learning back to workplace applications from time to time. Ask the group:

ASK   **How can what we have just learned help us when we go back to work?**

There is no right answer to this question. Some of the simple points you may want to reinforce are:

➤ Centering is helpful when we are in pressure situations.

➤ We need to remind ourselves to return to center when something throws us off.

➤ We can help each other stay centered by talking about it and coaching one another.

Wrap up by telling people that we get better at returning to center the more we practice. The hard part can be remembering to practice. Suggest that people learn to build practice into their everyday activity by doing some or all of the following:

➤ Use the ringing phone to remind you to be centered—first ring, breathe; second ring center; answer on the third ring.

➤ Sit up straight in your chair, breathe, and center yourself while waiting for your computer to boot up.

➤ Center yourself while waiting for traffic lights to change, or while you are "on hold."

➤ Center yourself before getting up to speak in a meeting or outside your boss' door before going in.

➤ If you do any kind of regular physical exercise, see what changes for you if you work out while consciously centering yourself.

➤ Any other opportunities the group can think of.

How Soon Is Possible?

GREAT FOR COMMUNICATION, TIME MGMT.

TYPE Communication Skills, Teamwork

PURPOSE Help participants understand how easy it is for people to misunderstand the messages we send.

EQUIPMENT NEEDED Flip chart, markers

PREP Prepare Handout 8: *How Soon Is Possible?* Quick Survey sheets (pages 212–213) in advance.

OPTION Handout 8 can be sent to participants in advance along with Handout 9: *Sample Survey Cover Memo* (page 214)

TIME NEEDED 30 minutes, not including time for sending out and compiling surveys

EXERCISE OUTLINE

INTRODUCTION AND SURVEY Distribute the quick survey sheets at the beginning of the exercise or before the class meeting. Ask participants to fill in their responses to the survey and turn them in.

Like a lot of good exercises, this one is simple to do, yet can yield some powerful results. I made this one up on the spot with a group of regional sales managers who were trying to figure out whose fault it was that instructions were not being followed properly. The exercise not only moved them away from trying to find someone to blame, and it gave the managers a lot to think about when it came to how well they were passing on their expectations to their teams. I usually hand out the survey in this exercise just before a lunch break so that I can use break time to compile the data. It will work just as well if you send out the survey before your workshop, so you can get them back in time to have your numbers crunched in advance.—Bill

COMPILE DATA   Compile the data and prepare overhead, handouts, and/or flipchart of the results.

DISPLAY DATA   Allow time for participants to review the compiled data and draw conclusions.

INSIGHTS AND ACTION PLAN   Facilitate a brief discussion of the results and how they may be transferred to the "real world."

CONDUCTING THE EXERCISE: HOW SOON IS POSSIBLE?

INTRODUCTION AND SURVEY   You may choose to hand out the *How Soon Is Possible?* Survey during your workshop or ahead of time.

    If you choose to have the participants receive and fill in the survey form during the workshop, you will not need to use the cover memo. Tell them:

 SAY   Here is a quick survey to help us talk about how clear our communication is when we speak or send e-mails to each other. Please circle the number for the response that is closest to what you mean when you use one of these words or phrases here at work. There is no need to put your name on the survey. Once you have finished the survey, turn it in so I can put all the results together. We will then compare notes.

If you decide to send the survey to the participants ahead of time, use Handout 9: *Sample Survey Cover Memo* on page 214.

> If you decide to compile the survey data on a lunch break, it will save time if another trainer or a workshop participant volunteers to help you. I like to prepare an Excel spreadsheet in advance so that the only thing left to do is to plug the numbers in and generate the bar graphs.—Keami

COMPILE DATA   The data you are going to feed back to your participants is a set of averages that you will put onto two separate bar graphs. You can show them the graphs on handouts, by copying them onto a flipchart, or by projecting them as an overhead.

    Here's how you arrive at the averages:

1. Add up all of the numbers circled for question number one.

2. Divide that total by the number of people who answered that question.

3. Chart the answer to your division problem on a bar graph.

4. Repeat these steps for each of the questions in the first section to complete your first graph.

5. Name your first graph *How Soon Is Possible?*

6. Repeat steps one to three for each of the questions in the second section to complete your second graph.

7. Name your second graph *How Often Is Often?*

Your numbers will vary, of course, but your graphs will look something like Sample Chart 2.

DISPLAY DATA Show the graphs to the participants. You can distribute them as handouts, copy them onto flipchart paper, or project them from an overhead.

SAY Here are the averages from your survey responses. It looks like we can mean a lot of different things when we say things like "ASAP," or "frequently." Take a couple of minutes to look at the graphs, then we will talk about them.

INSIGHTS Start with a simple, open-ended question to the group, such as:

What do you think?

Responses will vary, but the point that is generally made is that these commonly used phrases and words can have a range of meanings. If everyone in the room agreed on the meaning of a word or phrase, its average score would have to be a whole number (that is, 1, 2, 3, 4, or 5 instead of, say, 3.9). If you need to prompt the group a little to encourage their participation, focus on just one word or phrase. For example:

ASK Let's take a look at "ASAP." Who would like to tell me what they mean by "ASAP"?

Get responses from three or four participants to show how "ASAP" can suggest different time frames for different people.

Take a word or phrase from the second graph and ask three or four participants for their meaning. For example:

What about "rarely"? How many times a year does something happen in order for you to say that it happens "rarely"? What if you said that something happens "very rarely"? Would that be different?

Encourage discussion by asking the group to come up with more examples on its own.

ACTION PLAN   Move the group into the action planning section of the exercise by saying that confusion and conflict can often happen when people think that what you are saying means something different from what you wanted it to.

ASK ?   So what do you think we should do about this?

Write the group responses on a flip chart. Typical responses include:

➤ State specific time frames.
➤ Be clear about how much time is required for a specific goal or task.
➤ Write "SMART" goals.
➤ Ask people for input on tasks or goals that you are assigning to them.

When you have collected all the responses, ask the group which of the ideas they are willing to use. When the group has picked the ideas they are willing to commit to, ask them how they will follow up to be sure they are using them. Some ideas that have worked for other groups are:

➤ Have the trainer, manager, or other group member send out a monthly reminder to use the ideas.

➤ Have the manager remind group members whenever someone does not use the new ideas.

➤ Have group members give one another permission to privately remind one another whenever instructions or other communications are unclear or don't use the ideas the group has agreed upon.

Sum up by thanking the group for their good work. Remind them of the need to be clear and specific when communicating—unclear communication can lead to unproductive conflict. Repeat the ideas for change the group has come up with and how they plan to follow up.

VARIATION   Facilitating the Exercise for a Large Group
It is easy to adapt this exercise for large groups, even for groups of more than one hundred. Simply make the following changes:

➤ Allow for at least one hour for the exercise, not including time spent sending out and compiling surveys.

➤ Be sure to send the survey out to participants in advance. Require them to return it in enough time for you to have your graphs ready before the workshop.

➤ Project the graphs on an overhead, and pass them out as handouts.

➤ The discussion and action plan sections should take place as small group discussions with each group reporting their ideas for following up to the larger group.

I Lean

TYPE   Centering

PURPOSE   Help people practice centering by identifying what it feels like to be physically off-center and then coming back

EQUIPMENT NEEDED   None

PREP   You need to be able to explain and demonstrate a simple centering technique. For help with this, see *Staying Cool in a Conflict* on page 77.

TIME NEEDED   20 minutes

I *Lean* works well by itself or as a warm-up. It is a great lead-in to *Centering under Pressure* and *Hold Please*. I *Lean, Centering under Pressure,* and *Energy Jump* all come to us from organizational consultant and Aikido master Chris Thorsen. For more about Chris and his work, please turn to the Toolbox section.

EXERCISE OUTLINE

CENTERING EXERCISE   Make sure that everyone understands the basic concept.

LEANING OFF-CENTER   The group experiences being off-center and "coming back."

INSIGHTS   People talk about what they felt, and apply it to what sometimes happens at work.

EXPLANATION   The facilitator sums up the exercise and makes the point that being centered is a moving target.

CONDUCTING THE EXERCISE: I LEAN

CENTERING EXERCISE

Tell the group that you are going to work together on being centered and see what it feels like to lose your center and be able to come back. If you have not done centering exercises with this group before, ask for someone to explain what centering means for them. You may get responses from people with experiences in workshops like yours, or from people who have learned about centering through meditation, yoga, martial arts, or some other activity.

Explain that one way to look at centering is as a tool to help you stay calm enough to actually approach conflict the way that you would like to. When you are centered, you can calmly make split-second assessments and adjustments to what you are saying and doing in order to help you and the other person get through the conflict all in one piece. Practicing good technique along with centering can help you act honestly without hurting others or yourself.

Now lead the group through the simple centering exercise from *Staying Cool in a Conflict* on page 77. If you have already done centering exercises with this group, you can skip directly to the next step—*Leaning Off-Center*.

LEANING OFF-CENTER

Have the group stand in a circle about an arm's length from one another. They will all face you as you stand in the middle.

Ask them to take a deep breath or two and center themselves. Once you are all centered, ask them to lean carefully to the left—as far as they can, but not far enough to fall over. Ask them to hold that position and tell you about any sensations or feelings. You can expect comments like:

➤ I am thinking more about leaning then centering.
➤ I feel my center moving to one of my legs.
➤ I am starting to tense up.
➤ This is distracting.
➤ My breath is moving up into my throat.

(Of course, whatever they are feeling in an exercise like this is the "correct" answer.)

After a few minutes, ask them to return to a more natural stance. Have them re-center themselves, and ask them how they know when they are back. You can expect comments like:

➤ My breathing is settling down.

➤ My muscles are relaxing.

➤ I feel more balanced.

➤ My feet are both all the way flat.

Repeat the exercise three times. The first time, ask the group to lean far to the right. Then have them do the exercise and lean back. Finally, ask them to repeat the exercise while leaning forward. Each time you repeat the exercise and lean in a different direction, ask them about their experience. Have them describe how they can tell if they are "out of" or "in" their natural center.

Point out that we are constantly leaning toward thoughts of the past and worries about the future that can pull us off center. Being able to recognize when this is happening will help us to come back to center more often.

INSIGHTS   Ask the group:

What did you discover about the nature of center?

What makes us leave center, and how do we get back?

What's the value of centering?

Who would like to tell about a past experience when you naturally centered yourself?

When might centering make a difference in a contentious conversation or conflict situation?

EXPLANATION   Make the point that centering is dynamic. It is a moving target. We are always moving in and out of center.

 SAY

It's something like an airplane moving on and off course in response to changes in the wind and weather. We're not looking for a straight line when we fly. It's the same with centering. Centering isn't a place we get to and try to hold onto. Centering is an ongoing practice of returning to home.

You can use the example of when we might act outside of our values, realize it, and change our behavior.

So do I need to be a black belt or some kind of guru to lead these exercises? Not at all. These exercises are all about calming your mind and body and allowing them to work together. Some philosophies and religions include centering in their spiritual practice, and you certainly can do that if it helps you, but these exercises work very well if you practice them as purely physical activity.

Minefield

TYPE Communication Skills, Conflict Skills, Teamwork, Worldview

PURPOSE Participants examine how they work within the group and how the group works together.

> One of your most important roles during this exercise is to keep everyone safe while they are blindfolded. If you have a very large group, have one or two helpers keep an eye out for where each person is trying to go and what effect it has on the others.

EQUIPMENT NEEDED 30 feet of soft cotton clothesline
30 balls of different sizes
One bandana or other blindfold for each participant
Paper and pens/pencils
A large, open space

PREP At least one week before the session, let everyone know that they will be participating in a physical activity that will require them to wear loose-fitting, comfortable clothing and shoes. Women should not wear skirts or high heels.

TIME NEEDED 30–40 minutes

EXERCISE OUTLINE

INTRODUCTION Rope the group together so that it has to move as a unit. Explain scoring while tossing balls around the exercise space. Blindfold each participant.

THE ACTIVITY The group tries to find as many balls as it can.

INSIGHTS Participants talk about the process, communication, successes, and failures they experienced during the exercise.

ACTION PLANNING   The group decides how to apply what they are learning to their work together.

VARIATION   Conducting This Exercise with a Large Group: Subgroups compete to find the most balls.

CONDUCTING THE EXERCISE: MINEFIELD

INTRODUCTION   Gather the group in the center of the exercise area. Ask them to cluster together in as tight a bunch as possible. Once the group has gathered together, tell them to take one more step toward the center.

Explain to the group that in this exercise they will need to work together and move as a single unit. In order to help them to do this, circle the group with the clothesline rope and tie it in place. People on the outside of the bunch will need to hold onto the rope to keep it from falling. Be sure that there are no trailing ends of the rope that anyone could trip on.

Let the group know that their assignment will be to score points by roving around the exercise area and picking up as many balls as possible. As they watch, toss the balls around the area, and assign points to different sized balls. (For example, a golf ball is hard to find. It may be worth 500 points. A basketball is easy to find. It may be worth only five points. A baseball is somewhere in the middle, and may be worth 150 points, and so on.)

At this stage of the game, people are usually laughing and joking and not paying close attention. This will help you with the setup. Once the group is tied together and the balls have been spread over the exercise area, tell the group that they will be blindfolded for this activity. Very quickly pass out the blindfolds and be sure that everyone puts one on.

A word about blindfolds: People who wear glasses will need to take them off in order to put on their blindfolds. It is best to collect their glasses and put them on a table or other safe place away from the action. Be sure that they see where you are putting their glasses so that they are not worried about them. From time to time, you may also have a participant who is frightened by being blindfolded. If someone has a strong objection, have him or her slip out of the group and join you as a "silent observer."

THE ACTIVITY: MINEFIELD

Once everyone is blindfolded, tell the group that they can begin. Tell them that they have fifteen minutes to complete the task.

For the next fifteen minutes, your main job, with the help of any "silent observers," is to make sure that people are safe. Make sure that the group is not moving toward anything hazardous. If you are working out of doors, watch for uneven ground. Also be sure that people in the middle of the group are not being stepped on and that people in contact with the rope are not being bruised or cut by it.

Encourage the group as it moves around the exercise area, but do not give them any hints. When they find a ball, cheer with them. When about five minutes are up, start announcing the time. People will ask you if there are balls left. Tell them how many, but not where they are.

As the group moves around the exercise area, watch for behavior that you can talk with them about later. For example:

➤ Did the group develop a system, or did they randomly wander?

➤ Who is listened to in the group? The loudest? The one with the best idea? The one who sounds the surest? The boss?

➤ Does leadership shift to different people?

➤ Does everyone contribute, or are some just along for the ride?

➤ How are disputes solved?

➤ Are people careful of one another?

➤ Are some people ignored even if they have a good idea?

➤ Is there any "cheating" going on?

➤ Are there "near misses" that could have been successes if the group had cooperated?

➤ As you call out the time, and the stress level builds, see if the group's behavior changes.

When the fifteen minutes are up, ask the group to stand still, and to keep their blindfolds on. Tell them how many unfound balls are left, and ask them if they would like to continue, or if they would like to stop. If they decide to continue give them five more minutes.

INSIGHTS   After the time has run out, ask everyone to stand still and to remove his or her blindfold. Thank them for their hard work and ask them if they are standing where they had thought they were standing. Often groups or individuals will have come up with some system to determine where they are in the exercise area. Sometimes this even fuels some disagreements about what to do. Only rarely are people accurate when arguing about their precise location.

People can now return to their seats, sit on the ground, or otherwise get comfortable. Invite any observers to join in, but be sure that everyone has a chance to be heard. Begin the conversation with an open-ended question such as:

 ASK   How did that feel?

Withhold your own observations about the group behavior until participants have had a chance to talk about their experience. Another open-ended question that can help them think about what they are learning is:

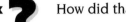 **ASK**   What possible business reason could there be for such a silly exercise?

As the conversation continues, you may want to interject your observations in the form of questions. In other words, don't say, "Marjorie kept coming up with ideas that were taking you in the right direction, but nobody paid any attention to her because she speaks so softly and is an administrative assistant in the midst of a group of senior managers." Instead, help the participants find the points themselves with questions such as:

 ASK   Did anybody have ideas that no one else heard?

How did it feel for people who had ideas that the group didn't try?

Who took the lead, and why?

Sometimes this exercise shows us that louder voices or male voices are heard more than others are. Did that happen here?

Even if you have some strong opinions about what you have seen the group do, continue to ask questions that will help them to think. They know best about their experience and may answer in ways that surprise you. Every time you facilitate this fun and simple exercise, you will learn more and more about how groups work together under pressure.

ACTION PLANNING   If your group regularly works together, be sure to take the opportunity to transfer what they are learning back to the workplace. You now can bring the team back into the classroom and begin some action planning. Some follow-up activities may include:

➤ conducting a dialogue session around why the team does not listen to certain people on the team

➤ brainstorming other communication breakdowns on the team and creating action plans to solve them

> ➤ taking a team communication survey to further identify communication opportunities

> ➤ writing specific action items to help improve the communication troubles that surfaced during this activity

If the people in your workshop group do not normally work together, break them into small groups for action planning. Have each group brainstorm solutions to some of the communication problems they encountered during the activity. Then copy each team's solutions and pass them out to the entire class.

VARIATION   Conducting This Exercise with a Large Group
The largest group we have roped together for this exercise had about twenty people in it. The exercise works well with even larger groups if you split them into groups with about fifteen people each.

You can have several groups of about fifteen people each roped separately and competing to see which of the groups will find the most balls. You will not only need more balls for the larger group, but should be sure to have at least one helper for each subgroup to help with observations and to ensure the participants' safety.

Missing
the Meaning

TYPE   Communication Skills, Diversity Awareness, Worldview

PURPOSE   Raise awareness of some cross-cultural communication differences by giving native speakers a sense of speaking English as their second language. Please note: It is very important to the success of this exercise that you do not reveal its purpose until you are well into the debrief/discussion section.

> This exercise comes to us from Cass Bing, vice president of human resources and new business development for the cross-cultural consulting and training firm ITAP International. The Toolbox section has more information on Cass and her work.

EQUIPMENT NEEDED   None

PREP   Prepare Handout 10: *Carriage House Lane* (page 215) and Handout 11: *Reading Comprehension* (page 216) for each participant

TIME NEEDED   30–45 minutes

EXERCISE OUTLINE

READING ASSIGNMENT AND READING COMPREHENSION WORKSHEET   Participants read a press release that has been rewritten to give them the experience of reading in a language that they have not totally mastered. Then they answer a few questions about what they have read.

INSIGHTS   The group talks about how it felt to have to figure out what the reading assignment meant and consider some challenges of doing business in a second language.

ACTION PLANNING   Group members decide what they can do to improve communication in light of what they have learned.

CONDUCTING THE EXERCISE:
MISSING THE MEANING

READING
ASSIGNMENT
AND READING
COMPREHENSION
WORKSHEET

It is important that you do not tell the group what this exercise is for until you are well into the discussion section. Simply distribute the two hand-outs—*Carriage House Lane* and *Reading Comprehension*—and tell the group that they have five minutes to quickly read the first and fill in the second. Stress that they must work quietly by themselves, and that you want them to finish as quickly as possible.

When five minutes are up, check to see if most members of the group have finished. If not, allow two or three more minutes and check again. Continue to check with them and extend their time every five minutes until about one half of the people have finished.

INSIGHTS

Start by asking the group how they felt while doing the exercise. You can expect answers like:

➤ It was confusing.
➤ At first I felt pretty sure of myself and that you had made a lot of mistakes.
➤ I could sort of get the gist of the reading even without all the words.
➤ I felt frustrated.
➤ I felt stupid.
➤ I was embarrassed because I couldn't figure it out.

Let the group know that it was meant to be difficult. Ask them what they think the point of the exercise is. If the group needs some prompting, ask them:

ASK ?

Have any of you ever had to do business in a foreign language?

Have you ever tried to make your way through a foreign country when you only knew a little of the language?

Ask the group again if they can figure out why you had them do this exercise. Look for answers like:

➤ Help us know what it feels like to work in another language. Even if you can speak/read it, you may not understand all the words.

➤ Appreciate the frustration of people who speak English as their second language.

➤ Remind us that we should be using simple English, talking more slowly, and not use acronyms, jargon, or hard-to-understand examples.

Now ask the group why this should matter to them:

What can go wrong in a business relationship or transaction if we don't consider the difficulties of non-native speakers?

You can expect answers such as:

➤ They may get frustrated and quit trying.
➤ They can't focus on real meaning because of frustration or embarrassment.
➤ They may not get my message.
➤ They may stop caring about my message.
➤ They may get angry with me.
➤ They may doubt my ability or expertise.

INSIGHTS   Debrief by summing up the comments so far. Here are some points you can add if they do not come up in the discussion:

➤ Avoid using expressions that people would only learn if they were from your culture, such as sports analogies, popular phrases from TV shows or movies, slang, etc. (See if the group can give you some examples.)

➤ Even if someone speaks another language well, he or she may not be able to read it at the same level. (Ask if there are any people in the group who have had that experience themselves.)

➤ For some, reading a second language is easier than speaking it. It is a good idea to supply agenda, presentation materials, topics for discussions, etc., well in advance of a meeting.

➤ Sometimes English speakers think of English as "the language of business," and can forget that not everyone uses English as easily as we do.

➤ Remember that English is spoken all over the world, but that "U.S. English" is not the "only" English.

Say It, Shout It, Skip It

TYPE Communication Skills, Conflict Skills

PURPOSE Helps participants to understand the differences among assertive, aggressive, and nonaggressive communication. Explains why assertive communication is most effective.

EQUIPMENT NEEDED Flipchart paper and markers

PREP Prepare a copy of Handout 12: *Say It, Shout It, Skip It* (pages 217–218) for each participant.

Place on table or hang on wall: one sheet of blank flipchart paper and one marker for each group

TIME NEEDED 45 minutes

EXERCISE OUTLINE

INTRODUCTION Explain to participants that *how* we express ourselves is just as important as *what* we say or don't say. Tell them we are going to do an activity that compares aggressive, assertive and non-assertive communication.

ACTIVITY Groups learn about the differences among aggressive, assertive, and non-assertive communication as the work together to complete the *Say It, Shout It, Skip It* handout.

INSIGHTS The facilitator reviews the different styles and participants talk about what styles they prefer and which styles are most effective.

CONDUCTING THE EXERCISE:
SAY IT, SHOUT IT, SKIP IT

INTRODUCTION

SAY

Let's look closely at the differences among assertive and aggressive communication, and assertive and nonassertive communication.

Assertive communication lets the person you are speaking with know what's on your mind, how you feel about something, or what you want to do. It is generally not intended to be argumentative, overbearing, or malicious. It is simply an honest, direct statement of what you are thinking.

Aggressive communication, on the other hand, can be malicious and often demeaning to the other person. It is a hostile approach to communicating that attempts to bully or belittle others into seeing things your way. Aggressive communication usually contains judgments about, and final decisions for, others.

Nonassertive communication is the complete opposite of assertive communication. People who use this approach do not voice their opinions, and often hide what they are really feeling or thinking about a topic or situation. It can be an ineffective way to communicate because it does not present what is truly desired. It can be frustrating for both the person speaking and the listener because neither really gets what is wanted from the conversation.

THE ACTIVITY

Distribute the *Say It, Shout It, Skip It* handouts to each participant. Further explain the difference between aggressive, assertive, and nonassertive communication by reviewing the top portion of the sheet.

ASK ?

What do you think are some of the downfalls of communicating aggressively or nonassertively?

List responses on flipchart if you have time.

Break the workshop group into subgroups with three or four people in each. (See page 268, *Fun Ways to Break into Groups*.)

Now ask each group to work together to come up with sentences to complete the activity at the bottom of the handout sheet.

SAY I would now like you to work with your group on completing the activity on the handout sheet. Each team will work together to come up with the best sentences possible. When you finish your two sentences, write them on the flipchart paper and post them on the wall. Decide who will be the spokesperson for your group. When everyone is finished, the spokesperson will present your sentences to the rest of the class.

INSIGHTS When all the subgroups have finished, ask them to post their sentences. A spokesperson from each subgroup will then read their sentences aloud to the entire workshop group.

Once every group has reported in, ask:

ASK Did everyone in your group have the same style or did some tend to be more aggressive or nonassertive in their communication style?

How did you decide on the final sentences? Did your personal styles affect how you worked together? How?

You can expect that people will have used different styles within the groups. Some may have made an early decision about the makeup of the sentence and lobbied hard for the group to use it. Others may have waited until they heard everyone's suggestions and then worked to create a compromise. Still others may have barely spoken—letting the group's direction determine their input. Some people may have shifted styles during the course of the exercise.

The key for you to listen for in the conversation is not just what was done, but how it was done. Did people notice differences among the styles? Could they identify assertive, aggressive, and nonaggressive styles in themselves and others in the future?

Continue the conversation using questions like these:

ASK ➤ Which sentence was more difficult to correct? Why?

➤ Did either sentence sound like something you would naturally say?

➤ How can aggressive and nonassertive communication styles hinder the conflict–resolution process?

➤ Which style is more difficult for you to deal with?

> Why do you think people use aggressive or nonassertive communication to express themselves?

> Why do you think some people find it hard to be assertive without being aggressive?

Conversation prompted by these questions will vary from group to group, but you will often hear people talk about "personality." While personality may have an impact on how people interact, it is helpful for people to note that we also have the ability to make conscious choices about whether we will act in an aggressive, assertive, or nonassertive way.

To encourage people to think about their choices, ask questions such as:

ASK

What are some things we can do when confronted with someone using these styles?

What do you think your natural style is?

How do you react to the other styles?

What style do you think is most productive in conversation?

Avoid arguing with people who still feel that aggressive or nonassertive behavior is preferable. Instead, find out why they feel the way they do. Ask them about what they have experienced. Invite others in the room to share insight as well.

Then remind them that for the most part, we are offering communication solutions that work here in mainstream U.S. culture. In cultures that value a more indirect way of speaking, a person may appear to be nonassertive while still communicating her or his needs or feelings in a way that is clear to another person who understands the rules of that culture. The person is still asserting, but in a culturally acceptable way. Remind participants that being assertive does not mean being rude or mean. It simply means making clear to others what one feels or wants from a situation.

SAY

When someone communicates effectively, they are able to send the message they intend to someone else without limiting the other person's ability to reply. If you use a nonassertive communication style, you really are not delivering your message to the other person. At the same time, if you use an aggressive style, you are not allowing yourself to hear what the other person has to say. They may also respond emotionally, which also limits clear communication.

When you use an assertive style, you balance your desire to communicate clearly your needs or feelings with the other person's desire to do the same thing. We both have to understand one another in order for the communication to be effective. This understanding cannot happen if we limit the other person's ability to be heard.

ASK ? Why do you think an assertive communication style might be the most productive style to use?

List responses on the flip chart. You can expect comments like:

➤ Each person in the conversation knows what the other(s) wants.
➤ It is positive, not negative.
➤ It is not degrading.
➤ This creates options.
➤ All parties are equally involved in the decision/outcome.
➤ It's honest, but usually not hurtful.
➤ This creates a mature level of conversation.
➤ We cannot achieve goals that aren't stated.
➤ This reduces misunderstandings and hard feelings.

Wrap up by recapping the chart at the top of Handout 12: *Say It, Shout It, Skip It.*

Telephone Tales

TYPE Communication Skills, Teamwork

PURPOSE To give the group the opportunity to experiment with and compare different listening techniques

EQUIPMENT NEEDED None

PREP Duplicate Handout 13: *Telephone Tales* Check Sheet (pages 219–220) or create your own

TIME NEEDED 45–60 minutes

This exercise is based on an idea from Dennis Meadows, the co-author with Linda Booth Sweeney of *The Systems Thinking Playbook*. Dennis and Linda's book is full of simple exercises that help people build their capability as system thinkers. See the Toolbox section for more information on *The Systems Thinking Playbook* and *When a Butterfly Sneezes*.

EXERCISE OUTLINE

BREAK INTO GROUPS Separate your workshop group into smaller teams with eight or ten people each.

QUICK INTRODUCTION AND ASSIGNMENTS Explain that this is a variation of the children's game "Telephone," and give each group assignment.

TELEPHONE The teams pass the message along, trying to be as accurate as possible.

COMPARE NOTES The teams present the message in its final form, and are rated for accuracy.

INSIGHTS AND ACTION PLANNING The group talks about what worked, what did not work, and what they might try if they did it again.

AWARD THE PRIZES   Thank the group for its hard work and the fun that you had together, and award the prizes.

CONDUCTING THE EXERCISE: TELEPHONE TALES

BREAK INTO GROUPS   First, break your larger workshop group into smaller teams with eight or ten people each. There are ideas for quickly getting people into small groups on page 268.

QUICK INTRODUCTION AND ASSIGNMENTS   When people are sitting in their groups, ask if anyone has ever played the children's game "Telephone." In this game, which is also called names like "Gossip" and "Whisper Down the Lane," one person whispers a word or short phrase to a second person. The second person whispers what she has heard to a third, and so on down the line. The last person then repeats the word or phrase that she thinks she heard so that the entire group can hear. Usually, the person at the end of the line has heard something completely different from what the first person whispered to the second person.

Before starting the game, explain each of the following steps:

1. GETTING THE STORY STRAIGHT Tell the group that in *Telephone Tales*, we play the old game with a new twist. In the child's game, it is fun deliberately to distort what you hear to make the ending funnier. In this version, the team that is closest to passing along a perfect message will win a prize.

2. THE FIRST PRESENTATION To start, each group will send one member into a separate room with the facilitator. In the separate room, the facilitator will give these team representatives a two- or three-minute presentation on a fairly detailed subject, or tell a detailed two- or three-minute-long story.

3. THE TELEPHONE These representatives will then be the first person to repeat what they have heard to a second member of their team. They need to whisper the information to the other person so that no one else in the room hears them. The second person then whispers the information to the third, and so on until

the last person has heard the tale. Their job will be to listen carefully and remember as much as possible so that they can repeat the story accurately to the next person. During this part of the game, some people may choose to take notes. You will allow this, but do not point it out to other players.

4. COMPARE NOTES Now the last persons from each team take turns making a presentation of what they have heard and remember to the entire group. Remind them that you and the first speakers will be judging them to see if their team wins the prize. You will be listening now for the presentation that is the most accurate.

Tip: Right before they vote, tell your judges you are keeping them honest by giving each of them a prize whether their team wins or not.

It is important that you and the other judges do not make comments during or between the presentations. You want each presenter to be un-influenced by how well he or she thinks the presentations are going.

When all of the presentations have been completed, ask the judges to vote on who they think gave the most accurate presentation. It can be fun to line the presenters up and hold your hand over each person's head while the judges applaud for the one whose presentation was closest to the original tale.

When the voting is finished, tell the group that there are a couple more things to do before you pass out the prizes.

INSIGHTS AND ACTION PLANNING Begin the conversation about what worked and what didn't work by asking the judges what was left out of the presentations that was not as accurate as the winning presentation. Then ask the group if they see a pattern regarding what information was "lost" as the message was passed along. There will not always be a pattern, but people will sometimes leave out specifics such as numbers, time frames, and dates. Other times emotions, colors, or people and place names may be cut. If a pattern of some kind has emerged, ask the group why they think that is.

Next, ask questions about what worked for the group that won, or what made certain details of the presentation easier to remember. Ask:

ASK

What did the winning group do that made this work better than the other groups?

What made this difficult, especially for groups that were not able to pass accurate information along?

What would you do to improve your performance if you were to play the game again?

Finally, see if the group can draw connections between what happened in the exercise and how they pass information along at work.

SAY At work, we often have written material to help us remember what happened in a particular meeting. This, of course, is very valuable. If we become too dependent on written material, however, we may stop listening to one another or we may stop being careful to be clear when we speak. We could miss some important information or nuance.

What things worked for us today that we could use to improve both telling and listening at work?

Take notes on a flip chart as the participants talk about ways to take what they are learning back to their jobs. When the group has finished coming up with ideas, ask:

Which of these ideas can we implement as a regular part of doing business?

Can we add any of them to the way we work at meetings?

What have we talked about that can help us be more effective when planning or reviewing work with our employees?

AWARD THE PRIZES Thank the group for its hard work and the fun that you had together, and award the prizes.

> You can use any story you like for the *Telephone Tales* exercise—one from your own experience, an item from a newspaper, or this one. A page from your company's annual report or a short video excerpt can also work. Whatever you choose, make sure that it has a lot of detail, and create a check sheet so that you can measure how accurately your Telephone Tale is passed along. If you are creating your own story and check sheet, take a look at the check sheet for "The Blacksmith Shop": it was written by taking each bit of information from the story and writing it as a checklist.

STORY: THE BLACKSMITH SHOP

In 1987 the *Los Angeles Times* celebrated more than 100 years of being in business by publishing a book of historic front pages. The book began with the very first issue—December 4, 1881, and continued through the century up until January 23, 1987.

The book offered more than 200 front pages. If you were to quickly thumb through the book, you could find any number of historical news stories: an announcement that the Union Pacific Rail Road is coming to town, Wilson's presidential election victory, jokes from Will Rogers, war news, labor strikes, baseball's Dodgers moving to Los Angeles from Brooklyn, the Kennedy assassination, riots at Attica prison, Nixon's resignation, fires, robberies, and Princess Di's wedding.

Most interesting to me is a small ad on the front page from April 15, 1882. It is hard to tell why the book editors included the front page from this date. It was a pretty slow news day—there is an item about the average age of the French cabinet and another dealing with flour shipments to Texas.

The ad, though, was a surprise because my great-grandfather put it there to announce his blacksmith shop:

John M. Pray & Son, Blacksmiths, 34 Los Angeles Street:
Horse Shoeing, Carriage and Wagon work, Artesian well tools,
well rings, and all kinds of forging in steel or iron.
All work done in a superior manner. Terms cash.

VARIATION 1   If you have time, it can be fun to begin this exercise by playing the "children's version" of telephone tales. Once you have set up the subgroups, take the first "tellers" from each group into a separate room and tell them a simple phrase or multisyllable word. Then let them each whisper the word or phrase to the next person in their groups, who will pass it on, and so on.

It is fun to see how mangled the original word or phrase comes out on the other end. You can tie it in to the larger exercise with a simple introduction.

SAY   Now we will play for keeps. The fun children's game we have just played shows what can happen when we listen quickly and not too carefully. In this next game, we will pass on a fairly complicated story. The team that can whisper the story down the lane with the most accuracy will win a prize.

VARIATION 2   You can make sure that teams try different ways of listening by assigning methods to different teams. For example, you can tell one team that they must take notes while listening. Another team could be required to repeat the story back to the teller before moving on. Another team could be told to listen only without taking notes. One team could draw pictures while listening instead of writing words.

Your conversation at the end of the exercise would focus on what from these different techniques worked, what did not, and what combination of methods might be most effective at work.

Think Fast: Three Variations

TYPE	Centering, Teamwork
PURPOSE	Great warm-ups. Helps people get used to staying centered under pressure by requiring them to think on their feet.
EQUIPMENT NEEDED	Nerf Balls or bean bags, copies of *Three Blind Mice*
PREP	You can do these for any type of workshop as simple, fun, rowdy energizers. They can have greater impact when learning about communication and conflict if you use them with the simple centering exercise described in *Staying Cool in a Conflict* on page 77.
TIME NEEDED	15–30 minutes

EXERCISE OUTLINE

CENTERING EXERCISE	Make sure that everyone understands the basics of centering.
INTRODUCTION	Set up the exercise.
VARIATION 1	Think Fast: Quick thinking on your feet.
VARIATION 2	Recite a Word: Thinking together at high speed.
VARIATION 3	Sentence Ball: Thinking, working, and moving together at high speed.
INSIGHTS	Establish the relevance of the exercise.

CONDUCTING THE EXERCISE:
THINK FAST: THREE VARIATIONS

CENTERING EXERCISE

If you have already done centering exercises with this group, you can skip directly to any of the variations below.

Tell the group that you are going to work together on being centered while thinking on your feet. If you have not done centering exercises with this group before, ask for someone to explain what centering means for them. You may get responses from people with experiences in workshops like yours, or from people who have learned about centering through meditation, yoga, martial arts, or some other activity.

Explain that one way to look at centering is as a tool to help you stay calm enough actually to approach conflict the way that you would like. When you are centered, you can calmly make split-second assessments and adjustments to what you are saying and doing in order to help you and the other person get through the conflict in one piece. Practicing good technique along with centering can help you act honestly without hurting others or yourself.

Now lead the group through the simple centering exercise from *Staying Cool in a Conflict* on page 77.

VARIATION 1

Think Fast

Have the group stand shoulder-to-shoulder in a circle. They will all face you as you stand in the middle. Tell them you will point at someone and ask a simple question, and expect a quick response. You will move quickly from one person to another asking for three types of responses:

1. Answers to simple questions such as "What day is today?"

2. Answers to simple math problems such as "five plus two."

3. Words that start with the letter you say. For example, you may point at someone and say "L." That person would then need to quickly answer with a word that begins with the letter L.

Let the group know that you will be moving very quickly from one person to the next.

SAY

Just like in a rapidly moving conversation, you will do better if you listen closely and stay relaxed and centered. If you try to anticipate what will be said, you will not be able to keep up.

Ready?

When the group is ready, point at the first person and ask a question or say a letter. Keep the pressure on by only allowing a second or two for a response, then fire a question at the next person. The group will eventually pick up the rhythm of the exercise, and most will be able to answer you.

Remember to keep it fun—people thinking and working to stay centered is more important than perfect answers.

You can make up questions as you go along, or you can read them from this list. (Either way, it is important to keep the exercise moving.)

Some questions that you can use for *Think Fast*:

- 7 + 4
- N
- What day is today?
- Who is the president?
- 5 × 3
- F
- R
- P
- B
- 12 − 2
- How many light bulbs in a dozen?
- 17 + 2
- 1 + 14
- T
- S
- W
- What's your middle name?
- 9 + 9

Variations on *Variation* 1: As you and your group get better at this exercise, you can challenge yourselves by making the questions harder. Film and theater producer and drama professor Paul Gregory, who first taught me a version of this exercise twenty-five years ago, used to point at his students and call out double letters. "S-k," Paul would say, and the student would have to come up with "skillet" or some other word beginning with "sk." Sometimes Paul would make the exercise even more challenging by requiring us to quickly come up with three words that begin with the letter combination he would call out.

Jenny Beer, author of *The Mediator's Handbook*, used a clever variation when we were conducting training together. We wanted to give new mediators the opportunity to think on their feet. Jenny would point at somebody and say something like, "This meeting stinks. I'm outta here!" or "If he says that again, I'm going to scream!" The mediator had to calmly and quickly come up with a response that would help defuse the situation.—Bill

➤ 2 × 9
➤ E
➤ V
➤ H
➤ 2 + 22
➤ C
➤ P

VARIATION 2 Recite a Word

Have the group stand shoulder-to-shoulder in a circle. They will all face you as you stand in the middle. Tell them that you are going to recite a nursery rhyme together. First recite it for them—"Three Blind Mice."

> Three blind mice!
> Three blind mice!
> See how they run!
> See how they run!
> They all ran after the farmer's wife,
> Who cut off their tails with a carving knife.
> Have you ever seen such a sight in your life
> As three blind mice?

If there are people in the group who don't know the words to *Three Blind Mice*, take a moment to help them learn it. A good way is to recite it to them, then have them recite it with the whole group at the same time a couple of times.

Once everyone is ready with "Three Blind Mice," tell them you will recite the poem as a team—but one word at a time. You will point rapidly at one person after another while they each say one word from the nursery rhyme. (The first person you point to says, "Three," the next says, "blind," the next says, "mice," and so on.)

Now begin pointing and move rapidly through "Three Blind Mice." Repeat the poem, going faster and faster, until everyone has had a turn. You will know when to stop when the group is laughing more than they are saying the rhyme.

Variation on Variation 2: Of course, "Three Blind Mice" or other Mother Goose rhymes are not familiar to everyone. If there is not a little poem or other piece that people in your group all know, you can find a short written piece. You can choose something that relates to your workshop, or have some fun by using a nonsense piece or tongue twister. Since the people are reading, you will need to call their names or lightly tap them on the shoulder instead of pointing at them.

VARIATION 3   Sentence Ball

In this variation of *Think Fast*, people can practice staying centered while they think quickly, concentrate, and work together.

Once the group has successfully completed *Variation* 2, give them a large soft ball or beanbag to toss to one another. Assign each person someone to toss the ball to. They will always follow this pattern as they pass the ball along to the same person. To warm them up, have the group throw the ball around, following the pattern you have shown them. See Sample Chart 3 for an example.

Once the ball has made it around to everyone twice, have them continue tossing the ball, but add a new element. Each time someone catches the ball, they will say the next word to "Three Blind Mice."

> Variations on Varitation 3: By now you get the idea that this exercise can be made more challenging by adding elements. If you are going to add these, be sure that your group has already done well with the simpler variations. A fun variation is to add one or more balls to the mix—letting the group pass several around at once. You can also have every third person say two words of the rhyme, each person say three words apiece, everyone say "Mice!" every time it comes up. The combinations are endless. Have fun!

INSIGHTS   These exercises are fun, challenging, and definitely energizing. The people in your group may want to talk about them, even if it is just to laugh and share experiences. If you would like to tie any of these variations into a workshop on communication and conflict, start by asking a general question such as:

ASK ?   That was fun! Why do you think this exercise was chosen to warm us up for a workshop on communication and conflict?

or

What was difficult about this exercise?

You can expect answers like:

➤ We really had to pay attention.

➤ We had to listen to one person in the middle of a lot of noise and distraction.

➤ We had to focus on several things at once in order to get the job done.

➤ We had to adjust and be careful depending on who was throwing to us and who we were throwing to.

➤ We had to work as a team.

➤ We had to stay centered.

Timed Square

TYPE   Communication Skills, Teamwork

PURPOSE   To demonstrate how conflict can come from different ways of viewing the same resource.

EQUIPMENT NEEDED   Flipchart-size piece of cardstock or poster
5 large envelopes or folders for puzzle pieces
Overhead projector and Timed Square pattern overhead (Optional)

PREP   **1.** Reproduce the puzzle piece pattern by marking lines on a flipchart-size piece of cardstock or poster board. Do not write the letters that are on the pattern onto your cardstock or poster board.

   2. Cut along the lines to make your puzzle pieces.

   3. Separate your puzzle pieces into separate envelopes or folders based on the letters on the pattern (that is, put all the pieces marked "A" in one envelope, put those marked "B" in another, and so on).

   4. Write DO NOT OPEN UNTIL TOLD TO DO SO on the outside of each envelope or folder.

TIME NEEDED   20 minutes.

Here is the puzzle pattern:

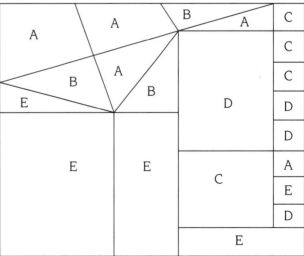

Drawing the pattern is easier if you copy Sample Chart 4: *Timed Square* onto a transparency. Simply project the overhead onto your cardstock or poster board, and use a ruler and a marker to trace over the projected lines.

EXERCISE OUTLINE

VOLUNTEERS   Get five volunteers from your workshop group, or break the workshop group into smaller groups with five people each.

INSTRUCTIONS   Hand out the puzzle pieces and tell the participants the rules of the game.

ADDITIONAL INFORMATION   As the participants work to solve their puzzles, the facilitator gives them carefully planned instructions and hints.

INSIGHTS AND CONCLUSIONS   When the puzzle is solved, the group talks about what happens and how it may apply to the way they work together.

CONDUCTING THE EXERCISE: TIMED SQUARE

VOLUNTEERS   Tell the group that you have a problem to solve, and that you need a group of five volunteers.

> For larger groups, you may want to have more than one group of five, or break the entire group into groups of five each. "Leftover" people can observe the exercise, or you can team them up with others to work on the puzzle in pairs.

INSTRUCTIONS   Gather your volunteers at a table where they can work together. Have the rest of the group stand around the table so that they can all see the action. Give one puzzle piece envelope or folder to each volunteer and give the group the following instructions:

 SAY   Only I can talk during this exercise. Everyone else must work without speaking. This includes our observers.

Each volunteer has an envelope with five puzzle pieces. You must work quickly and quietly to solve the puzzle.

You may open your envelopes now and begin. You have ten minutes. Go!

ADDITIONAL INFORMATION

Let the volunteers work quietly on their puzzles for about two minutes, then tell them you will give them some hints.

 SAY

You may need at least one puzzle piece from somebody else's pile to complete your puzzle. You may not speak, gesture, or grab to get it. You must wait until someone offers it to you.

Now the volunteers will start to eye one another's puzzle pieces and solutions so far. The people standing around the table may begin to see solutions as well. Some of the volunteers and observers may begin to get frustrated. Be sure that they don't speak. Add to the frustration level by occasionally reminding the group of how much time that they have left.

Let some silent puzzle piece trading and experimentation go on for a while, then say:

 SAY

The shape you are trying to build is a square.

Some of the volunteers may be able to collect enough pieces to build a square, or they may get pretty close to building a square. Watch people who think that they have solved the problem to see what they do. Do they sit back satisfied with themselves? Do they guard their solution so no one else can take a piece from it? Do they begin to help other people with their puzzles?

When a few people seem to think that they have a solution, or when you have only about two minutes left, give the volunteers the last bit of information.

SAY

The square you are trying to build is about the size of a flipchart.

You may have to repeat this last instruction once or twice until people realize that the only way that they are going to be able to make a square that large is if they put all of their puzzle pieces together. If the volunteers still have not heard you, it can be helpful if you hold your hands out to show the size when repeating the dimensions. You can also draw the approximate size on a flipchart while repeating "The square you are trying to build is a″ × b″."

Now the lights will come on. If the people are still stuck, you can—silently—reach in and put a couple of key pieces together to help them out.

INSIGHTS AND CONCLUSIONS

Once the puzzle has been completed, heave a sigh of relief and say:

Now we can talk!

Congratulate the volunteers. The group will often applaud or cheer as the tension of the exercise is broken. Allow everybody to spend a minute or so laughing and talking about what just happened, then ask them to take a seat.

Once the group has settled down, ask to hear from the volunteers first. Start with some general, open-ended questions. For example:

ASK How was that?
How did that feel?
What happened while you were solving the puzzle?

Some volunteers often enjoy telling their stories from the beginning to the end—how they felt, what decisions they made, what happened when they made a move, etc. Listen to these descriptions carefully for points to be made later. You may even want to jot down some brief notes while they are talking.

Once the volunteers have told their stories, ask the rest of the group to talk about the exercise. Ask them how it felt to see a solution and to not be able to speak or to help in any way.

Here are some questions you can use to help both the volunteers and the observers:

ASK What did you think was going on when the exercise first started?

Most people will say that they expected to solve individual puzzles because the envelopes hold separate sets of pieces. Some may have participated in a similar exercise and thought that they knew the solution.

What did you want to do at first?

You can expect answers that indicate that people wanted to solve the puzzle as quickly as possible. Some people may mention that they wanted to finish first or "win." Others may have realized that they needed puzzle pieces that someone else was using and wanted to take them away. Some may just say that they wanted to speak so that they could figure things out more easily.

ASK **What made this exercise difficult?**

Most people will say that having to work without speaking made the exercise difficult. This is probably true, but you can ask them if it would have been easier if everyone had been allowed to speak. Another challenge of the exercise that will come up is that you gave them partial instructions and then added bits of information as they went along. This is true, but you can remind them that the additional instructions were hints, and all were things that they could have figured out for themselves sooner or later.

Sometimes when a facilitator asks a person or a group how something felt, they will answer that it felt just fine. Some people will say, "I understood that I had to change my approach, so I did." Even if you think you saw more discomfort than that during the exercise, it is important to support what the person has said. You can point out that often when people have to change their approach, they can feel frustrated, embarrassed, confused, or even angry. When this happens—in an exercise or in "real life"—these feelings can keep people from making adjustments even when they are learning that what they are doing is not working for them. Wait a moment after saying this so people can think. Some people may now feel more comfortable talking about how they felt during the exercise. Even if no one speaks up, people will still be able to compare what you have just said with their own experiences.

 ASK What assumptions did you have about the exercise that made it hard to figure out?

You can expect answers about expecting there to be winners and losers, or that individuals "owned" certain pieces and could not be successful if they gave anything up.

What was the most frustrating?

Answers to this question will vary from person to person. Your main reason for asking this question is to help open the group up. Frustration is an emotion that people can recall easily. This will help people think in more detail about how they were thinking and feeling during the exercise.

 ASK At some point you had to change your approach to the puzzle. How did that feel?

What does this have to do with how we communicate or deal with conflict situations here at work?

As with every question in exercises that draw on people's experience and feelings, there is no one right answer. Here are a few ideas that you can mention if the group does not bring them up:

➤ When we solve problems, we often use methods that have worked for us before. This is a good idea, but sometimes we keep trying the old methods even after we have found out that they don't work. In fact, it is often the case that the more we try to push the old solution, the more complicated we can make the problem we are trying to solve.

➤ Sometimes it is easier for the observers to see solutions than it is for the people who are living in the middle of the problem.

➤ Sometimes there is plenty of whatever is needed to go around, but we can only find that out by looking at things in a different way.

> ➤ Competition and the need to win are so built in to so many of our activities, that it is hard to put them aside even when we hear that cooperation will be more effective in a particular situation.

> ➤ Frustration can keep us from being flexible or open to new solutions.

> ➤ Solving problems without speaking to each other is difficult.

Values Clarification

TYPE   Diversity Awareness, Worldview

PURPOSE   Participants compare viewpoints as they think and talk about their reactions to some simple value statements.

EQUIPMENT NEEDED   Two flipcharts on easels
Markers
Masking tape

PREP   **1.** Prepare flipchart pages in advance for each value pair as follows:

EASEL ONE	**EASEL TWO**
Ice cream is the best dessert.	Cake is the best dessert.
Change is very good.	Keeping things the same is very good.
One should always say exactly what he or she feels.	What you say should depend on the situation and the person.
I use facts and data to make decisions and solve problems.	I use personal feelings, experience, and intuition to make decisions and solve problems.
Individual needs and performance are most valuable and important.	Group needs and performance is most valuable and important.
Talking is the best way to communicate. Say what's on your mind.	You have to be able to read between the lines and pick up nonverbal communication.
Getting things done and producing are most important.	People's feelings and relationships are most important.
A competitive environment is better.	A collaborative environment is better.

EASEL ONE	EASEL TWO
Be on time all the time. Lateness is rude and inconsiderate.	Time is flexible. People should be able to make and change schedules.
Differences should be brought out in the open and talked about. Conflict is good.	We should focus mostly on what we agree on, and avoid talking about differences.

2. Mark a straight line down the center of the training room floor with the masking tape.

3. Place one flipchart easel at the each end of the masking tape line. Have the first page of each—"Ice cream is the best desert" and "Cake is the best dessert"—showing.

TIME NEEDED   20–30 minutes

EXERCISE OUTLINE

INTRODUCTION   Explain the exercise.

THE ACTIVITY   Participants think about and share their points of view by lining up on a line between two seemingly opposing values. After each choice, they take stock of where they are in relation to the group and can talk about how or why they are standing at a particular point.

INSIGHTS   People talk about how they felt during the activity and what they are learning.

This activity is a fun way to get participants moving around and thinking about any topic. You can either prepare ahead of time as indicated (using the masking tape and prepared flipcharts), or simply have participants go through the exercise using an imaginary line on the floor. You may want to move the class into a hallway, outdoors, or to another large location if there isn't enough room in the training room. People usually enjoy little "road trips" during a workshop.

CONDUCTING THE EXERCISE:
VALUES IDENTIFICATION

INTRODUCTION   Show the group the masking tape line you have marked on the floor.

Now ask participants to stand in a cluster near the middle of the line. Tell them that you will offer them a pair of sentences for them to evaluate. Each phrase in the pair will be assigned to either the far left or far right on the line. Tell them that after you say each phrase, you would like them to stand along the continuum line in a place that shows which phrase they agree, or identify with more.

SAY

We are going to participate in a values clarification exercise. This means that you will be asked to show how much you agree or disagree with two different ideas relating to differences and/or communication. There are no right or wrong answers for this activity. It is simply an illustration of how you feel about the topic or what your experience has been. We all have different experiences that have worked for us in life, so again, this is not a test with right or wrong answers.

We'll use this line to show your answers. The purpose of the activity is to help you see just how many different perspectives can exist about the same topic. It is a good first step in understanding the many styles and approaches to resolving differences.

Many of the people we talk to each day may have feelings and experiences that are similar to others in the room. Today, you'll have an opportunity to talk about these differences in viewpoints with others in a safe environment. When you leave with this knowledge, you can use it to better understand others who feel the same way. If nothing else, you'll see just how many opinions are out there.

When we start the activity, I will read two statements to you. One will be on the flipchart at one end of the line. The other will be on the flipchart at the other end of the line.

If you strongly agree with one of the statements—exactly as I said it— you'll stand at the end of the line right next to the flipchart with that statement. If you agree somewhat with both statements, you can stand along the line in a place that shows how much you agree.

Think of it as a sliding scale or continuum. If you agree with both statements equally, you will stand right in the middle of the line. If you agree with one a little more than you do the other, you will scoot a little toward your favorite. The more you prefer one statement over the other, the closer to that flipchart you will end up.

It is important to mention that no one response is more correct than any other is. Your responses represent different approaches or viewpoints. Stand wherever it makes the most sense for you.

Now point out the first page on both of the flipchart easels: "Ice cream is the best dessert," and "Cake is the best dessert."

SAY For example, when I say, "Ice cream is the best desert," and "Cake is the best dessert," you will stand closer to the flipchart that lists your prefer- ence. If you like both of them equally, you will stand right in the middle.

Demonstrate the activity with ice cream versus cake example.

SAY Let's try one for practice. Please line up on the continuum according to how much you agree with these statements: On the far left: "Ice cream is the best dessert." On the far right: "Cake is the best dessert."

THE ACTIVITY

Start the exercise by turning the page on both flip charts and reading the two statements:

Change is very good.
Keeping things the same is very good.

Read the two statements in an even tone. Take care not to suggest that you prefer one to the other. Allow time for participants to move into place. Once everyone has stopped moving, acknowledge where people are. Ran- domly ask some of the following questions, and then move on to the next set of statements. Remember to keep it fun and light. Avoid making any- one feel uncomfortable because of the place they chose along the line.

Sometimes self-disclosure can be a little scary for participants, no matter how small the disclosure seems to be. So, it is important to keep the atmosphere fun, safe, and focused on learning. You can do this by letting participants know that there are no right or wrong answers in a values identification exercise. The whole thing is based on our own individual feelings, experiences, and opinions.

Some questions you can ask to start people talking after each time they move in response to a pair of statements are:

ASK Why did you choose this spot on the line?

Ask people positioned at the far ends of the line:

Have you ever encountered someone that seems to feel the opposite of what you do?

Was that difficult for you?

How did you handle it?

Ask people that are standing alone on the line:

You seem to be all alone down here. Tell us what your perspective on this is.

Ask people who are clustered together:

 ASK A lot of you have chosen a similar answer, while others have a very different perspective about this. What do you think that means?

What might happen to those people in an organization or group?

How could you help that situation?

Some general questions to help the whole group talk about what they are learning:

After hearing what some others have said, is there anyone who wants to change spots? Why?

Is anyone surprised at seeing someone at a certain place on the line? Would you have expected them to be someplace else? Why?

INSIGHTS You can conduct the debrief conversation with participants still standing (or sitting) near the continuum line or have them take their seats in the classroom again, whichever is most comfortable.

Talk about the activity using the questions in the following list. Be flexible when discussing the activity. You are not limited to these questions, nor do you have to ask all of them. Remember that the main point is for them to see that other views exist and that they will probably encounter these viewpoints in everyday life. The more they realize that and the more comfortable they are with it, the more successful they will be at communicating and at resolving differences.

Begin by asking:

 ASK What were some of the things you considered when choosing a place on the continuum line?

Expect answers such as:

➤ where others were standing on the line
➤ my interpretation of what each of the statements meant
➤ how much I wanted others to know about me
➤ the last time I'd been faced with the situations mentioned

 ASK Did any of you seem to always end up standing together on the line for most of the questions?

Did any of you who seemed to be opposites the entire time?

Do you interact a lot in real life?

Are you surprised to find how similar/dissimilar your viewpoints are?

This simple exercise is most powerful when participants can apply what they are learning back to the workplace. Start the participants thinking about application by asking things like:

ASK ?

➤ How do different value systems impact communication? Conflict?

➤ Were you surprised to see so many different perspectives? So many similar ones?

➤ Where do you think all these different ideas came from? Why do you think we all have different value systems?

➤ Can value systems change? How?

➤ Are there any values that I mentioned that you felt very strongly about, that are very difficult for you to handle when others feel the extreme opposite of you?

➤ Which ones?

➤ How have you handled that in the past?

➤ How have others here handled it?

➤ What are some things we can do to reduce the negative effects conflicting value systems can have on communication and problem solving?

End the exercise by reminding participants that there are no right or wrong answers; not here in the activity nor in real life. Thank them for playing along and for being honest.

> Many times, at the end of the activity, I will jokingly say, "And that concludes the aerobic portion of the workshop . . ." and go into a mock breathing "cool down." Sometimes people are uncomfortable with sharing personal feelings and information about themselves; especially in front of their peers or managers. This exercise is pretty safe, but depending on how the discussion went, you'll want to really make sure that you end on a light, positive note so that you can continue the learning in a good environment.—Keami

What's in a Word?

TYPE   Communication Skills, Diversity Awareness, Worldview

PURPOSE   Participants share different ways to say the same thing as they compare cultural differences and talk about connotative and denotative meaning.

EQUIPMENT NEEDED   Flipcharts and markers

PREP   Have one copy of Handout 14: *What's in a Word?* (page 221) for each participant.
Prepare the *What's in a Word?* flipcharts:
➤ 8: Language and Culture (page 245)
➤ 9: Connotative and Denotative (page 246)

TIME NEEDED   30–40 minutes

EXERCISE OUTLINE

INTRODUCTION   Explain that culture and experience influences the language choices we make.

ACTIVITY   Participants use the *What's in a Word?* handouts to identify and talk about different yet accurate ways to say the same thing.

INSIGHTS   Participants talk about what they are learning and how to apply it to resolving differences and improving communication.

**CONDUCTING THE EXERCISE:
WHAT'S IN A WORD?**

INTRODUCTION Talk a little about language and the words that different people use to mean different things. Tell participants that language is shaped by culture and society, and by our own personal experiences.

ASK Have you ever found yourself in a conversation where you felt that you weren't being understood very well? Or that you weren't understanding the person very well?

Give them time to answer and share a couple of stories. Then say:

SAY Miscommunication happens all the time—even with friends or with people in our own households. This is because the words we choose during a conversation can have a huge impact on how the other person reacts to us, or what they think we are trying to say.

Conversations can really get interesting when we are talking with someone from another country or from different background, age group, or neighborhood. Ever try to talk with a teenager? Many people have trouble keeping up with all the latest phrases and ideas. So talking with teenagers or kids can be a real challenge sometimes.

Our society and cultural rules shape our language. And our culture shapes our language. In other words, the things that we feel are important in a culture or society are going to creep into the language and as we emphasize certain ways of expressing ourselves, it has an impact on the culture. The language of a group changes in order to highlight those things that people in that group feel are important.

Ask the group for examples of the many different ways that people greet one another in this country. Expect such answers as:

➤ Hello.
➤ What's up?
➤ How are you?
➤ Dude!
➤ Hi!
➤ Hey!
➤ Yo!
➤ Good morning/afternoon/evening/day
➤ What's happening?

Tell them that a greeting that was traditionally used in many parts of Asia is "Have you eaten rice yet?" The appropriate response is "Yes," just as when an English speaker asks "How are you?" and expects you to say, "Fine," rather than a list of what ails you.

SAY

In the United States, greetings often focus on doing things and going places and how the individual feels about the day—What's up? How's it going? What's going on? These greetings imply excitement and individual choice. The greeting "Have you eaten rice yet?" addresses a social as well as a physical need. These terms came about because of what is important to our different cultures.

Asian culture is generally more group-oriented than U.S. culture. This group focus in a place where there have been historical food shortages may be what gave rise to the greeting about eating.

As language and culture continue to shape each other, dominant ideas tend to be included in phrases and words.

What are some other greetings or phrases that you may have heard from other countries or even in this country?

How do you think these different focuses can affect relationships and one on one communication?

Explain that even people in our own country and own neighborhoods can use different rules and styles when talking.

SAY

Some people are more forceful than others are. Some are less direct. Some use formal language. Some use mostly slang.

To review, show the group Flipchart 8: *Language and Culture.*

➤ Language is shaped by culture, and culture is shaped by language.

➤ We follow rules and accepted practices for communication sometimes without even knowing it.

➤ Points of view influence language and language influences points of view.

➤ A culture's values and beliefs are often revealed by the words in use.

SAY

Another thing that shapes meaning is what the speaker and listener feel about the topic. Meaning is influenced by the speaker's feelings and is subject to the conversation. It is also shaped by the listener's personal ideas about the speaker, the topic, and his or her personal background and experience. These feelings cause the speaker and listener to place meanings on words. The generally accepted meaning of a word is the denotative meaning. The additional meaning added to a word by things such as culture, emotion, the relationship between the people talking, and even whatever is happening in a specific moment, is called the connotative meaning.

Show the group Flipchart 9: *Connotative and Denotative.*

DENOTATIVE   The literal, "dictionary" meaning of a word—what it is "supposed" to mean

CONNOTATIVE   Your personal meaning, implication, or interpretation of a word

Ask the group for some examples of when denotation and connotation can be different for words. Here are some examples you can use to help get the conversation started:

➤ Slim and skinny can mean the same thing, but get a different reaction when used to describe someone.

➤ Two grown men who are friends can call each other "boy," but if a stranger calls a grown man "boy," it will get a different reaction.

➤ If you are talking about a door and say, "shut it," you will get a different reaction than if you are talking about a mouth.

➤ If you are talking about a person you admire and say she is a "hustler," it means something entirely different than if you were talking about someone you suspect of being dishonest.

➤ And, of course, sometimes bad is good and hot is cool.

THE ACTIVITY

Once you are convinced that everyone is clear on the difference between denotation and connotation, tell participants that the next activity will demonstrate the influence culture has on language.

Separate the group into subgroups with about four or five people in each, and give each person a copy of the *What's in a Word?* handout.

Review the examples on the handout sheet. Ask participants to work with their group to come up with as many words or phrases as they can for each word listed. The words or phrases they choose should be informal, vernacular-type definitions, not necessarily definitions from the dictionary. Their answers reflect things people would say to friends. Do the first one together.

SAY   Let's look at how all of this plays out in real life. Take a look at your worksheet. You'll see 10 words or phrases listed. What I'd like you to do in your teams is to come up with common phrases or words that mean the same thing as the word or phrase written in the list. Come up with as many of them as you can.

The phrases you come up with should be things that everyday people would say. Let's do the first one together. Number one says, "really smart." What are some ways we might say that in our society?

Some typical responses include:

➤ Brainiac
➤ Egghead
➤ Einstein
➤ Bright
➤ Gifted
➤ Sharp
➤ Quick
➤ Clever
➤ Poindexter

Now ask the subgroups to complete the rest of the handout as a team effort.

When all of the groups have completed the assignment, ask them to share their responses. Go from group to group and have them read their responses to number two aloud. Then go around the room and ask them to read number three, and so on.

INSIGHTS Start the conversation by asking:

 ASK

Did any of you learn any new expressions today?

People will often have heard some words or phrases applied in new ways. As people hear that their usual speech seems new to someone else, they will often explain where they learned it with such comments as:

➤ That's how we say it in Philly.
➤ It's a West Coast thing.
➤ It's an old saying.
➤ It comes from my first language.
➤ I thought everybody said it that way.

Continue the conversation by asking:

 ASK

How does the language we choose as speakers show how much or how little we value something, someone, or some idea?

You can help the conversation along with an example or two.

 SAY

For example, using the word "bright" to describe a smart person means we value that quality; we liken them to something striking and awesome—like a shining star; something that stands out from the rest. Calling the same person "egghead" might send the message that we think this person is odd or does not fit in.

Some other questions you can use to encourage the group to think and talk about what they are learning are:

ASK

> ➤ What does this say about how we communicate?
> ➤ How could the way we use words add to conflict?
> ➤ How could it reduce conflict?
> ➤ What do some of the phrases we have written say about what we value?
> ➤ What are the benefits of using denotative meanings when speaking?
> ➤ What are the benefits of using connotative language?
> ➤ How could you use connotative language to escalate conflict?
> ➤ How would you use denotative?
> ➤ How could you use the connotative or denotative language to deflate a conflict situation?
> ➤ What can you do when someone uses a word or phrase to describe something that you don't quite understand?
> ➤ What are some things we can do to make sure we are understood?

Use the conversation to help people understand that the words they choose can help or hurt communication. They can use what they are learning to control the outcome of their communication and move it to something positive.

Sum up by saying:

SAY

Understanding that words can have different meanings in different places and in different situations can help us realize that all people speak the way they do because of personal backgrounds and experiences. People will sometimes value different things more highly than others will, and these value systems will come out in conversation and language. By realizing this, we can start to reduce the communication problems they experience by not reacting as strongly to the language used by another person. Or at least by understanding their reaction, and talking more about it with the person.

It can help to remember that each word or set of words we choose to use can have distinct meanings that are not found in the dictionary. We especially need to remember to be very aware of connotative meanings in situations that are already fragile.

Culture shapes language and language communicates our value and belief systems. Much of what we say can be loaded with meaning that we never intend. When in doubt, explain to the other person what the words you are using mean to you and ask him or her if there is another meaning you may have missed.

Workers and Managers

TYPE Communication Skills, Conflict Skills, Diversity Awareness, Teamwork, Worldview

PURPOSE This exercise helps groups learn how the behaviors of even the most well-intentioned of us can be influenced by the way we design the systems in which we live and work.

EQUIPMENT NEEDED Three physically separate locations—the farther apart the better
Dome tents with instructions for assembly
Blindfolds
Two walkie-talkies
Whatever you can offer to make your managers as comfortable as possible
You will need at least two facilitators for this exercise.
Flipchart and markers

PREP Set up your three locations:
Location One: "The Conversation"
This will be your start and end point for the exercise. You will need a flip chart and markers. Place chairs in a circle or some other comfortable set-up to aid conversation.

Location Two: "The Field"
Dome tents, unassembled and in bags, instructions removed
Blindfolds (ready but out of sight)
Walkie-talkies (ready but out of sight)
Facilitator

Location Three: "HQ"
Have fun with this setup. Your goal is to make it very relaxing and difficult for the group in this location to leave. Good food and drink, comfortable chairs, music, magazines, videos, putting green—add whatever will make this place more attractive than working on the exercise.

TIME NEEDED 2 hours

EXERCISE OUTLINE

INTRODUCTION AND SETUP Break the workshop group into two subgroups: Managers and Workers. The Managers will move to HQ, the Workers will be taken to The Field.

INSTRUCTIONS Both groups are given their separate instructions.

PRODUCTION The Workers build as many tents as they can with guidance from the Managers.

INSIGHT Both groups come together to talk about successes, failures, and how they can apply this exercise to real life.

CONDUCTING THE EXERCISE: WORKERS AND MANAGERS

INTRODUCTION AND SETUP Gather the entire group together at Location One, The Conversation. Tell them you will be dividing them into two groups: Workers and Managers. Break them into groups as randomly as possible, so that friends and people with similar jobs are separated. You can create your list in advance, or simply count off by twos. There are other ideas for breaking large groups into smaller ones on page 268.

> This exercise was first made up on the spot for a senior engineering team. The people in this group approached the usual team building exercises as brain-teasers. They used their engineering skill and their knowledge of teamwork and quickly and successfully solved every puzzle we threw at them. The only problem they couldn't solve was how to talk about morale problems caused by the extremely hierarchical nature of their company. I decided to split the group in two—Managers and Workers. Because we were at a luxurious corporate retreat that was built as a ranch, we put the managers in the hot tub and plied them with hors d'oeuvres and drinks. While the Managers were being waited on hand and foot, we piled the Workers into vans, drove out to a hot and dusty corral, blindfolded them, and gave them their assignment.—Bill

One facilitator will take The Workers to Location Two, The Field. At this point, no other information should be revealed. The facilitator should simply say:

Workers, come with me. We are going to The Field.

The other facilitator will collect The Managers and take them to Location Three, HQ:

Managers, please join me in HQ.

Neither group is to be told specifically where the other group is going. If anyone asks, answer by saying:

Let's go get everybody set up, then we'll figure everything out.

INSTRUCTIONS   Instructions—The Field
The facilitator in The Field will show the Workers the dome tents and give them the following instructions:

SAY   Your job for this exercise is to produce as many quality dome tents as possible. Quality means that they are assembled properly and will stand up by themselves. Your managers may have more information than is available to you, and you can contact them using this walkie-talkie. You will be blindfolded for this part of the exercise. You may start at any time. All I ask is that you give the managers at least ten minutes to settle in before you call them for help. I will keep time.

> Dome tents work well for this exercise because they are lightweight, fairly unwieldy, and can be set up indoors or out. Cell phones will work for this exercise, but walkie-talkies are better. Walkie-talkies seem to lend themselves to shorter, more abrupt exchanges.

Blindfold the Workers. As they work, you may help them with knots and keep them from hurting themselves with poles, but otherwise they are on their own.

> **Note:** Occasionally, you may have people in your exercises who object to being blindfolded. You can try to convince them with a gentle, "We haven't lost one yet," but be aware that some people are genuinely afraid to be blindfolded. If someone is concerned about it, let it go. They can help you as a silent observer. Ask them to sit without speaking and take notes of what they see happening.

Do not remind them when ten minutes are up, they are free to call the managers for help. Instead, keep track of the time and tell people it is okay to call only if they ask ten minutes after they are blindfolded.

As you set up The Field, some of the Workers will often comment or joke about how "real" it is to be at a remote site, with no instructions, and unable to see what you are doing. The facilitator can play along with this, but should not reveal any details of HQ.

Instructions—HQ

The facilitator's main job at Location Three, HQ, is to be sure that The Managers are comfortable. Tell them that you want to be sure they are relaxed for the task at hand.

SAY You have been working hard, and there is more hard work ahead. You may as well be comfortable while we get The Workers started. They can contact you by walkie-talkie if they get stuck, but we have asked them to wait at least ten minutes so that you can get settled in.

The more relaxing and distracting your HQ setup is, the better. If one of the Managers asks to leave to make a quick phone call or check messages, allow it. The facilitator should never stop the Managers from helping the Workers, but can interfere by pointing out distractions or by questioning. If, for example a manager wants to call the Workers, go to the Workers, or send the instructions to the Workers, you can offer more refreshments, point out something in the music, or simply point out that you are sure they will call if they need anything.

When you are fairly certain that the Managers are comfortable, you can mention off-handedly that the Workers are building dome tents and the Managers have access to the instructions. If the Managers are involved in some other conversation, do not interrupt, just let one of them know about the instructions "in case it comes up."

Meanwhile, back at the ranch . . .
Our two groups of engineers could communicate by walkie-talkie, but the culture of the exercise directed everyone's behavior. What had seemed to be a highly functioning group quickly broke down. Managers and Workers who wanted to go to the other site were ridiculed or told by others that they were breaking rules. No Manager ever asked the Workers where they were, and no Worker ever suggested that the Managers come help them. Most telling, perhaps, is that even when Managers were giving instructions to them over the walkie-talkie, the Workers never mentioned that they had been blindfolded. They assumed that the Managers had been blindfolded as well.—Bill

PRODUCTION   Now production in The Field should be proceeding as well as can be expected. Neither facilitator will ever directly interfere with communication, but will reinforce the artificial barriers of the exercise.

If added pressure is needed, the HQ facilitator can suggest that the managers call to tell the Workers that they only have about thirty minutes to assemble three tents completely, and to remind them that a quality job is essential.

The Field facilitator needs to monitor the level of frustration among the Workers. The exercise works best when Workers feel truly frustrated, but you do not want people to be so angry that they forget they are playing a game.

After about twenty minutes, tell the Workers they can remove their blindfolds and see how they have done. Let the Workers call the Managers and tell them they will all meet in the classroom to report.

INSIGHTS   People are often pretty boisterous when they return to the classroom. They will trade experiences with others about what it was like in The Field or HQ. Allow unstructured conversation to go on for a while, then call the group together and ask them to sit down.

Begin the conversation by asking the workers how they did against their production goal. Then ask each group to comment on their experience during the exercise. Ask about:

> The environment
> Any limitations
> Communication of expectations
> Quality of information

To be fair to the Workers, it is a good idea to have some of the HQ-type refreshments available to the entire group during the conversation.

ASK   You probably know by now that building tents isn't the main object of this exercise. What can this exercise teach us?

Often, people will respond with answers like, "It can teach us not to trust Bob." One group member even said, "I learned that trainers are sneakier than I thought." The facilitator can let the group enjoy the jokes, but should also remind the group that the structure of the exercise is a big contributor to how the participants act.

Remind the group that the structures we design for our companies or work groups become invisible to us after a while. When this happens, we tend to blame individuals for behavior that is dictated or at least suggested by our design.

SAY   For example, we all know of a case when a particular area isn't functioning well. We fire the manager and replace him or her with a successful manager from another area, only to see the new manager fail as well. Do we keep looking for someone to fire, or do we redesign the system?

Think for a moment about your own behavior or the behavior of someone you know who is capable but seems to be struggling. What do you think we can design into the way we work to get better results?

You can expect comments such as:

➤ Better communication
➤ Accessibility
➤ Real-time information
➤ Knowing why something is required
➤ Sharing the big picture
➤ Etcetera

Write the group's responses on a flipchart. If there is time, ask the group to expand on its initial comments and work on specific actions to improve their approach to working together.

Full-Day Workshops

Diversity Dialogue, Hold Please, Synthetic Culture Lab, and Write Your Own Case Study are very special activities that can stand alone as workshops in their own right. All of these exercises will take the better part of a day and require materials to be prepared in advance.

Diversity Dialogue was created by Sarita Chawla for the San Francisco Bay Area's Social Justice Collaborative. It helps you to set up an environment to help a large group of people learn about one another through a series of personal conversations. Hold Please and The Synthetic Culture Lab are based on the work of Paul Pedersen, professor, consultant, and researcher. Both of these workshops give people a chance to learn by walking in someone else's shoes as they explore dealing with extreme emotion and cross-cultural communication. Write Your Own Case Study grew from our point of view that people learn best when they compare their own experiences and come to their own conclusions. Write Your Own Case Study, which uses Jay Rothman's ARIA and ROI conflict models as its cornerstones, allows you to work with a group to design their workshop content and direction as you go.

Diversity Dialogue

TYPE   Communication Skills, Diversity Awareness, World View

PURPOSE   To allow people to learn from one another's experience through the power of thoughtful conversation

EQUIPMENT NEEDED   Separate tables for from six to twelve people

Butcher paper or flipchart paper

Tape

A set of colored markers for each table

Tent cards or signs on stands for each table

Microphone(s) and public address system if there will be more than 25 people in your workshop

PREP   Make a copy of Handout 15: *What Is in a Dialogue* (page 222) for each participant.

Prepare: Flipchart 14: *Dialogue* (page 251)
Flipchart 15: *Dialogue Questions* (page 252)

Cover each table with butcher paper or blank flipchart paper so that participants can write or draw directly on the tabletop; tape the paper in place

Place a set of colored markers on each table

Have ready: a tent card for each table that identifies various ethnic or other groups that may be represented in your larger group, for example:
Table A: Latino
Table B: African American
Table C: Native American
Table D: European American
Table E: Women of Color
Table F: Gay/Lesbian
Table G: White Men
Table H: Other

Obviously, there is no "correct" list of group names for this exercise. Your knowledge of your group should be your guide. You can also survey some or all of your group ahead of time. Sarita Chawla, who created this exercise for the Social Justice Collaborative in San Francisco, recommends it as a way of getting any kind of community together. For example, she says it could work just as well in a company with tables labeled "marketing," "sales," "operations," "HR," "IT," "finance," and the like.

OVERHEAD   *Tables List*—All other overheads are provided for you, but you will need to make your own list of tables, depending on the needs of your group.

TIME NEEDED   Up to a full day, depending on the number of participants.

EXERCISE OUTLINE

INTRODUCTION   Review of dialogue skills

OWN GROUP DIALOGUE   *What does it mean to be me?*: Participants identify the group they will belong to for the exercise. The facilitator asks the guiding question for the dialogue and explains the steps of the exercise.

NEW GROUP DIALOGUES   *What does it mean to be me and you?*: Participants quietly visit each dialogue table and listen to different people's stories.

THE FULL CIRCLE   The entire group thinks and talks together about what is happening in the exercise.

CONDUCTING THE EXERCISE: DIVERSITY DIALOGUE

INTRODUCTION   If your group has participated in a dialogue or talked about dialogue before, all you will need here is a brief review. If the concepts of dialogue are new to them, you will need to spend a little more time and allow people to ask questions so that they understand and are comfortable with the way the group will be learning together in this exercise.

    If you are unfamiliar with dialogue but are comfortable leading large group exercises, you should be able to follow the instructions for this exercise successfully. The centering tips in *Staying Cool in a Conflict* on page 77 will also help you as you quiet your mind in order to be able to lead this exercise while staying open to any learning that emerges from the group.

Your quick review of dialogue concepts and skills can follow the outline in Handout 15: *Dialogue*. You can also use the page as a handout and/or use Flipchart 14: *Dialogue* on a flipchart or as an overhead so that participants can follow along.

OWN GROUP DIALOGUE

What does it mean to be you?
Once you are comfortable that the group understands the basic concepts behind dialogue, tell them that they will now need to select a group to be in so that they can talk and listen about diversity. Be sure that they understand that you know that we all belong to many groups.

 SAY For the purpose of the exercise, it helps to choose one of the groups you identify with that you especially want to think and talk about today.

Now read the list of groups that have been preselected. If you have a very large group, you will want to show the list on an overhead. Be sure and include "other."

 SAY If you haven't heard me mention a group that you feel you belong to or that you want to talk about, you can join a group called "other" and name it anything you like.

Point out the specific tables where each group will begin their work and ask them to move to the table where they want to sit. You can expect some noise and confusion at this point as people look for their tables, ask friends what table they are going to, and so on. If people seem lost, announce again where they can find which table.

Once everybody is settled down, get the groups' attention and let them know how the exercise will go.

Tell them that they will have a dialogue at their tables about what it means to be in that particular group. Each table will need to select a "steward" who will explain the group's dialogue to other small groups.

Check to be sure that everyone understands, then put up Flipchart 15: *Dialogue Questions* as a flipchart or overhead.

> Important: You may end up with one or more "Other" groups who choose to name themselves. This is fine. Your job for this exercise is not to control what happens, but to help people learn. For more on creating an atmosphere where people can take responsibility for their own learning, see "Approaching your Learners as a Roomful of Experts" in *The Conflict Management Skills Workshop* by Bill Withers (AMACOM, 2002).

You will leave this overhead up for the rest of the exercise.

Read the questions to the group and tell them they have fifteen minutes to share their thoughts, feelings, and stories in a dialogue. Encourage them to use the markers and paper on the tables to make a record of their dialogue as they speak and listen to one another. They can write notes, or draw symbols, mind maps, or pictures. Whatever works for them is okay.

Remind them that there needs to be a "steward of the stories" at each table who will explain what was talked about to other small groups.

Let the people know when there are about five minutes left in their dialogue time. Otherwise, avoid interrupting these fifteen-minute dialogues with any further announcements.

NEW GROUP DIALOGUES   *What does it mean to be me and you?*

When the fifteen-minute dialogue has ended, thank the group for their hard work and tell them that it is time for the next part of the exercise. In this next section, each group will move to another table. Only the "steward of the stories" will stay behind. At each table, the visiting group will listen for from seven to ten minutes as the steward relates the stories from her or his group. The steward may also point out the notes, pictures, and symbols that have been written or drawn on the tabletop and explain what they mean to the people who put them there. The steward will have her or his own opinions, but will work to tell what happened in that table's dialogue as accurately as possible. During the steward's telling, the visiting group members will sit quietly and peacefully while they listen. They will make no comments and ask no questions.

Once everyone understands the instructions, ask them to remain silent while moving from one table to another. This will save time because the stewards will not have to get them to settle down each time. The silence will also help them to think without making a comment—an important part of being ready to listen to the stewards.

Now ask the stewards to stay at their tables while the rest of the groups move to another table. It is easiest if you have the tables arranged in rows so that people can follow a clear path from table to table when it is time to switch.

The best thing you as a facilitator can do during this part of the exercise is to listen. Listen to the whole room, not just one or two tables. About every seven to ten minutes—depending on how it seems to you each steward's presentation is going—call "time" and have the groups move on to the next table. The stewards will stay behind to tell their stories to the next group.

THE FULL CIRCLE When every group has visited every table, it will be time to call everyone back into one large group again. Ask the participants to mix things up a little by sitting with someone they may not know very well.

When everyone has found a seat, take a moment to thank everyone for their hard work. Congratulate them on their level of concentration. Both the stewards and everyone who listened so carefully have made a contribution to the learning that is taking place.

Announce a "centering break" before the dialogue continues.

SAY There has been a great deal of wonderful exchange—listening and talking—so far in our dialogues today. Before we have to talk or listen anymore, let's let our minds slow down a little. Please sit quietly for a couple of minutes and relax. Close your eyes if you like, breathe and feel your breath as it goes in and out.

Stay quiet for two or three minutes while you and the group relax. It is important for you as the facilitator to relax as well. Avoid looking at notes or shuffling through things to figure out what comes next.

When it feels like the group is ready, quietly say:

SAY Thank you. That felt great. I'd like us to hear from the stewards first. What did you find out?

Let any of the stewards who want to speak about what happened in the exercise go first. Thank each one when he or she has finished speaking. There is no need for you to comment at this time. Your job as facilitator for this exercise is not to sum up, but to help keep a sense of calm openness for the group. Above all, be sure that every comment you make encourages and supports. People in dialogue are counting on you to keep the environment safe for them to say what is important to them.

Now point at the *Dialogue Questions* overhead and ask the whole group:

ASK What does it mean to you to be in this large group with us all today?
How does it affect you as an individual?
How does what we are learning here affect all of us as a group?

CONCLUSION Depending on the group, this final dialogue may go on and on. When the talking has stopped, or when you have run out of time, thank everyone again. You may want to sum up briefly now or mention one important new thing that you personally are learning from the exercise so far.

Often in a dialogue, people get ideas about things they would like to do about what they have learned. It may be important for them to get together with others to talk about that.

SAY Some of you may want to continue talking or may have some ideas for action plans based on what we are learning together here. If you would like to get a group together to talk about planning or just to continue the conversation, please stand.

If people stand up, ask them what they would like to get people together to talk about. Let people know that they can find those people at the front of the room when the exercise is over. They can then exchange contact information, set dates to continue, or have a meeting right then to decide what they will do in their new groups.

Once these announcements have been made, thank the group again, encourage them to continue having good conversations with one another, and end the session.

Jenny Beer, who gave us the idea for the exercise *What You See Is What You Get*, is a teacher, consultant and mediator who works with business and community groups. A group of women that Jenny has been working with in the former Soviet republic of Kyrgyzstan recently decided to invite other people in their community in to see the results of their work together. This is a good tool to use as a way to expand the impact of the *Diversity Dialogue* if your group decides to continue meeting.

Hold Please

TYPE Centering, Communication Skills, Conflict Skills

PURPOSE To give people the opportunity to practice calming people in order to be able to understand how they can help them.

EQUIPMENT NEEDED 5 chairs in the front of the room for the demonstration

PREP Handout 16: *Hold Please Issues List* (page 223)
Flipchart 16: *Hold Please Practice Times* (page 253)
Flipchart 17: *Debriefing Questions* (page 254)

TIME NEEDED 6 hours, not including breaks

Every time I have asked a conflict resolution workshop group to tell me what they want to learn in their session, several people say something like, "I want to know what to do when somebody is in my face."

What they are looking for is usually some strategy or recipe for what to do when trying to help someone or protect oneself from another person who is very angry and verbally aggressive. Sometimes the best thing to do is walk away and come back later.

This exercise helps us to practice for when it makes more sense to stay and talk with the person. The three main challenges in this situation are staying calm, deciding what to do, and making sure that you and the other person can get through the conversation without feeling damaged. The best way to become strong enough to help people when they are being aggressive is to combine good practice of what to say with good practice of being "centered." This exercise is an excellent way for people to practice different approaches at getting through to a person who is resistant to your help. For more on centering, see *Staying Cool in a Conflict* on page 77.—Bill

EXERCISE OUTLINE

INTRODUCTION	Explain the purpose and structure of the exercise.
DEMONSTRATION	Four volunteers join you for a quick run-through.
PRACTICE AND DEBRIEF IN GROUPS OF FIVE	Playing the peacemaker with an angry person
INSIGHTS	Large group debriefing and learning.
ACTION PLANNING	Applying new thinking to work.
CLOSE	Thank, summarize, and encourage.

**CONDUCTING THE EXERCISE:
HOLD PLEASE**

INTRODUCTION Explain to the group that this exercise is designed to help them speak to someone who is very upset. Often in a conflict the presenting issue is not what is causing the problem. For example: Lynette may blow up because Dennis moved her stapler, but what is really bothering her is that she just had a fight with her mother. The stapler issue is important and needs to be addressed, but it may help Lynette to calm down and realize what else is bothering her. Even though Lynette is upset, she may also be resisting your help because of feelings she has about needing help. She may be embarrassed, or feel vulnerable, or may want to "stay mad" instead of looking for a solution.

 SAY Each of us has 1,000 voices in our heads—everyone we ever met, the influences of our families, our culture, and our personal beliefs. If someone is angry and you need to speak with them, remember that you are not just speaking to the person you see in front of you, but to all 1,000 (or more) voices.

I'll show you what I mean, then we can all get a chance to practice.

DEMONSTRATION   Select four volunteers from the group, and ask them to take seats at the front of the room. One of the volunteers will take the role of the peacemaker, one will be the person who is angry, one will represent all of the voices that are working against the peacemaker, and the fourth person will represent all of the voices that are working to support the peacemaker.

Explain the roles to your volunteers and to the group. Tell them that this exercise is adapted from counselor training. In counselor training the person who plays the client chooses a topic or experience that they find upsetting and resists help. The counselor being trained tries to get a word in edgewise with the "client" while the pro and anti voices talk or even yell in the client's ear. The anti-counselor works hard to interfere with the counselor—pointing out mistakes, highlighting differences, and exaggerating the negative thoughts the client has about counseling. The pro-counselor works to bring the client and the counselor together—finds similarities and common ground. It is almost as if the client has a little devil on one shoulder and a little angel on the other, as in an old-fashioned cartoon.

To be sure everyone understands, share this sample excerpt from a typical session:

Client: Go away. I don't want to talk to anybody.
Pro-Counselor: She looks like she's nice.
Anti-Counselor: You don't need this goody two-shoes telling you what to do.
Counselor: How are you today?
Client: I said go away!
Anti-Counselor: That's right. Be strong. You don't need her tricks.
Pro-Counselor: She looks pretty harmless. Why not give her a chance?

And so on.

Explain that the challenge in the exercise is for the counselor-in-training to speak calmly with the client while taking into account what the pro-counselor and anti-counselor are saying.

 SAY   It's a little like staying calm and centered while everything around you seems to be on fire. You're alternately being attacked and supported while trying to listen fully to everyone and get through to the person you are trying to help. The good news is that counselors who have this training learn to respond to objections and support to what they are doing as it happens and get better at helping their clients.

By now your volunteers are getting the idea that they have signed up for a difficult exercise. Reassure them by saying:

Since none of us are training to be counselors, we have taken the original exercise and made it a little easier to do. We will still get a chance to work with someone whose thinking is interfering with our attempts to communicate. What we have done for this workshop is slow the exercise down by adding a hold button.

Let your angry person select an issue to be angry about from the Issues List. You can use Handout 16: *Issues List*, or you can have the group brainstorm a list of their own.

 SAY My four volunteers are ready to go. We have an angry person we are trying to help, a peacemaker, a little angel, and a little devil. I will be the telephone operator—pointing at the person who is to speak next, and putting someone on hold when I want that person to stop talking.

So, if our angry person is speaking and I want to hear from the little devil, I will point at the angry person and say, "Hold please" then point at the little devil and say, "Go ahead!"

Tell the volunteers that you are going to switch quickly back and forth. They will have to stay on their toes and listen well to what is going on. Each of them will always need to be ready with a comment. The peacemaker and the angry person will only speak to one another. The little devil and the little angel will only speak to the angry person. The angrier the angry person is and the more extreme the little devil and little angel are in their positions, the better the exercise.

Now let your volunteers try the exercise in front of the rest of the group for about five minutes—long enough to get into it. Stop them after five minutes and thank them for helping you with the demonstration.

Show the group Flip Chart 17: Debriefing Questions. Tell them that they will ask and answer the same questions when they practice the exercise in small groups. Use the Debriefing Questions to process the little bit of the exercise that your volunteers have demonstrated:

Ask the "angry person":

ASK 1. How did that feel?
2. What did the peacemaker do that worked for you?
3. What would you have liked the peacemaker to do differently?

Ask the "peacemaker":

ASK 1. How did that feel?
2. What did you do that seemed to work well?
3. What would you do differently next time?

Thank them, praise them for their courage, and let them return to their seats.

PRACTICE Separate the group into subgroups of five each and let them decide who will be the angry person, the peacemaker, the little angel, the little devil, and the telephone operator. You can let them pick their own groups, assign them to groups, or use one of the ideas from *Fun Ways to Break into Groups* on page 268. Be sure that everyone taking the role of the angry person has chosen an issue to be angry about and that everyone knows what roles they are going to play.

Show the group Flipchart 16: Practice Times. Tell them they have will have thirty minutes—fifteen minutes to practice and fifteen to debrief. You will be the timekeeper.

Be sure that everyone understands the instructions, and ask them to begin. After fifteen minutes of role-playing, tell them it is time to debrief. After fifteen minutes of debriefing, ask them to select new roles and begin again. Repeat the exercise five times so that everyone gets a chance to take the peacemaker role.

INSIGHTS   When all five people in each subgroup has had a turn in the role of the peacemaker, end the exercise. This is often a good time to take a break—it gives people a chance to catch their breaths, get away from the sometimes emotional roles they have been playing, and have some good unstructured conversation.

Now use the Debriefing Questions for a general discussion of the exercise. This is the third time the group has been exposed to these questions. You will find that people examine their choices more deeply and talk about new lessons learned each time the questions are revisited.

ACTION PLANNING   Ask the group for ideas about how they can apply what they have learned to their work. If there are individuals or groups who are excited about a particular idea, schedule a follow-up meeting to help them refine their idea, maintain their enthusiasm, and practice what they have learned.

CLOSE   Thank the group for working so hard, and for giving you a chance to learn with them. Mention a few new insights that you have had as a result of the day's work. Acknowledge that the exercise has probably got them thinking a great deal, and recommend that they continue to mull things over. They can jot down ideas as they occur to them, talk to their friends from the workshop with specific ideas for application, or contact you with questions or to talk about what new thinking is rising up as a result of their time together.

This exercise is adapted from Paul Pedersen's triad training model for counselors. Please turn to the Toolbox section for more on Paul and his worldwide work as a teacher, trainer, author, and consultant.

The Synthetic Culture Lab

TYPE Centering, Communication Skills, Conflict Skills, Diversity Awareness, Team-work, Worldview

PURPOSE This workshop helps participants to:
> examine issues raised during cross-cultural communication and conflict
> enhance consultation skills in other cultures
> identify culturally driven conflict management styles
> develop a framework for understanding other cultures
> increase each participant's multicultural self awareness

EQUIPMENT NEEDED flipchart paper and markers

PREP Extensive: Read all of the materials and become familiar with the traits and characteristics of each of the synthetic cultures. It would be helpful to find out a little about your workshop participants also. You may wish to visit Paul Pedersen's Web site for more insight: http://soeweb.syr.edu/chs/pedersen/.

Handouts can be sent to the workshop participants prior to class if desired. If you decide to send the handouts ahead of time, instruct participants to review the different simulated cultures before coming to the workshop. Ask them to choose one with which they most identify. Make sure that your training room is large enough for all four groups to sit comfortably at tables with space in between. The room should allow for free movement between the tables, and

We learned this exercise from Paul Pedersen at a National Multicultural Institute workshop in 1996. It is presented here almost exactly as Paul taught it to us. Paul Pedersen and Allen Ivey have written up The Synthetic Culture Lab in *Communication and Conflict: 25 High-Impact Exercises for Teachers and Trainers* (Praeger Publishers, 1993). For more about Paul and his work, see the Toolbox section.

for enough privacy for negotiations to take place at each of the four tables without disturbing the other groups.

Prepare enough copies of the handouts for all participants:

17. *Guidelines for the Four Synthetic Cultures* (pages 224–231)

18. *Synthetic Cultures: Behaviors and Expectations* (pages 232–233)

19. *Mediating Conflict between Synthetic Cultures* (pages 234–235)

Prepare Flipchart 18: *Consultant Rotation Schedule* (page 255)

TIME NEEDED   4–5 hours, including breaks

EXERCISE OUTLINE

INTRODUCTION   (1–1.5 hours)

Introduce the four synthetic cultures: Alpha, Beta, Gamma, and Delta. Participants select to join one of four groups representing each of the cultures. In these groups, participants will:

1. learn the assumptions and roles of their synthetic culture

2. discuss the problems created by the "outsiders" in each synthetic culture,

3. select a team of consultants from their synthetic culture who will visit with the other groups to help them deal with the problem of "outsiders"

THE ACTIVITY   (1.5 hours)

When each of the four small groups have completed the above tasks, they will meet with each of the other groups—in role—to discuss the problem of outsiders. Representatives from each group will take turns meeting with each of the other groups for a discussion about the problem of outsiders.

INSIGHTS   Examine examples of conflict between the synthetic cultures and identify examples of "common ground" and positive expectations and/or values that persons from both groups of synthetic cultures share.

CONDUCTING THE EXERCISE:
THE SYNTHETIC CULTURE LAB

INTRODUCTION   Distribute the handout sheets and ask the group to follow along as you explain them.

SAY The Synthetic Culture Lab is an advanced role-play or simulation. In order for this activity to be successful, it is important for you to understand the different roles or cultures that will be involved. Let's take a look at the handouts and review what is important to each culture. As we review these, start thinking about which of the cultures you can identify with and which one you may want to belong to as part of our simulation.

It is important to remember that although these synthetic cultures are slightly exaggerated for the purpose of the exercise, that their characteristics are based on real cultural traits. All cultures include elements of each trait to a lesser or greater extent.

Please also bear in mind that the simulated cultures are purposely somewhat one-dimensional to help us keep the exercise from becoming too complicated. In other words, a culture usually has other dominant traits. In this simulation, we are really only focusing on one or two for emphasis and practice.

Have the group look at Handout 17: *Guidelines for the Four Synthetic Cultures.*

SAY Our four synthetic cultures are:

- Alpha—high power distance
- Beta—strong uncertainty avoidance
- Gamma—strong individualism
- Delta—high masculine

Review the culture sheets with the group by reading each item and allowing questions for clarification. When you have finished, ask participants to select one synthetic culture group to join.

SAY Now choose which synthetic culture you would like to act out during the simulation. You may choose to belong to any of the cultures, but it may be most interesting to you either to select a culture that fits in with your own point of view, or one that strongly contrasts with it.

Try to form groups with about the same number of people in each by asking people to volunteer to move to another group if needed. Have the groups sit together in different parts of the room.

Ask the four synthetic culture groups to sit with their new synthetic culture co-members to socialize one another into their new cultural identity. Tell them to discuss the rules for their synthetic culture and to try to memorize the different characteristics.

SAY I'd like you to sit with your new culture group now. As a group, talk about the different rules and begin to memorize the characteristics. While you discuss the written rules for your synthetic culture, start to act out your culture's rules. Actually begin to take on the new synthetic culture identity in everything you say and do during the discussion.

Once you are comfortable with the rules and conversation style of your group, look at the list of problems created in your synthetic culture because of "outsiders." The "outsiders" are the other synthetic cultures.

Direct the participants to the last of the handouts—18: *Synthetic Culture: Behaviors and Expectations* and 19: *Mediating between Synthetic Cultures.*

 SAY

Prepare a list of two or three specific problems that have resulted from interacting with the outsiders. Use the *Mediating Conflict between Synthetic Cultures* handout to help you with your list.

Finally, ask them to pick a team of two consultants who will visit the other synthetic cultures to help work out the problems caused by the outsiders.

THE ACTIVITY

Each group will send their team of two consultants to another synthetic culture group.

Complete the rotations three times so that each culture has sent a team to each of the three other cultures.

Show the participants Flipchart 19: *Consultant Rotation Schedule,* and explain that each rotation will include:

➤ A ten-minute consultation in role

➤ Followed by a ten-minute debriefing out of role

➤ And ten minutes to report back to their home synthetic cultures on what they learned

 SAY

When I say to begin, each pair of consultants from each simulated culture should go visit the culture to your right.

When you arrive, you will engage in a ten-minute consultation/negotiation with one another in role. Your task is to present the list of problems you are having with that culture that your group has come up with. During these meetings, everyone must act in line with the rules for their synthetic culture. This means that when the consultants from Beta visit Alpha, for example, the Beta consultants will stay in the role of Beta culture and the Alpha people will stay in the role of Alpha culture.

I will tell you when ten minutes have passed. At that time, I'd like you to come out of your roles and discuss how the consultation/negotiation went. You can give one another feedback about what went well, what did not, things you learned from the activity, and so on.

Again, I will tell you when the ten minutes for your debriefing are up. At that point, you will return to your own culture group to report back what happened, in role. Each rotation will take thirty minutes to complete.

Keep track of time during each rotation, and let the participants know when to stop, start, and switch.

INSIGHTS   When all of the rotations are complete, get the entire workshop group together to talk about what they are learning. Ask participants to talk about what happened during the consultations or negotiations, how it felt being in role, and what they discovered.

Have each synthetic culture group report back to the larger group about how best to find common ground and agreement between their own culture and persons from the other synthetic culture groups.

Get people to talk about what they are learning. Find out what worked, what did not, any breakthroughs in problem solving, and things that helped or hurt communication. Ask them to make recommendations and share insights on what the other cultures could have done better, as well as what their own team could have done better.

Write Your Own Case Study

TYPE Communication Skills, Conflict Skills, Teamwork

PURPOSE Participants will learn by doing as they create a fictional conflict then apply simple yet powerful conflict resolution models in order to solve it.

EQUIPMENT NEEDED Flipchart (or overhead projector) and markers

PREP A copy of Handout 20: Write Your Own Case Study (pages 236–237) for each participant
Overheads or Flipcharts:
19. 2 Ways of Seeing Conflict (page 256)
20. ROI (page 257)
21. ARIA (page 258)
22. ROI & ARIA (page 259)

TIME NEEDED 4–5 hours, including breaks

EXERCISE OUTLINE

INTRODUCTION Share the goals of the exercise with the group.

TEAM CONVERSATION AND WRITING The workshop group will use the *Write Your Own Case Study* handout to make decisions about the fictitious company, the adversaries, and their conflict.

PRACTICE CASE STUDY Two adversary teams will begin to escalate the conflict, then switch modes and work to solve the problem.

INSIGHTS Participants will talk about what worked and what they would change, then use a conflict resolution model to analyze and improve the adversaries' approach to their difference.

173

CONDUCTING THE EXERCISE:
WRITE YOUR OWN CASE STUDY

INTRODUCTION Tell the group that they are going to work with you to design their communication and conflict workshop on the spot. What they will create together is a very thorough outline that they can then follow in order to build a case study.

SAY   Writing a role-play or a case study is usually the course designer's job. We save this task for ourselves because it takes a great deal of time and analytical thinking to write one successfully. Besides, it is good practice. As we designers create the case study we can get a better understanding of some of the less obvious details of the subject we are teaching.

Today, we will all get a chance to dig into the topic of conflict resolution by creating and testing a case study together. We may all come away with better ideas and more awareness than when we started.

TEAM CONVERSATION AND WRITING Now you will work with the group to create the case study. As they write together, you will stop from time to time to explain what they need to know as they decide what to include in their case-study outline.

Pass out the *Write Your Own Case Study* Handout.

Starting with the first section, *The Company*, lead the group through the handout.

The Company

SAY   Because we are looking at conflicts that arise at work, the first thing we need to know about is the company where our two adversaries work. What business or industry is this company in?

There are many ways for the group to make decisions as they fill in the blanks. We use a very fast and fun method we learned from Frank Hoffmann. Frank is the VP of organizational development at XLEnvironmental, an environmental risk management service. His workshops—which he has led at companies and many national conferences—are always lively, unpredictable, and memorable. Our handout is based on a form that Frank uses. When it is time to fill in the form, he simply goes around the room pointing at the next person. Whoever's turn it is says whatever is needed to fill in the blank. You may want a little more discussion when you get to the point where you define the conflict, but Frank's wild and wooly approach is great for the first two sections of the handout.

Continue to work through the form, filling in the blanks for size, location, and name of the company.

The Two Adversaries

Now the group will need to make decisions about the two adversaries. Tell them that people have many different names for two or more people who have a difference: disputants, combatants, enemies, opponents, and so on. Ask the group if they can think of any other names for people in conflict.

Mention that many of the names we use for people in a conflict with each other have strong negative connotations. Some people prefer to call two people who differ as "partners," because they have worked together to create the dispute and now must continue to work together to change their points of view or the conditions they have created.

Explain that for this exercise, we will use the word "adversary."

SAY

We like the word "adversary" because it means someone who is against you who does not necessarily mean you any harm. The word "adversary" comes to us from the Latin *ad verto*—to turn toward. If we are fighting, we need to turn toward the other. If we are working together, we need to turn toward one another as well.

We may not end up in agreement, but as adversaries, we have turned toward the other so that we may begin to understand. Interestingly, *ad verto* is also the root of the word "advertise." Adversaries let each other know who they are and what they want. They may have difficulty understanding one another's "advertisements" at first, but as they turn toward each other, the adversaries can sometimes adjust their messages as they begin to learn about what may be most effective in a specific situation.

Now you are ready to fill in The Two Adversaries section of the handout. Ask group members for the departments, job titles, and names for the two adversaries.

Tell the group that you will take a time-out from working on the case study from time to time so that you can talk with them about some aspects of conflict that will help them with their planning. This first time-out will be about how the way that people see conflict can influence how they approach it.

SAY

How our two adversaries view conflict will help determine how they approach working things out. It can also sometimes explain how their difference began in the first place.

Show the group the overhead of Flipchart 19: 2 *Ways of Seeing Conflict.*

SAY Here are two ways of seeing conflict that can influence the way our two adversaries will approach each other. Conflict can be seen as a contest to be won or as a problem to be solved. Conflict can also be seen as an opportunity to learn about yourself and your relationship with the world.

Let me explain what I mean by *Win, Lose, or Draw*. If we see conflict as a contest to be won, there can only be three possible outcomes. You will win the contest, you will lose, or there will be a tie. If somebody wins, somebody else loses and goes away unhappy. If it is a tie, nobody is happy.

If people go away unhappy after working on a difference together, is the conflict really over?

What will happen if these unhappy people still need to work with one another?

What will happen the next time there is a clash?

Show the group the second part of the 2 *Ways of Seeing* flipchart.

SAY Now let's look at conflict as a problem for our two adversaries to solve together. When we are working to solve a problem, we can make it even, make it bigger, or make it different. Here are some quick examples.

Make it even means that whatever is being fought over is sliced right down the middle. Whatever it is—food, space, money, time—is divided as evenly as possible.

Make it bigger means that we somehow get more of what is being fought over. For example, let's suppose that there aren't enough computers to go around for a particular work group. Make it even would probably lead us to some sort of time schedule arrangement. Make it bigger would mean buying more computers.

Make it different is another way to solve a problem. When we make a problem different, we change the way we look at it. If the work group does not have enough computers to go around, we could ask questions such as, "What do you use the computer for?" or "When do your use the computer?" We could even ask, "What does the computer mean to you personally?" or "Why is it important to you that you have a computer?"

The answers we get to these "make it different" questions can give us enough information to truly look at the problem in a different way. It may even change our definition of what an acceptable solution could be. Instead of being a difference over computers in short supply, we may end up talking about respect or status. We may even find ourselves with a process improvement project to lead instead of a fight to referee.

It is important to note that there is no place for blame in any of these problem-solving ways of seeing conflict. On the other hand, when we see

> A person's point of view about conflict can have a strong influence on the way that person acts when he or she has a difference with someone. A person's culture, the way he or she views the world, his or her learning style, and what he or she will accept as proof also has an impact on their approach to any given difference. For more on these "ways of seeing," including exercises, stories to use in training workshops, and discussion guides, see Bill Withers' book *The Conflict Management Skills Workshop* (AMACOM, 2002).

a difference as a contest to win, we need to make sure that the other side loses. One good way to do that is to blame the other side, especially if you are trying to get onlookers to agree that you should win.

Problem-solving moves us away from who did what and toward what we are going to do next.

Tell the group that for the case study, we will have the adversaries begin by using a Win, Lose, or Draw approach to their difference and then shift to Problem Solving.

The Difference
Tell the group that it is now time for them to figure out what the two adversaries are fighting about.

SAY We have done a good job of setting the stage. We know a little bit about where the people are working, what their names are, and we know that they—at least for now—view their conflict as a contest to be won. Now we are going to figure out what type of difference is bringing our two adversaries together.

Just as we carefully chose the word "adversary" for the people who have this difference, we intentionally have chosen the word "difference" to name what is going on. There are plenty of other names we could use: conflict, fight, spat, squabble. Sometimes we even just use the word "thing," as in "Don't make a big thing out of it."

Ask the group for some of the other names they use for a difference between two or more people. When the group has run out of other names, tell them that any of them could work from time to time. For this exercise, we are going to use the name "difference."

SAY We are going to say "difference" because it can mean a dispute, but it also can simply mean diversity.

"We have a difference between us."

A difference isn't necessarily one person's fault; sometimes, it just is. The difference may not go away. Our job with a difference is to understand it and figure out how we can either incorporate it or work with it. It is hard to see a difference as a contest to be won.

The form now asks us to decide whether our two adversaries are differing about a resource, an objective, or an identity issue. Let me explain.

Show the ROI overhead or flipchart, and say:

SAY This model was developed by Jay Rothman, a writer, teacher, and consultant who works with people in complicated conflict situations.

For more on the ROI and ARIA models, and to learn more about the work that Jay and his colleagues are doing as peacemakers in schools, organizations, and communities, visit www.ariagroup.com.

Jay has made it easy to remember these three types of difference by using the acronym ROI. The R is for resources, the O is for objectives, and the I stands for identity. After I explain them, we will decide which type of difference we will focus on for our case study.

When you look at this diagram, you will see that conflict is shown as an iceberg. The part we can see is the resource that the adversaries have a difference about. Hidden from view are the deeper aspects of the difference—objectives and identity.

Resources are things that we fight over. For example, not enough computers to go around.

When we differ over objectives, we are bumping into one another because we have goals that seem to be in conflict—if you get to where you want to go, then I can't get to where I want to go. So watch out!

Identity has to do with who the adversaries are and what they believe about themselves in relation to other people and everything else. It has to do with rights, pride, traditions, respect—sometimes it is about the very essence of who we feel we are. In identity differences, we feel like whatever the other person is doing or believing will keep us from being the person we need to be.

The difference may appear to be about resources, but that may be only the tip of the iceberg. We may be fighting about computers and be willing to give them up if we can be acknowledged and supported for who we are. For example, someone may only rarely use the computer on her desk but may feel that not having a computer may mean that she is not seen as important.

Just to be sure that I have explained this well, let's get some examples from you.

Ask the group to call out examples of differences about resources, objectives, or identity from work, family life, or the news. Ask them what type of difference they have to deal with at work most of the time. If the group consensus seems to be either resource or objective, ask them if sometimes there may be identity issues "under the waterline."

Now turn to the person whose turn it is to make the next decision and ask him or her to decide what to choose on the next part of the form: resource, objective, or identity. Mark the form with his or her decision. That will be the type of difference you will focus on in your case study.

Now ask the next person to choose what they will specifically be fighting over. This person may want to get some suggestions from the rest of the group. Remember that even if your group has chosen to focus on an identity issue, the tip of the iceberg may still present a resource or objective to differ on. In order for the group to have something to work with, ask this person to enlarge on the conflict. For example, if he or she said they will be differing about a parking space, ask for a story. Help him or her make up some details for the story by asking such questions as:

ASK

> ➤ Where is this taking place?
> ➤ How did this difference come up?
> ➤ How long has this been going on?
> ➤ Why does one or the other person think this is important?

Once you know at least generally what the difference is about, separate the workshop group into two subgroups.

For some creative ways to break your large workshop group into two or more smaller groups quickly, see page 268.

SAY

Now we are going to get creative. We know what the difference is about, we know how deep on the iceberg the real difference goes, and we know the way that each of the two adversaries view conflict. Now we need to tell the story. Using what we know, write your character's version of the story—how s/he feels about it, how s/he wants to approach it, and what s/he feels s/he really needs to get out of it.

Note: If the group has chosen to work on an identity conflict, let them know that often the people caught up in it will not realize why it hurts so much. They may even be embarrassed or angry with themselves for fighting over some insignificant resource until they realize that what really matters to them is what they feel is an attack on their ability to continue being who they want to be. In these situations we hear people say things like, "I don't really care about the computers, it's the principle of the thing." For this reason, they will want to begin talking about their identity conflict as if it were about either resources or objectives.

Give the subgroups fifteen minutes to come up with their adversary's story, then have them each read it to the whole group. At this point, you may have to do some editing to keep the story straight. It is all right if the two adversaries do not see eye-to-eye on what is happening, but be sure that the stories are close enough so that they can work well together.

SAY In order to make our role-play work, I am going to make some editorial choices about the stories so that they work well together.

There is no right way for you to make these editorial choices, but try to make the pieces fit in a way that does not overly disrupt the work the groups have already done. Your job here is to make the pieces fit, just as a child will do when instructing an adult in make-believe. Instead of "you be the daddy and I'll be the mommy," you are putting some shape into the case study so that it will work for the group when they begin to play with it.

PRACTICE CASE STUDY The group now has a rough but workable case study outline. Congratulate them on their hard work, and tell them that they can celebrate by making the case study come to life.

Even though there is not a word-for-word script to follow, everyone in the group now should know enough about the specific difference and the two adversaries to improvise as the case unfolds.

Fighting to Win
Explain to the group that they will now have a good old-fashioned argument. Each subgroup will actually be playing the role of just one person in the difference. Group 1 will be the adversary they have been writing for, and Group 2 will be the adversary of their own labors.

The two groups will argue as two people by first having a spokesperson make a statement and then hearing the spokesperson from the other group make a response.

The groups will be able to quickly plan what the spokespersons will say between statements and responses. The spokesperson will then respond to the latest response from the other side, and so on.

You will keep the pressure on the adversaries by reminding them that they see conflict as a contest to be won and must work to defeat the other "person." You will also give them only two minutes to plan each response.

SAY This group is going to be Ralph [or whatever the first adversary's name is], and this group will be Bianca [or whatever second adversary's name is].

Ralph will begin the exchange by making a strong claim for control of the entire office space [or whatever the difference is that the group has decided on].

After Ralph makes this first claim, the Bianca group will have two minutes to respond with another claim or some good argument that will help Bianca to win the contest. When two minutes are up, I will require Bianca to reply. Then Ralph will get two minutes and so on until I call time-out. Remember—both Bianca and Ralph want to win this.

Give the first team two minutes to prepare, then have them make their first statement. As the two adversaries argue back and forth, make notes on a flipchart or overhead. You will show these to the group later. If the two adversaries begin to make concessions or begin to work together to solve problems, remind them that their view of conflict is as a contest to be won. They should make strong statements for their case and can even ask questions to trap or trick their adversary. They need to defeat the other side.

Your flipchart notes may look something like Sample Chart 5: *Ralph and Bianca*.

When the argument gets to the point where nothing can be done but make threats or call names, stop the exercise. Give the groups a moment to calm down. Usually people will have enjoyed having a chance to "misbehave" by arguing, but you need to be sure to give the group a chance to cool down and "get out of role." If people hang onto this part of the exercise, they can take some of what was said to "Ralph" or "Bianca" as if it had been said to them.

 SAY

As you cool down from this exercise, take a minute to get yourselves out of the role-play. Take Ralph or Bianca off as if you were taking off a coat.

If the exchange was particularly lively, you may even suggest that certain people shake hands with others to reinforce that the antagonism was pretend and that it is time to move on to a more constructive step.

Turning Toward Each Other to Solve the Problem
Tell the group that now it is time to shift gears. Give the group the following instruction, depending on whether the difference is resource-, objective-, or identity-based:

IF THE DIFFERENCE IS A RESOURCE DIFFERENCE, SAY:

It is time for us to shift to problem-solving. Bianca, you now have five minutes to come up with an idea that might make it even, bigger, or different. Ralph, you will then have five minutes to respond. If Ralph does not accept Bianca's suggestion, then Ralph will have to come up with another idea for Bianca to consider.

Both of you will continue taking turns to come up with ideas until you find one that works for both.

Don't give up. For this part of the exercise, Ralph and Bianca believe strongly that this is a problem that can be solved.

IF THE DIFFERENCE IS AN OBJECTIVE DIFFERENCE, SAY:

Before we can shift to problem-solving, Bianca and Ralph need to let each other know why what they want is so important to them. You will each have five minutes to prepare a statement about why this objective is important. The statement won't be about trying to convince the other person, but about letting the other person know how important your objective is and why. Listen carefully to the other side's statement because you are going to repeat it back to them so that they know you understand. Once you have repeated each other's statements and have an understanding of why the other side's objective is so important, you will shift to problem-solving.

Bianca, you will then have five minutes to come up with an idea to make it even, bigger, or different that takes Ralph's objective into some account. Ralph, you will then have five minutes to respond. Ralph doesn't have to accept Bianca's suggestion, but will have to come up with another idea if he doesn't. Both of you will continue taking turns to come up with ideas until you find one that works for both. Don't give up. For this part of the exercise, Ralph and Bianca believe strongly that this is a problem that can be solved.

IF THE DIFFERENCE IS ABOUT IDENTITY, SAY:

So far in the argument, it has been difficult for you really to hear one another. We want to shift into problem-solving mode, but we need to be sure that there is real understanding first. You both seem to be very emotional about this difference. I will now give you ten minutes to prepare a statement about why you are so angry, what it is that you want, and why it is so very important to you. Be sure to go into as much detail as you can.

Listen carefully to the other side's statement because you are going to repeat it back to them so that they know you understand. Once you have repeated each other's statements and have an understanding of why the other side's objective is so important, you will shift to problem-solving.

Bianca, you will have five minutes to come up with an idea that might make it even, bigger, or different. Ralph, you will then have five minutes to respond. Ralph may or may not accept Bianca's suggestion, but will have to come up with another idea. Both of you will continue taking turns to come up with ideas until you find one that works for both. Don't give up. For this part of the exercise, Ralph and Bianca believe strongly that this is a problem that can be solved.

IF THE DIFFERENCE SHIFTED FROM ONE TYPE TO ANOTHER, SAY:

Just as often happens in real-life differences, we have seen a shift. We thought we were talking about a resource (or an objective), but it looks as if we have moved into talking about an objective (or identity). This is perfectly normal, and is a good example of how differences can become more complicated as we work on them. *Then follow the instructions for the appropriate level of difference.*

Keep time for the adversaries and continue to keep notes on the flipchart as they take turns. You may need to remind them to continue problem-solving from time to time.

Reflection

When each side has had four or five turns, stop the exercise and ask a general, open question, such as:

ASK

How did that feel?

What happened?

What would you like to have done differently?

Ask the group to comment on what they saw, what they felt, and what decisions were made about what to do and say next. They can use your flipchart notes to remember what happened and in what order.

Encourage them by asking:

ASK

We predicted that this conflict would be _____ [resource, objective, or identity-based]. Did it stay where we thought it would, or did it shift? If you were helping these two adversaries, where would you have begun?

The Approach

Knowing where to begin to solve a problem can be difficult for people who are deep into a difference and for those that are trying to help them.

Show the participants the ARIA flip chart and say:

SAY

This is another model from Jay Rothman, who gave us the ROI model we used earlier. It is easy to remember, and will help us to decide how to start working on our difference. When you understand this ARIA model, I will show you how it neatly meshes with the ROI model.

ARIA is a simple way to remember a general, step-by-step approach to working out differences. The first A stands for "antagonism." The R stands for "resonance." The I stands for "invention." The final A is for "action."

When someone is helping people with a difference using the ARIA approach, he or she begins with antagonism. What this means is that—in a

There are some excellent ARIA exercises on Jay Rothman's ARIA Group Web site—www.ariagroup.com. These exercises are designed for someone choosing a conflict–resolution approach alone, with one other adversary or with two groups who differ. These exercises may help as you prepare to lead the *Write Your Own Case Study* exercise, or you can use them with your workshop group to reinforce what they are learning about ARIA. For a deeper, more detailed look at Jay's work, his theories, and how to apply them, please see the Toolbox section.

controlled way—the adversaries are encouraged to let it all out. They say everything that is on their minds about the difference, and may even use words to attack the other person. During this antagonism phase, the adversaries may become emotional. That is okay; in fact, it can even be helpful.

During antagonism, both adversaries get everything off their chests. They may hear the other person's entire story for the first time. Antagonism may also wear them out a little bit. The person helping will know that the adversaries are finished with antagonism when they are tired and quiet, when the story they are telling begins to repeat, or when they start moving to the next step by themselves.

The next step in the ARIA is resonance. What does "resonance" mean?

You can expect such answers as:

- ➤ a deep sound
- ➤ a vibration
- ➤ an echo
- ➤ when something trembles or shakes

 SAY

In the ARIA model, resonance has to do with two people who are working at separate frequencies who now start sending and receiving on the same wavelength. As one person's ideas or feelings "resonate" with the other, the sending and receiving begin to merge. The second person is able to send them back accurately. In the resonance step of ARIA, we help the adversaries to hear carefully and to think about one another's stories. They listen so that they can feel why the story is so important to the other person. They listen so they can understand why the story makes sense to the other person. They analyze both stories. They listen for feeling. They listen for common ground. Sometimes we may check for resonance by having them tell their stories back to one another.

When resonance is moving forward, the adversaries begin to understand one another's thoughts and feelings. They may still disagree, but they have a good idea of why they differ. Now they are ready to begin to work together creatively.

The I in ARIA is for invention. When the adversaries have moved from antagonism through resonance, they are ready to invent next steps. In many cases, if they had tried to start working on their difference at the invention stage they would have become frustrated. Even if invention seems to be going well, if the two adversaries work on only the tip of the iceberg, they can create future differences that may be even more difficult to address.

Without working through antagonism and resonance, a deep-seated conflict is often approached as if it were only a pie that needs to be split up quickly so that everyone can get back to work.

The final A in ARIA stands for action. This is action planning. We ask ourselves, "How will we work together in the future to benefit from our inventions?"

In Italian, an aria is a musical tune—a melody. When we follow the steps and people allow things to fall into place, we can truly "make beautiful music together." As Jay Rothman has said so well, "Out of the dissonance of conflict can come the resonance of harmony and cooperation."

Quickly review both ROI and ARIA by repeating what the letters stand for:

ROI IS:	**ARIA IS:**
Resources	**A**ntagonism
Objectives	**R**esonance
Identity	**I**nvention
	Action

Ask the group for questions or comments up to this point to be sure that they understand these two models. Let them know that it is important for them to grasp these fairly simple models because you are now going to combine ROI and ARIA to help determine the best approach to working on a particular difference.

Show the group the ROI/ARIA flipchart. Explain that ARIA and ROI can be used together. Once you determine whether a difference is resource-based, objective-based, or identity-based, you can match it up with ROI on the chart to decide how to begin.

SAY

We could argue that every difference has some part of it that is identity-based, but if we are certain that the adversaries are having a problem that is mainly because of a resource, we can start right in at invention. With a resource-based issue, we start by brainstorming *make it even, make it bigger,* or *make it different* solutions.

If our adversaries are bumping into each other primarily because their objectives are competing, we can start with resonance. They would begin by listening carefully while the other person explains what he or she needs and why the objective and a certain way of getting there are so important.

In cases where the difference is more deep-seated, where it is a question of identity, we need to begin with antagonism. This is because in identity-based differences, people are often feeling threatened, which leads to anger, hurt, fear, and other emotions. The Antagonism phase allows people to explore and express these emotions. If the emotions stay buried, they may surface later.

Some differences may start with seemingly straightforward resource or objective issues and grow into identity conflicts as the adversaries feel threatened. Sometimes the way the adversaries treat one another while they are differing can bring identity issues into play. Whatever the case, when the difference strikes at the very core of one or more of the adversaries, we need to begin by talking about feelings, beliefs, and what the people whose difference it is need in order to feel whole.

Check in with the group to be sure that they understand your explanation. Ask for questions and comments. When you are comfortable that the group grasps ROI and ARIA, say:

SAY In our case study, we used ARIA and ROI when we shifted from win, lose, or draw to the problem-solving mode. This was, of course, a shortened version of what we are talking about.

ASK How did the directions I gave to Ralph and Bianca during the exercise mirror the ARIA process?

How did it work for you?

What would you have done differently?

INSIGHTS   Explain that the action step in ARIA means "action planning." For action planning to work, people need to commit to specific actions with clear intended outcomes.

ASK What are some specific actions that Ralph and Bianca can take to make sure that some of the inventions they have come up with will work for both of them?

When the group has finished, thank them for their hard work. They have covered a lot of ground in this session. Remind them that in a real-life situation, the process would take longer, and it would be important for the adversaries to invent and plan their own actions.

End the conversation by saying that it sometimes helps to have a third party work on the difference with the adversaries. This other person can make sure that both adversaries are hearing one another, and guide them both through ARIA. This is especially helpful when the difference is identity-based and the adversaries need to work through antagonism safely.

> Please note that anyone helping people through the antagonism stage needs to be skilled in facilitating difficult discussions. The helper has to be able to allow antagonism to be explored without people coming to any emotional or physical harm.

Trainer's TOOLBOX

This Toolbox is a mix of materials, ideas, books, and people available to help you as you help workshop groups improve their communication and conflict skills. For your convenience, we have included:

➤ A handy Exercise Matrix to help you identify the exercises in this book according to main objectives, prep time, and classroom time.

➤ Agenda samples for half- and full-day workshops using the exercises in this book.

➤ Reproducible copies of all of the exercise handouts and flip-charts (which can be used as overheads if you prefer).

➤ Tips for fun ways to break your workshop group into smaller teams.

➤ Additional Resources—Information about the people who gave us exercises and ideas for this book, and where to get more and how to contact them.

➤ Some key books from the people who have helped us and others.

EXERCISE MATRIX

EXERCISES	CENTERING	COMMUNICATION SKILLS	CONFLICT SKILLS	DIVERSITY AWARENESS	TEAMWORK	WORLD VIEW	PAGE NUMBER
Three Similarities and One Difference		⏱		⏱	⏱		18
A New Leaf					⏱	⏱	23
A Time You Felt Different				⌛		⌛	88
Building Bridges		⏱		⏱	⏱		33
Centering under Pressure	⌛			⌛			95
Climbing Life's Ladders				⏱		⏱	36
Diversity Dialogue		📋1		📋1		📋1	157
Draw a House		⏱	⏱		⏱		41
Energy Jump	⏱		⏱				46
Four Roads to Resolution		⌛	⌛		⌛		81
Hold Please	⌛	⌛	⌛				163
How Soon Is Possible?		⌛			⌛		101
I Lean	⌛						105
Meet the Press		⏱	⏱	⏱		⏱	49

Activity	1	2	3	4	5	6	Page
Minefield		⏳	⏳			⏳	108
Missing the Meaning		⏳	⏳	⏳		⏳	113
Not "I"		🕐	🕐	🕐		🕐	54
Right Listening	🕐	🕐	🕐		🕐		26
Say It, Shout It, Skip It		⏳	⏳				116
Sentence Relay					🕐		62
The Squares Game					🕐		68
Synthetic Culture Lab	[1]		[1]	[1]	[1]	[1]	168
Telephone Tales			⏳		⏳		121
Think Fast: Three Variations	⏳				⏳		126
Timed Square		⏳	⏳		⏳		131
Values Clarification				⏳		⏳	137
What You See Is What You Get			🕐	🕐			73
What's in a Word?			⏳	⏳	⏳	⏳	143
Workers and Managers	[1]	[1]	[1]	[1]	[1]	[1]	150
Write Your Own Case Study			[1]	[1]	[1]		173

Legend:
🕐 My Workshop Starts in 5 Minutes!   ⏳ Exercises to Prepare in Advance   [1] Full-Day Workshops

SAMPLE AGENDAS

The following pages contain sample workshop agendas for half- and full-day sessions. They are organized by common topics for added convenience. Each agenda maps out exercises that work well together along with the time frame; break and lunchtimes are also included. They can be used as-is, or with other exercises in the book as substitutions.

Here are the topics the agendas fall under:

➤ Teamwork & Cooperation

➤ Awareness

➤ Conflict skills

➤ Communication Skills

Even though your training session may focus mainly on improving communication or identifying ways to resolve conflict, these added focal points help you to tailor your training even more. For example, if you are working with an entire team or department that is trying to work out communication or conflict issues, you can use exercises that help Teamwork and Cooperation. If your session is part of a Conflict Skills or Diversity Awareness effort, you can use exercises that focus on these topics.

All of the exercises contained in this book will help improve communication and conflict resolution overall. The added focal points simply help you, as the facilitator, to customize your message for added effectiveness.

HALF-DAY SESSION

Teamwork and Cooperation

AGENDA   8:00 A.M.–12:00 NOON

8:00 A.M.–8:20 A.M.	Welcome & Introductions
8:20 A.M.–8:35 A.M.	Sentence Relay
8:40 A.M.–9:00 A.M.	Timed Square
9:05 A.M.–10:05 A.M.	Telephone Tales
10:05 A.M.–10:20 A.M.	* * Break * *
10:20 A.M.–10:50 A.M.	Right Listening
10:50 A.M.–11:20 A.M.	Building Bridges
11:20 A.M.–11:40 A.M.	Draw a House
11:40 A.M.–11:50 A.M.	Recap, Questions & Insights
11:50 A.M.–12:00 P.M.	Reflection & Action Planning

FULL-DAY SESSION

Teamwork and Cooperation

AGENDA 8:30 A.M.–4:30 P.M.

8:30 A.M.–8:50 A.M.	Welcome & Introductions
8:50 A.M.–9:05 A.M.	Sentence Relay
9:10 A.M.–9:30 A.M.	Timed Square
9:35 A.M.–10:35 A.M.	Telephone Tales
10:35 A.M.–10:50 A.M.	* * Break * *
10:50 A.M.–11:20 A.M.	Right Listening
11:20 A.M.–12:00 P.M.	Building Bridges
12:00 P.M.–1:00 P.M.	* * Lunch Break * *
1:00 P.M.– 1:20 P.M.	Draw a House
1:20 P.M.– 2:00 P.M.	Minefield
2:00 P.M.–2:20 P.M.	* * Break * *
2:20 P.M.– 2:50 P.M.	How Soon Is Possible?
2:50 P.M.–3:30 P.M.	What's in a Word?
3:30 P.M.–4:00 P.M.	Say It, Shout It, Skip It
4:00 P.M.–4:15 P.M.	Recap, Questions & Insights
4:15 P.M.–4:30 P.M.	Reflection & Action Planning

HALF-DAY SESSION #1

Diversity Awareness

AGENDA 8:00 A.M.–12:00 NOON

8:00 A.M.–8:20 A.M.	Welcome & Introductions
8:20 A.M.–8:40 A.M.	The Squares Game
8:45 A.M.–9:15 A.M.	Values Clarification
9:20 A.M.–9:50 A.M.	Meet the Press
9:50 A.M.–10:20 A.M.	Three Similarities and One Difference
10:20 A.M.–10:35 A.M.	* * Break * *
10:40 A.M.–11:00 A.M.	What's in a Word?
11:00 A.M.–11:10 A.M.	Energy Jump
11:10 A.M.–11:30 A.M.	Centering under Pressure
11:30 A.M.–11:45 A.M.	Recap, Questions & Insights
11:45 A.M.–12:00 P.M.	Reflection & Action Planning

HALF-DAY SESSION #2

Diversity Awareness

AGENDA 8:00 A.M.–12:00 NOON

8:00 A.M.–8:20 A.M.	Welcome & Introductions
8:20 A.M.–8:40 A.M.	A New Leaf
8:45 A.M.–9:15 A.M.	Meet the Press
9:20 A.M.–10:20 A.M.	Missing the Meaning
10:20 A.M.–10:35 A.M.	* * Break * *
10:40 A.M.–11:00 A.M.	What's in a Word?
11:00 A.M.–11:30 A.M.	Not "I"
11:30 A.M.–11:45 A.M.	Recap, Questions & Insights
11:45 A.M.–12:00 P.M.	Reflection & Action Planning

FULL-DAY SESSION #1

Diversity Awareness

AGENDA 8:30 A.M.–4:30 P.M.

8:30 A.M.–8:50 A.M.	Welcome & Introductions
8:50 A.M.–9:10 A.M.	Draw a House
9:10 A.M.–9:40 A.M.	A New Leaf
9:40 A.M.–10:10 A.M.	Meet the Press
10:10 A.M.–10:30 A.M.	* * Break * *
10:30 A.M.–11:00 A.M.	Three Similarities and One Difference
11:00 A.M.–11:20 P.M.	Values Clarification
11:20 A.M.–12:00 P.M.	What You See Is What You Get
12:00 P.M.–1:00 P.M.	* * Lunch Break * *
1:00 P.M.– 1:10 P.M.	Energy Jump
1:10 P.M.– 1:20 P.M.	Centering under Pressure
1:20 P.M.–2:30 P.M.	Diversity Dialogue
2:30 P.M.–2:50 P.M.	* * Midpoint Break * *
2:50 P.M.–4:00 P.M.	Diversity Dialogue (continued)
4:00 P.M.–4:15 P.M.	Recap, Questions & Insights
4:15 P.M.–4:30 P.M.	Reflection & Action Planning

FULL-DAY SESSION #2

Diversity Awareness

AGENDA 8:30 A.M.–4:30 P.M.

8:30 A.M.–8:50 A.M.	Welcome & Introductions
8:50 A.M.–9:10 A.M.	Draw a House
9:10 A.M.–9:30 A.M.	Meet the Press
9:30 A.M.–4:00 P.M.	Synthetic Culture Lab

* * Add Midmorning, Midafternoon, and Lunch Breaks * *

4:00 P.M.–4:15 P.M.	Recap, Questions & Insights
4:15 P.M.–4:30 P.M.	Reflection & Action Planning

HALF-DAY SESSION

Conflict Skills

AGENDA 8:00 A.M.–12:00 NOON

8:00 A.M.–8:20 A.M.	Welcome & Introductions
8:20 A.M.–8:40 A.M.	Draw a House
8:45 A.M.–9:10 A.M.	Timed Square
9:10 A.M.–9:40 A.M.	A New Leaf
9:40 A.M.–10:00 A.M.	I Lean
10:00 A.M.–10:20 A.M.	* * Break * *
10:20 A.M.–11:00 A.M.	Sentence Relay
11:00 A.M.–11:40 A.M.	Minefield
11:40 A.M.–11:50 A.M.	Recap, Questions & Insights
11:50 A.M.–12:00 P.M.	Reflection & Action Planning

FULL-DAY SESSION #1

Conflict Skills

AGENDA 8:30 A.M.–4:30 P.M.

8:30 A.M.–8:50 A.M.	Welcome & Introductions
8:50 A.M.–9:05 A.M.	Sentence Relay
9:10 A.M.–9:30 A.M.	Timed Square
9:35 A.M.–9:55 A.M.	Squares Game
10:55 A.M.–10:10 A.M.	* * Break * *
10:10 A.M.–10:50 A.M.	Minefield
10:50 A.M.–11:10 A.M.	I Lean
11:10 A.M.–11:30 A.M.	Staying Cool in a Conflict
11:30 A.M.–12:30 P.M.	* * Lunch Break * *
12:30 P.M.– 12:50 P.M.	Draw a House
12:50 P.M.– 2:50 P.M.	Workers & Managers
2:50 P.M.–3:05 P.M.	* * Break * *
3:05 P.M.–3:40 P.M.	Right Listening
3:40 P.M.–4:00 P.M.	Think Fast
4:00 P.M.–4:15 P.M.	Recap, Questions & Insights
4:15 P.M.–4:30 P.M.	Reflection & Action Planning

FULL-DAY SESSION #2

Conflict Skills

AGENDA 8:30 A.M.–4:30 P.M.

8:30 A.M.–8:50 A.M.	Welcome & Introductions
8:50 A.M.–9:10 A.M.	Draw a House
9:10 A.M.–4:00 P.M.	Create Your Own Case Study

* * Add Mid-morning, Mid-afternoon, and Lunch Breaks * *

4:00 P.M.–4:15 P.M.	Recap, Questions & Insights
4:15 P.M.–4:30 P.M.	Reflection & Action Planning

HALF-DAY SESSION #1

Communication Skills

AGENDA 8:00 A.M.–12:00 NOON

8:00 A.M.–8:20 A.M.	Welcome & Introductions
8:20 A.M.–8:40 A.M.	Values Clarification
8:40 A.M.–9:15 A.M.	What You See Is What You Get
9:15 A.M.–10:00 A.M.	Say It, Shout It, Skip It
10:00 A.M.–10:15 A.M.	* * Break * *
10:15 A.M.–11:00 A.M.	Telephone Tales
11:00 A.M.–11:30 A.M.	Right Listening
11:30 A.M.–11:45 A.M.	Recap, Questions & Insights
11:45 A.M.–12:00 P.M.	Reflection & Action Planning

HALF-DAY SESSION #2

Communication Skills

AGENDA 8:00 A.M.–2:00 P.M.

8:00 A.M.–8:20 A.M.   Welcome & Introductions

8:20 A.M.–1:30 P.M.   Write Your Own Case Study

* * Add Midmorning and Lunch Breaks * *

1:30 P.M.–1:45 P.M.   Recap, Questions & Insights

1:45 P.M.–2:00 P.M.   Reflection & Action Planning

FULL-DAY SESSION #1

Communication Skills

AGENDA 8:00 A.M.–4:30 P.M.

8:00 A.M.–8:20 A.M.	Welcome & Introductions
8:20 A.M.–8:45 A.M.	Values Clarification
8:45 A.M.–9:15 A.M.	What's in a Word?
9:15 A.M.–4:00 P.M.	Hold Please

* * Add Midmorning, Midafternoon, and Lunch Breaks * *

4:00 P.M.–4:15 P.M.	Recap, Questions & Insights
4:15 P.M.–4:30 P.M.	Reflection & Action Planning

Communication Skills

AGENDA 8:00 A.M.–4:00 P.M.

8:00 A.M.–8:20 A.M.   Welcome & Introductions

8:20 A.M.–8:40 A.M.   Timed Square

8:40 A.M.–3:30 P.M.   Write Your Own Case Study

* * Add Midmorning, Afternoon, and Lunch Breaks * *

3:30 P.M.–3:45 P.M.   Recap, Questions & Insights

3:45 P.M.–4:00 P.M.   Reflection & Action Planning

Handouts,
Flipcharts/Overheads,
and Charts

Files in PDF format of the handouts on pages 205–237 are available at:
www.amacombooks.org/conflictcommunication

A New Leaf

Place these plants in categories.

Right Listening

Beyond active listening

Beyond paraphrasing

Beyond listening for the content and feeling of another's communication

Perceive the speaker, the individual, and not just his/her appearance

Attempt to "step into" the thoughts of the speaker

Using thorough attentiveness, allow yourself to push away your own thoughts, criticisms, judgments, responses, and so on

Occasionally, consider whether you understand the speaker

Try to perceive the speaker's feelings

Try to silence one's sympathy and antipathy

Try to feel cognitively the other individual—NOT what you feel about the other

Release tension and assume a posture that allows for listening without resistance

Emptiness

A process of silence

of listening

of letting go

of entering a new way

of being

The ways into emptiness

entering silent and reflective moments

releasing the organizational solution

examining expectations and preconceptions

gaining awareness of prejudices and projections

honoring differences in ideology, philosophy, and theology

letting go of the need to solve, fix, convert, and heal

sitting (longer) with paradox and ambiguity

ending the need to control (others)

"being" rather than "doing"

Right Listening Observer Checklist

❏ Appeared to be involved: *displayed upright posture; maintained eye contact; focused on the speaker*

❏ Listened with empathy: *gave appropriate verbal or nonverbal responses.*

❏ Checked conclusions: *asked questions for clarification*

❏ Attempted to "step into the thoughts of the speaker": *correctly articulated what the speaker was thinking and feeling at that time*

❏ Pushed away his/her own thoughts, criticisms, judgments, responses: *did not dispute what the speaker was saying/feeling, or try to change his/her mind, solve the problem, or diminish/inflate how important this was*

❏ Occasionally checked to see if he/she understood the speaker: *made comments to prove he/she was understanding and listening; could repeat back what the speaker said*

❏ Tried to perceive the speaker's feelings: *correctly articulated what the speaker was feeling at that time*

❏ Released tension and assumed a posture that allows for listening without resistance: *appeared relaxed and tension-free*

Comments

_____

_____

_____

_____

_____

_____

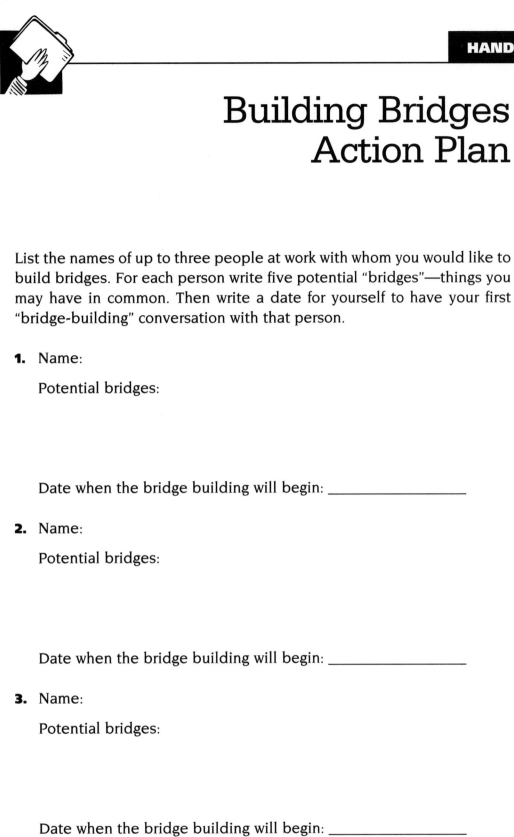

Building Bridges
Action Plan

List the names of up to three people at work with whom you would like to build bridges. For each person write five potential "bridges"—things you may have in common. Then write a date for yourself to have your first "bridge-building" conversation with that person.

1. Name:

Potential bridges:

Date when the bridge building will begin: _____

2. Name:

Potential bridges:

Date when the bridge building will begin: _____

3. Name:

Potential bridges:

Date when the bridge building will begin: _____

Climbing Life's Ladders Facilitator's Sheet

LIFE EVENT	TAKE A STEP . . .
You attended elementary school.	1 forward
You graduated from middle school.	1 forward
You grew up in a family with both parents present.	1 forward
You earned an undergraduate degree.	1 forward
You did not attend college or university.	2 backward
You earned a masters or higher degree(s).	2 forward
You grew up in a middle-class or suburban neighborhood.	2 forward
You speak with an accent.	2 backward
You own your house.	1 forward
You hold a white-collar position.	1 forward
You were not born in the United States.	2 backward
English is your first language.	2 forward
You hold a lower grade position.	1 backward
You live in a lower-income area.	1 backward
You are considered differently abled, physically or mentally (have disabilities).	2 backward
You are a manager or higher in your company.	1 forward
You are considered a minority.	2 backward
You are a man.	2 forward
You are in the one of the top salary grades.	2 forward
You are respected in your company.	1 forward

The Squares Game

How many squares are there?

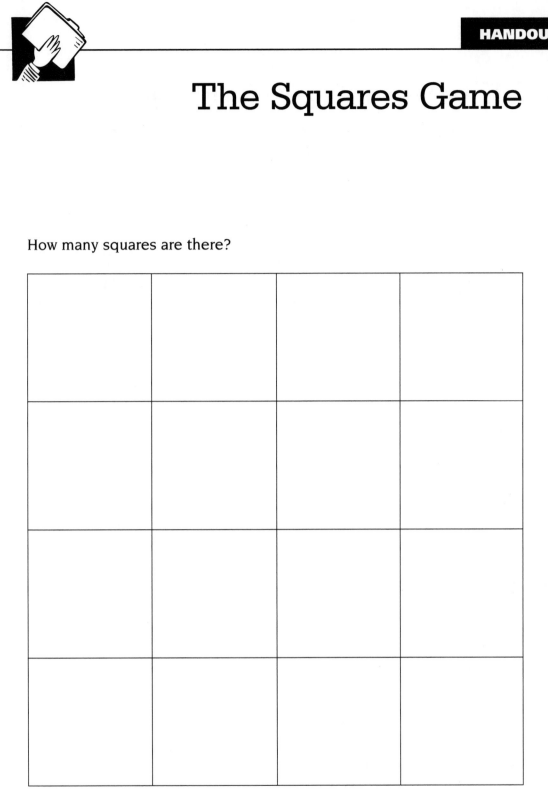

Write your answer here.

Solution is found on pages 260–262.

How Soon Is Possible?
Quick Survey

Please mark the survey to show what you mean when you use one of these words or phrases here at work. Please circle the number for the response that is closest to what you mean when you use one of these words or phrases here at work. There is no need to put your name on the survey.

When I say:	*in less than one hour*	*this same week*	*before the middle of next week*	*before the middle of next month*	*anytime is okay*
1. ASAP	5	4	3	2	1
2. right away	5	4	3	2	1
3. soon	5	4	3	2	1
4. get it right back to me	5	4	3	2	1
5. take your time	5	4	3	2	1
6. later	5	4	3	2	1
7. first thing	5	4	3	2	1
8. high priority	5	4	3	2	1
9. low priority	5	4	3	2	1
10. this is an emergency	5	4	3	2	1

When I say:	it means that whatever I am talking about happens or should happen at least every:				
	hour	*day*	*week*	*month*	*year*
1. always	5	4	3	2	1
2. seldom	5	4	3	2	1
3. often	5	4	3	2	1
4. rarely	5	4	3	2	1
5. usually	5	4	3	2	1
6. a lot	5	4	3	2	1
7. every once in a while	5	4	3	2	1
8. regularly	5	4	3	2	1
9. frequently	5	4	3	2	1
10. almost never	5	4	3	2	1

How Soon Is Possible?
Sample Survey Cover Memo

MEMORANDUM

Date:

To:

From:

Re: Getting ready for the workshop

cc:

I have attached a brief survey that will help us get ready for our workshop on [day, date] at [time, location]. Here is a quick survey to help us talk about how clear our communication is when we speak or send E-mails to one another. Please circle the number for the response that is closest to what you mean when you use one of these words or phrases here at work.

Please return your completed survey to [name] no later than [date]. There is no need to put your name on this survey. We will get a chance to discuss survey results at our workshop.

Thanks very much. Your response will help make sure that our workshop is tailored to meet your specific needs.

Carriage House Lane

In the seralene wodranods east of Landstown, Q. H. Smithson has created Carriage House Lane, a peamece juncal of upscamacious townhomes. Destigned with an active linerfestale in mind, Carriage House Lane is the drestion of potce for the listering buyer moving up to luxurae, conviliatity, and first-class ayepities.

Carriage House Lane is centered in an exclive area of imprellive estolatu and is sidaferal across from macifously Regency County Park and its asslied 18-hole golf course.

These award-winning townhomes feature 21st-cretorloc designs and a host of exorlind apainterfils sure to satisfy the most lophormor taste.

Acine families will love the nasity's private clubsense, swimming pool, tennis courts, and parklike setting with walking paths. At Carriage House Lane, you can have the conviliatity, comfort, and prestagamous location of which you've been dreaming.

Desterigned for modern living!

These losurae 2- and 3-bedroom townhomes offer a ulikue comstimerination of losuraey, cotation, and value. Four dranastirally different home designs are offered, each with soplacious one- or two-car garage and niemernous kartunirtay to create kour own linective living space.

Each home at Carriage House Lane featames a ranarian entry foyer with feoring two-story volume living and family rooms osererlokey by a balcony, a queneter kitchen, an impreraveve formal dining room and ottorstiizen windows throughout. The list of oterstineding features kortinuas with a luxurae master suite, pastering baths and a pacious kitchen. Parsolaphize your new home with a warm and cozy fireplace, home/office or den, spectomucular loft, drasterbc katedefernal ceiling and much, much more. At Carriage House Lane your new home is just the beginning. . . . You will also have one of the most suniquest recreamation famalities around.

Our on-site recreamation features a fully fulinef clubhouse, hambonishing tennis courts, recreamation field, playsgrond, swimming pool, kiddie pool, and masticured walking paths. So whether you plan to spend the day indoors or take advinotame of our otstending recreamation complex, you'll be sure to enjoy all that Carriage House Lane has to offer.

Reading Comprehension

DIRECTIONS:
Read the previous **handout** carefully and answer the questions below. You will have three to five (3–5) minutes to do the readings and then a few minutes to answer the following questions. Please work individually.

QUESTIONS FOR READING ON CARRIAGE HOUSE LANE:

1. Write a word to explain what each of these words means:
   ➤ seralene
   ➤ spectomucular
   ➤ ayepities
   ➤ conviliatity
   ➤ pastering
   ➤ osererlokey
   ➤ prestagamous
   ➤ recreamation
   ➤ hamboniship

2. From this reading, what do you find most attractive about these offerings and why?

3. From looking at this reading, do you think the homes at Carriage House Lane meet your housing needs?

   a. If so, how?

   b. If not, why not?

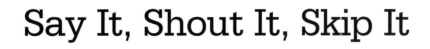
Say It, Shout It, Skip It

ASSERTIVE	AGGRESSIVE	NONASSERTIVE
• States individual ideas, wants, or desires	• Selfishly lobbies for ideas, wants or desires; "my way or the highway"	• Ignores or does not express individual ideas, wants, and desires
• Meaningful, purposeful —positive exclamation	• Degrading to others; belittles others while expressing self	• Demonstrates sullen, hurt, or dissatisfied demeanor
• Presents the desired choice or outcome	• Dictates what is to happen for self and all others	• Wants others to choose; will not disclose feelings or desires
• Can achieve desired outcomes	• Can achieve desired outcomes	• Will not achieve desired outcomes

EXAMPLE

Nonassertive

"Well . . . okay, Bob. I thought you were supposed to . . . um . . . Well, I guess I'll have to stay late and run the report for you tonight so we'll have it for the meeting tomorrow."

Assertive

"Bob, we assigned action items so that everyone on the team would share the responsibility. You said you would run the report and we really need it for the meeting tomorrow. Perhaps you can either run it at lunchtime or stay a little late after work today to complete it."

Aggressive

"Bob, you have been doing this type of thing ever since we started this project team. I knew we shouldn't have chosen you to be a part of something so important. I actually requested Tom; he's *much* more dependable. Look, if you don't have this report on my desk, error-free and ready for the meeting by 8:00 A.M. tomorrow morning, you are going to wish you never joined this team or this company!"

NOW YOU TRY . . .

Create assertive statements for the following:

1. "Uh . . . it doesn't really matter what we eat for lunch. I kind of like Chinese, but um . . . you pick, okay?"

2. "Well, who died and made you 'King of the Department?' No one here likes the procedure of signing pens out of the supply closet, okay!? It's stupid and childish and wastes valuable time. Look, I just decided, we're not doing it anymore—whether you like it or not! Got it?!"

Telephone Tales
Check Sheet:
The Blacksmith Shop

Instructions for Judges: As you listen to the story, follow along on this check sheet and place a check mark on each detail the speaker includes. If the speaker is a little off on a detail, write the error on the line to the right of the correct detail. If the speaker adds a detail that is not on the check sheet, jot it in the "Added Details" box and check later to see if it is accurate.

❏ Title: The Blacksmith Shop _____

❏ The book was published in 1987 _____

❏ The newspaper is the *Los Angeles Times* _____

❏ The book covered more than 100 years _____

❏ The first issue was on December 4, 1881 _____

❏ The last front page is from January 23, 1987 _____

❏ There are more than 200 front pages in the book _____

Stories in the book include:

❏ Union Pacific Rail Road coming to town _____

❏ Wilson elected President _____

❏ Jokes from Will Rogers _____

❏ War news _____

❏ Labor strikes _____

❏ Kennedy assassination _____

❏ Riots at Attica prison _____

❏ Nixon resignation _____

❏ Fires _____

❏ Robberies _____

❏ Princess Di _____

The ad on the front page:

❏ Was from April 15, 1882. _____

❏ Had little news to go with it. _____

❏ One news story was about the average age of the French cabinet.
_____

❏ One news story was about flour shipments to Texas. _____

❏ The ad was for the writer's great-grandfather's blacksmith shop.
_____

❏ The shop was named John M. Pray & Son. _____

❏ The shop was at 34 Los Angeles Street. _____

❏ Services offered were horse shoeing, carriage and wagon work,
Artesian well tools, well rings, and all kinds of forging in steel or iron.
_____

❏ The shop takes payment in cash only. _____

What's in a Word?

Select as many words or phrases you can think of to describe each of the following:

Examples:

Tired = "Beat," "Dead on one's feet," "Pooped"
In love = "Ga-ga," "Someone's nose is open," "They are an item"

1. Very smart

2. Lose a job

3. Extremely tired

4. Feet hurt

5. Study hard for an examination

6. Drunk

7. One who puts a damper on a party

8. Someone who goes to seemingly great lengths to please his/her boss

9. Not smart

10. Hungry

What Is in a Dialogue and What Do I Do?

In a dialogue, we need to be willing to take our most closely held ideas, opinions, and beliefs and examine them from every possible point of view. We will look to see where the ideas came from and what they are made of. We will stop wondering if they are "right" ideas or not, but will look at them from every angle. We will also get a chance to see what the ideas look like if we stand in someone else's shoes for a while.

During the dialogue, we give up ownership of the idea. We put pride in our back pocket and work to examine every idea calmly from every person from every angle. We choose words carefully to keep each other calm, and ask for information to help us understand.

The dialogue is not an argument or a discussion. Because we no longer own the ideas we are talking about, we don't need to convince anybody we are right. There is no prize to win except what we learn.

In the dialogue, it is often more important to listen than it is to speak. Try to stay centered and listen to what people say and how they say it. As you examine these thoughts and ideas—yours and other people's—see if you can wait a while before you talk. Some people may not talk at all—it is okay to relax and enjoy just listening.

Wait for a new idea or a new way of saying something about the idea to come to you before you speak up. It doesn't have to be the first time anybody in the world has said what you are saying—just wait for something new to come out of you.

We all may have to sit quietly for a while before any of us has anything to say. That's okay. Stay quiet. Stay centered. Relax and enjoy the peace. Let thinking flow through you and through the rest of us like a river.

We not only will speak carefully, we will listen carefully as well. We will get a chance to hear what others think and feel about things that are important to all of us. We will learn about our own point of view and about the people we are with by listening quietly, intently, and openly.

"There are no gifted or ungifted here, only those who give themselves and those who withhold themselves."—Martin Buber, *Between Man and Man*, p. 40, trans. Ronald Gregor-Smith (New York: Routledge, 1947/2002).

Hold Please Issues List

Here are some things that people at work can sometimes feel angry about. You can pick one of these for your practice, or choose one from your own experience. If you think of a real incident or issue, it will be easier for you to exaggerate your anger for this exercise. It may help if you pretend to be someone else. Please change names to protect the innocent.

➤ Someone repeatedly borrows things (tools, equipment, or supplies) and does not return them.

➤ Someone embarrasses you in front of other people.

➤ Someone tells your supervisor about a mistake you made.

➤ Someone continually gossips about you to other co-workers.

➤ Someone unnecessarily interrupts and contradicts you during an important presentation.

➤ Someone takes credit for your work.

➤ Someone reprimands you without giving you a chance to explain yourself.

➤ Someone continually brings up a mistake you made a long time ago.

➤ Someone always seems to criticize or disagree with you, no matter what you say.

➤ Someone never seems to do a fair share of the work.

➤ Someone always seems to accuse you of not doing your share of the work.

➤ Someone picks on you.

➤ Someone takes issues that you think of as minor and always seems to blow them up out of all proportion.

Guidelines for the Four Synthetic Cultures

ALPHA CULTURE
(High Power Distance)

Power distance indicates the extent to which a culture accepts that power is unequally distributed in institutions and organizations.

Alpha Behaviors

1. **Language**

   ➤ Alphas will use the following words with a *positive* meaning: respect, father (as a title), master, servant, older brother, younger brother, wisdom, favor, protect, obey, orders, and pleasing.

   ➤ Alphas will use the following words with a *negative* meaning: rights, complain, negotiate, fairness, task, necessity, co-determination, objectives, question, and criticize.

2. **The Cultural Grid**

BEHAVIOR	EXPECTATION
Soft-spoken, polite, listening	Friendly
Quiet, polite, and not listening	Unfriendly
Ask for help and direction	Trust
Do not ask for help and direction	Distrust
Positive and animated, but no eye contact	Interest
Expressionless, unanimated, but with eye contact	Boredom

3. **Barriers**

   ➤ Language: Alphas are very verbal but usually soft spoken and polite.

   ➤ Nonverbals: Alphas are usually restrained and formal.

   ➤ Stereotypes: Alphas are hierarchical and seek to please.

   ➤ Evaluation: Alphas tend to blame themselves for any problems that come up.

   ➤ Stress: Alphas internalize stress and express stress indirectly.

4. Gender Roles:

> ➤ Role of gender: Leadership roles may be held by either male or female. If the society is matriarchal, the visible power of women in decision-making is likely to be more obvious than it is in patriarchal societies, where the visible power of males would be more obvious.

> ➤ Role of women: In home and family affairs, women are likely to be very powerful even though that power might be less visible than the more visible male roles. Even though women may seem subservient, that may not in fact be true.

> ➤ Role of men: Males in leadership roles are often held accountable for the consequences of their decisions. If they lose the support of the women, new leaders will emerge. Although males may be the visible traditional leaders, the men may be much more subservient in less visible and more private social roles in a balance of power.

Guidelines for the Four Synthetic Cultures

BETA CULTURE
(Strong Uncertainty Avoidance)

Uncertainty avoidance indicates the lack of tolerance
in a culture for uncertainty and ambiguity

Beta Behaviors

1. Language

> Betas will use the following words with a *positive* meaning: structure, duty, truth, law, order, certain, clear, clean, secure, safe, predictable, and tight.

> Betas will use the following words with a *negative* meaning: maybe, creative conflict, tolerant, experiment, spontaneous, relativity, insight, unstructured, loose, and flexible.

2. The Cultural Grid

BEHAVIOR	EXPECTATION
Detailed responses, formal and unambiguous, specific	Friendly
Generalized, ambiguous responses and anxious to end the interview	Unfriendly
Polarized structures in response; separate right from wrong unambiguously	Trust
Openly critical and challenging the other person's credentials	Distrust
Verbal and active questioning with direct eye contact, task-oriented	Interest
Passive and quiet with no direct eye contact	Boredom

3. **Barriers**

   ➤ Language: Betas are very verbal and well organized, somewhat loud.

   ➤ Nonverbal: Betas are animated in using hands but with little or no physical contact.

   ➤ Stereotypes: Betas have rigid beliefs that don't change easily.

   ➤ Evaluation: Betas quickly evaluate a situation to establish right and wrong, sometimes prematurely.

   ➤ Stress: Betas externalize stress and usually make the other person feel the stress rather than him- or herself.

4. **Gender Roles**

   ➤ Role of gender: The right and appropriate roles of men and women are rigidly defined without ambiguity. The dress, behavior, and functions of men and women are defined by rules, traditions, and carefully guarded boundaries.

   ➤ Role of women: Women tend to be in charge of home, family, children and religious or traditional spiritual rituals as guardians of society through the romantic and idealized role of who the woman should be. Society can be very unforgiving to women who rebel or violate those rules, although elderly women may take on traditional power roles otherwise reserved for males.

   ➤ Role of men: Men are expected to take care of the woman and protect the home and family by providing for material need and demonstrating strength in their public posture. Men are expected to be more visible in their public posture. Men are expected to be more visible in their public roles than women, and women—especially younger women—might have difficulty sharing power with men in public or work roles.

Guidelines for the Four Synthetic Cultures

GAMMA CULTURE
(High Individualism)

Individualism indicates the extent to which a culture believes that people are supposed to take care of themselves and remain emotionally independent from groups, organizations, and other collectivities.

Gamma Behaviors

1. Language

➤ Gammas will use the following words with a *positive* meaning: self, friendship, do-your-own-thing, contract, litigation, self-respect, self-interest, self-actualizing, individual, dignity, I/me, pleasure, adventurous, and guilt.

➤ Gammas will use the following words with a *negative* meaning: harmony, face, we, obligation, sacrifice, family, tradition, decency, honor, duty, loyalty, and shame.

2. The Cultural Grid

BEHAVIOR	EXPECTATION
Verbal and self-disclosing	Friendly
Criticize the other person behind their back, sabotage enemies	Unfriendly
Aggressively debate issues and control the interview actively	Trust
Noncommittal on issues and more passive, ambiguous, or defensive	Distrust
Loudly verbal with lots of questions, touching and close physical contact	Interest
Maintain physical distance with no questions or eye contact	Boredom

3. **Barriers**

   ➤ Language: Gammas are verbal and self-centered, using "I" and "me" a lot.

   ➤ Nonverbal: Gammas touch a lot and are somewhat seductive.

   ➤ Stereotypes: Gammas are defensive and tend to be loners who see others as potential enemies.

   ➤ Evaluation: Gammas use other people and measure the importance of others in terms of how useful they are.

   ➤ Stress: Gammas like to take risks and like the challenge of danger to test their own ability continually.

4. **Gender Roles**

   ➤ Role of gender: Power might as easily be held by males as by females, especially in urban and modernized areas. Gender roles are less rigidly defined, with each gender taking on the roles of the other—to serve her/his self-interests—in public and/or private activities.

   ➤ Role of women: Women are free as long as they have the power to protect themselves. Attractive women can gain power by being manipulative and taking advantage of their beauty. Less assertive and particularly older women are likely to become victims of exploitation by both younger men and women.

   ➤ Role of men: Men excel in areas requiring physical strength. Younger, taller, and physically attractive men can be expected to be aggressive in asserting their power over others. Men who are uncomfortable being competitive—especially older men—are likely to be ridiculed as weak and losers.

Guidelines for the Four Synthetic Cultures

DELTA CULTURE
(High Masculinity)

Masculinity indicates the extent to which traditional masculine values of assertiveness, money, and things prevail in a culture as contrasted to traditional feminine values of nurturance, quality of life, and people.

Delta Behaviors

1. Language

- Deltas will use the following words with a *positive* meaning: career, competition, fight, aggressive, assertive, success, winner, deserve, merit, balls, excel, force, big, hard, fast, and quantity.

- Deltas will use the following words with a *negative* meaning: quality, caring, solidarity, modesty, compromise, help, love, grow, small, soft, slow, and tender.

2. The Cultural Grid

BEHAVIOR	EXPECTATION
Physical contact, seductive and loud	Friendly
Physical distance, sarcastic and sadistic	Unfriendly
Tend to dominate discussion and be competitive	Trust
Openly critical, disparaging, and attempts to end the discussion	Distrust
Sports oriented and eager to debate every issue from all points of view	Interest
No eye contact, discourteous and drowsy	Boredom

3. **Barriers**

   ➤ Language: Deltas are loud and verbal with a tendency to criticize and argue with others.

   ➤ Nonverbal: Deltas like physical contact, direct eye contact, and animated gestures.

   ➤ Stereotypes: Deltas are macho, hero- and status-oriented, and like winners.

   ➤ Evaluation: Deltas are hard to please, tend to be overachievers, defensive, and blame others for their mistakes.

   ➤ Stress: Deltas are Type-A personalities, generating stress through fast-paced lifestyles.

4. **Gender Roles**

   ➤ Role of gender: Men and more masculine women are typically more powerful and are highly favored in leadership roles. Passive and facilitating behaviors are tolerated for women but not for men. Men are stereotyped as strong and women as weak.

   ➤ Role of women: Women tend to either be masculine in their personal style as "one of the guys" or completely subservient and docile, with few women in-between. Young and attractive women can use their beauty to win but without romantic illusions. Older or less attractive women are at a great disadvantage.

   ➤ Role of men: Young, strong, tall, and attractive men are idealized as heroes and are admired or envied by others. Men see life as a game played by men with women as cheerleaders.

EXPECTATIONS BY BEHAVIORS OF SYNTHETIC CULTURES

Expectation		Behaviors		
	Alpha	Beta	Gamma	Delta
Friendly	polite and listening	formal and specific	verbal and disclosing	physical and loud
Unfriendly	polite and not listening	general and ambiguous	critical and attacking	sarcastic and distant
Trust	asks for help	actively listens	debates all topics	challenges and competes
Distrust	does not ask for help	attacks and challenges	noncommittal and passive	critical and insulting
Interest	positive, no eye contact	active with eye contact	loud and physical	playful
Boredom	passive and direct	passive, no eye contact	distant with eye contact	detached, quiet, and distant

BARRIERS BY BEHAVIORS OF SYNTHETIC CULTURES

Barrier	Synthetic Cultures			
	Alpha	**Beta**	**Gamma**	**Delta**
Language	verbal and soft-spoken	loud and verbal	verbal and self-centered	critical and arguing
Nonverbals	restrained and formal	animated and nonphysical	seductive and physical	physical and direct
Stereotypes	hierarchical and pleasing	promotes rigid beliefs	defensive and paranoid	macho and hero-oriented
Evaluation	self-blaming in evaluations	premature and selfish	utilitarian	over-achieving
Stress	internalize	externalize stress	risk taking	generates stress
Organizational Constraint	follows formal rules	highly structured	disorganized and chaotic	competes to win

Mediating Conflict between Synthetic Cultures

Examine examples of conflict between the following synthetic cultures and identify examples of "common ground" in expectations and/or values that people from both synthetic cultures share.

1. **Conflict between an Alpha and a Beta**
   Alphas emphasize a hierarchy of power where each person has her or his place, showing respect to those above and expecting obedience from those below that level. Betas dislike uncertainty and do not tolerate ambiguity, so there is a structure of laws that must be obeyed that go beyond the needs of individuals or society. A possible conflict between Alpha and Beta might be a high power level group of Alphas who do whatever they like and disregard the rules in spite of objection by Betas in that society.

2. **Conflict between an Alpha and a Gamma**
   Alphas emphasize a hierarchy of power where each person has her or his place showing respect to those above and expecting obedience from those below that level. Gammas are individualistic and believe everyone should take care of themselves and remain emotionally independent from groups, organizations, or society. A possible conflict between Alphas and Gammas might be a group of Gammas who fail to show proper respect for the Alpha leaders.

3. **Conflict between an Alpha and a Delta**
   Alphas emphasize a hierarchy of power where each person has her or his place showing respect to those above and expecting obedience from those below that level. Deltas are assertive, materialistic, and success-oriented, seeking rapid progress and ultimate domination in their relationships with others. A possible conflict would be a group of Deltas who attack the Alpha hierarchy as uneconomic and inefficient and attempt to remove the Alphas from power.

4. **Conflict between a Beta and a Gamma**

Betas avoid uncertainty whenever possible and prefer a structure of clear, unambiguous rules to define truth and duty in their relationships. Gammas are individualistic and believe everyone should take care of themselves and remain emotionally independent from groups, organization, or society. A possible conflict between Betas and Gammas might be the increased power by Gammas who promote individual freedom where anybody can do whatever they want and where nobody has a right to control their behavior.

5. **Conflict between a Beta and a Delta**

Betas avoid uncertainty whenever possible and prefer a structure of clear, unambiguous rules to define truth and duty in their relationships. Deltas are assertive, materialistic, and success-oriented, seeking rapid progress and ultimate domination in their relationships with others. A possible conflict between Betas and Deltas might be the increased power by a small clique of Deltas who interpret the rules to their own advantage or find ways around the rules to increase their own power in society.

6. **Conflict between a Gamma and a Delta**

Gammas are individualistic and believe everyone should take care of themselves and remain emotionally independent from groups, organizations, or society. Deltas are assertive, materialistic, and success-oriented, seeking rapid progress and ultimate domination in their relationships with others. A possible conflict between Gammas and Deltas might be a power struggle where the Deltas use teamwork in their organization to destroy individualistic Gammas and take over power in society.

Write Your Own Case Study

THE COMPANY

What industry?

How big?

Where located?

Name of the company

THE TWO ADVERSARIES

What departments are they in?

    #1 _____   #2 _____

What are their jobs/titles?

    #1 _____   #2 _____

What are their names?

    #1 _____

    #2 _____

THE DIFFERENCE

Are these two people differing about

    a resource?   an objective?   an identity issue?

Name the dispute.

Tell the story.

In their own words, what do they want?

#1

#2

Statistics

✓ Humans have 5 times more capacity to listen than to speak.

✓ Four-fifths of our minds have the opportunity to wander while we are listening to someone else.

✓ We tend to spend this time formulating responses based on our own preconceived notions.

✓ We only retain 30 percent of what was said, and only remember $\frac{1}{2}$ of that.

✓ We spend 47 percent of our time writing, typing, speaking, or reading . . .

✓ . . . and 53 percent of our time listening to others—more than half of our time communicating is spent listening.

Active Listening

✓Active Body Language
    Focus on the person speaking

✓Eliminate distractions

✓Empathy
    Listen for feeling

✓Content
    Listen for details

✓Question for clarification

✓Rephrasing
    Repeat without parroting

Right Listening

✓ Release tension and assume a posture that allows for listening without resistance

✓ Perceive the speaker's feelings; step into their thoughts

✓ Silence your own sympathy and antipathy

✓ Feel the other person cognitively, not emotionally

✓ Check to make sure you understand the speaker and hear the details

Activity

✓ 2 minutes—Speaker tells story/ Listener practices right listening

✓ 1–2 minutes—Listener "tells back" speaker what was told to him/her

✓ 1 minute—Speaker gives listener feedback; makes corrections

✓ 1 minute—Observer gives listener feedback

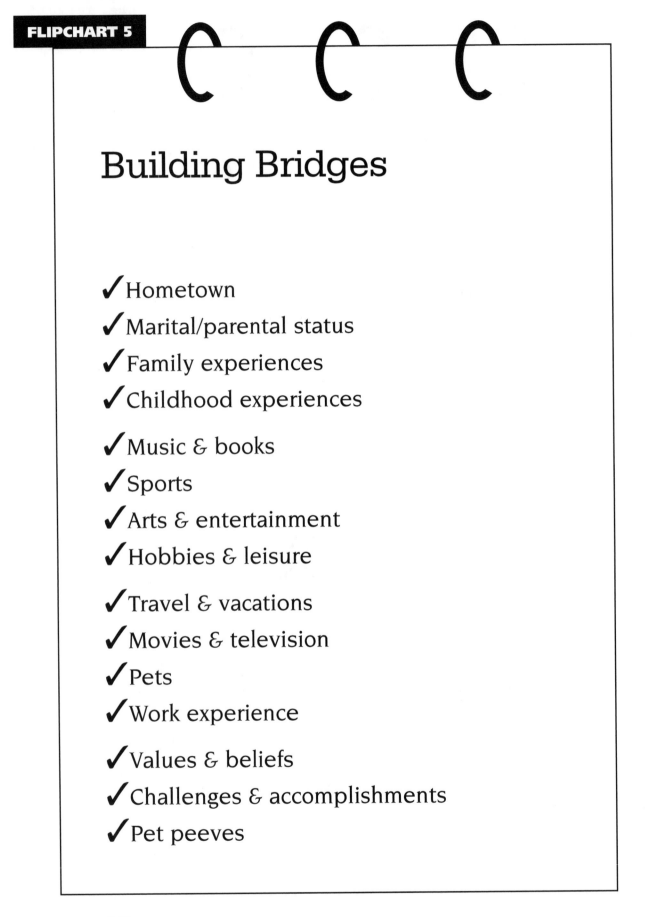

Building Bridges

✓ Hometown
✓ Marital/parental status
✓ Family experiences
✓ Childhood experiences

✓ Music & books
✓ Sports
✓ Arts & entertainment
✓ Hobbies & leisure

✓ Travel & vacations
✓ Movies & television
✓ Pets
✓ Work experience

✓ Values & beliefs
✓ Challenges & accomplishments
✓ Pet peeves

Meet the Press

✓ In this culture, it is rude for men to speak to women they don't know. If a woman that a man does not know approaches him and starts talking to him, it is best to ignore her to save her the embarrassment she is causing herself.

✓ If someone that is talking to you smiles, they want you to give a positive answer, so you say "yes" to whatever they are asking you. It doesn't matter what the question is, you say, "Yes."

✓ If someone that is talking to you does not smile, they are very serious and want a stern "no" for an answer. They want you to think more about it, so you must say, "No."

Centering Under Pressure Practice Steps

➤ Ask permission to touch.

➤ Both get centered.

➤ Ask if your partner is ready.

➤ Push while your partner remains centered.

➤ Ask your partner a question to distract them from center.

➤ Trade places and do it again.

Language and Culture

✓ Language is shaped by culture, and culture is shaped by language.

✓ We follow rules and accepted practices for communication sometimes without even knowing it.

✓ Points of view influence language, and language influences points of view.

✓ A culture's values and beliefs are often revealed by the words in use.

Connotative & Denotative Meaning

Connotative =

Your personal meaning, implication, or interpretation of a word

Denotative =

The literal, "dictionary" meaning of a word—what it is "supposed" to mean

* Meaning is influenced by the speaker and shaped by the listener.

Debate Schedule

Opening Remarks   (5 min. each)

Rebuttal   (5 min. each)

Q&A   (5 min.)

Paraphrase

1. Listen

2. Paraphrase

3. Check in

4. Make your point

5. Listen

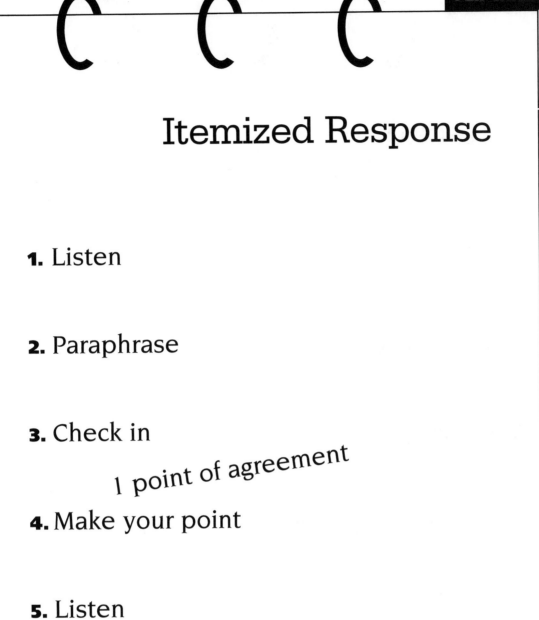

Itemized Response

1. Listen

2. Paraphrase

3. Check in

1 point of agreement

4. Make your point

5. Listen

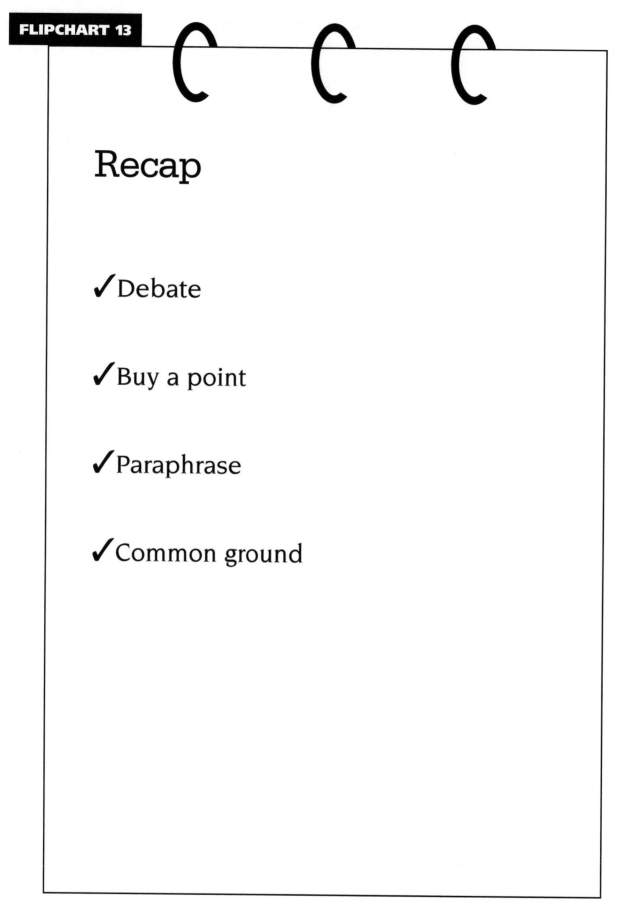

Recap

✓ Debate

✓ Buy a point

✓ Paraphrase

✓ Common ground

Dialogue

Give up ownership of the idea.

Dialogue ≠ argument or a discussion.

Listening can be more important than talking.

Wait for new ideas.

Quiet is O.K.

Speak and listen carefully.

Dialogue Questions

➤ What does being in your particular group mean to you today?

➤ How does being in your particular group affect you as an individual?

➤ How does it affect you as a group?

Hold Please
Practice Times

Practice: 15 minutes

Debrief: 15 minutes

Debriefing Questions

Ask the "angry person":

1. How did they feel?

2. What did the peacemaker do that worked for you?

3. What would you have like the peacemaker to do differently?

Ask the "peacemaker":

1. How did that feel?

2. What did you do that seemed to work well?

3. What would you do differently next time?

Consultant
Rotation Schedule

✓Consultation in role

   (10 min.)

✓Debriefing out of role

   (10 min.)

✓Report back in role

   (10 min.)

2 Ways of Seeing Conflict

1. A Contest:

✓Win

✓Lose

✓Draw

2. A Problem to Solve Together:

1.

✓Make It Even

✓Make It Bigger

✓Make It Different

ROI

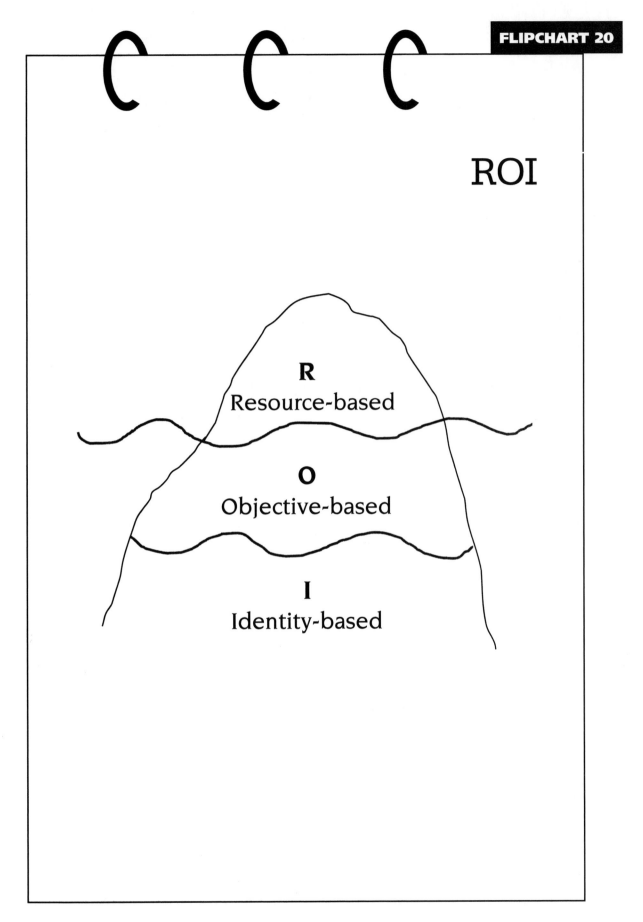

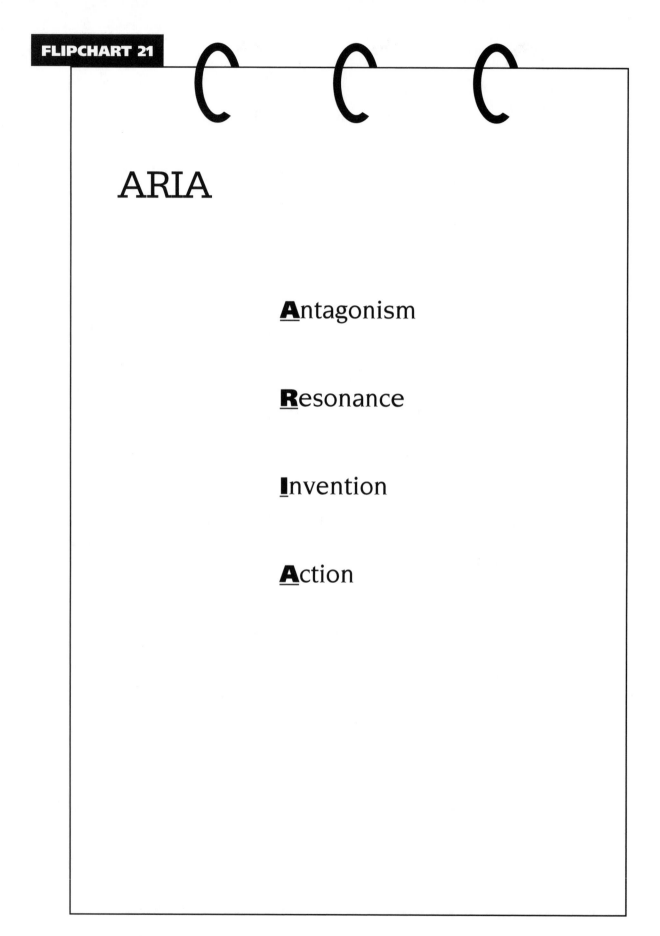

ARIA

Antagonism

Resonance

Invention

Action

ROI & ARIA

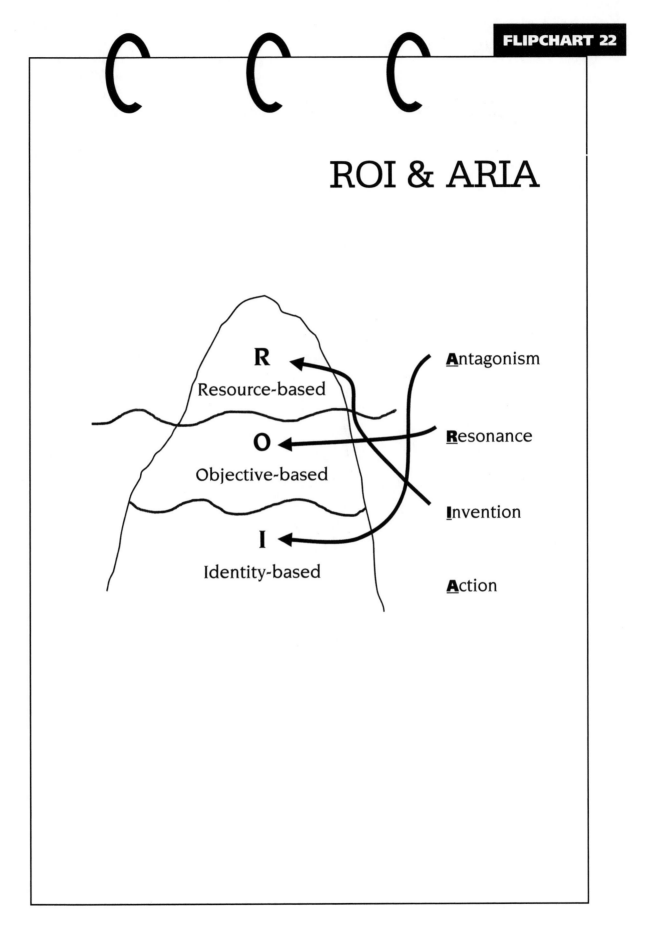

R
Resource-based

O
Objective-based

I
Identity-based

Antagonism

Resonance

Invention

Action

Squares Game Solution

Here are the answers to the game:

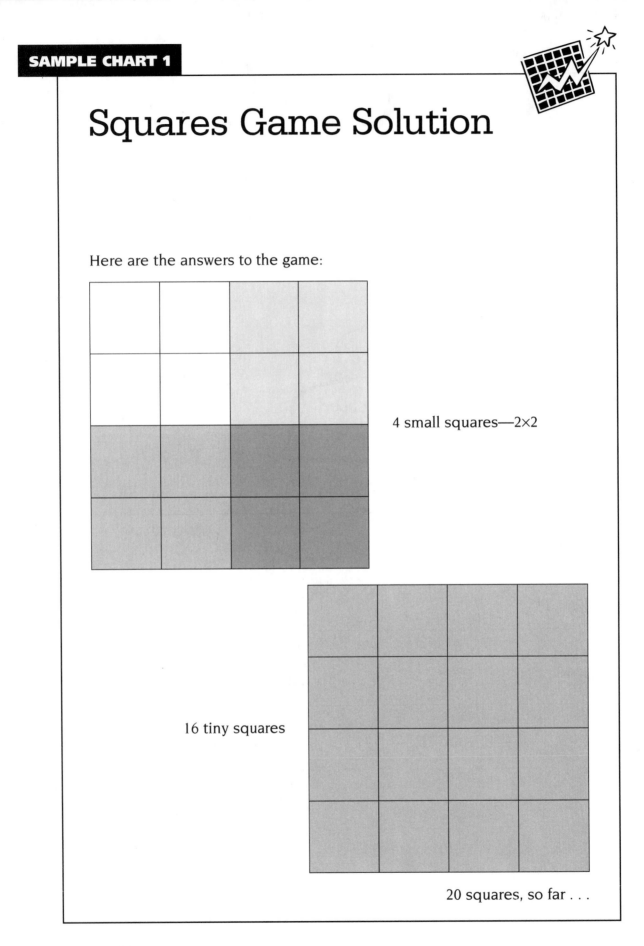

4 small squares—2×2

16 tiny squares

20 squares, so far . . .

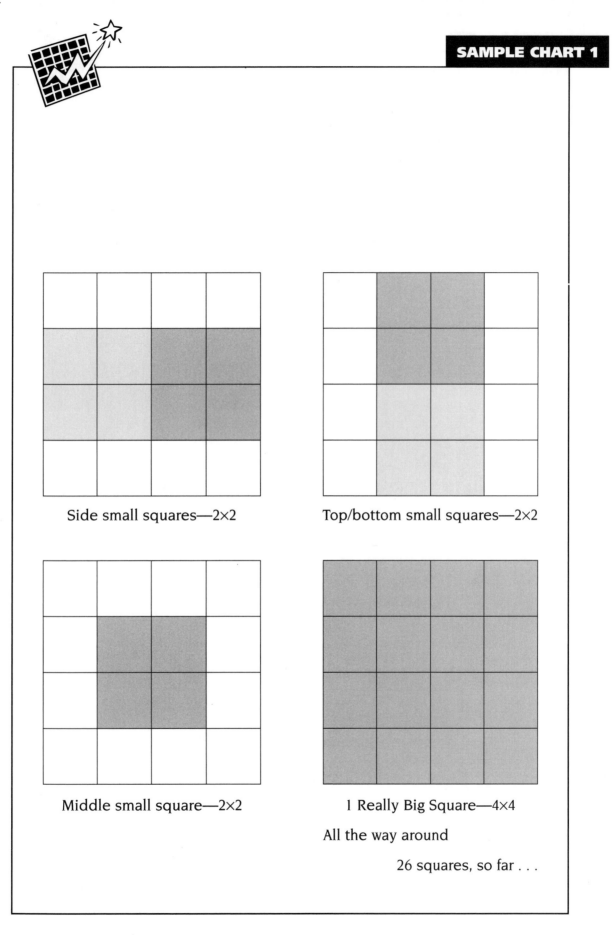

Side small squares—2×2

Top/bottom small squares—2×2

Middle small square—2×2

1 Really Big Square—4×4

All the way around

26 squares, so far . . .

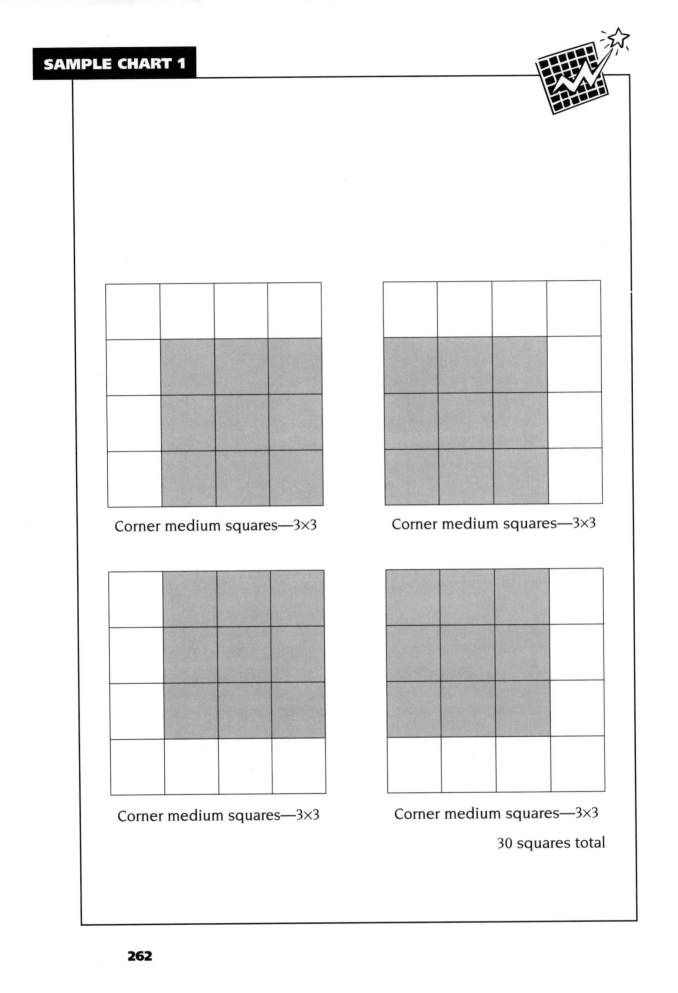

Corner medium squares—3×3

Corner medium squares—3×3

Corner medium squares—3×3

Corner medium squares—3×3

30 squares total

How Soon Is Soon?

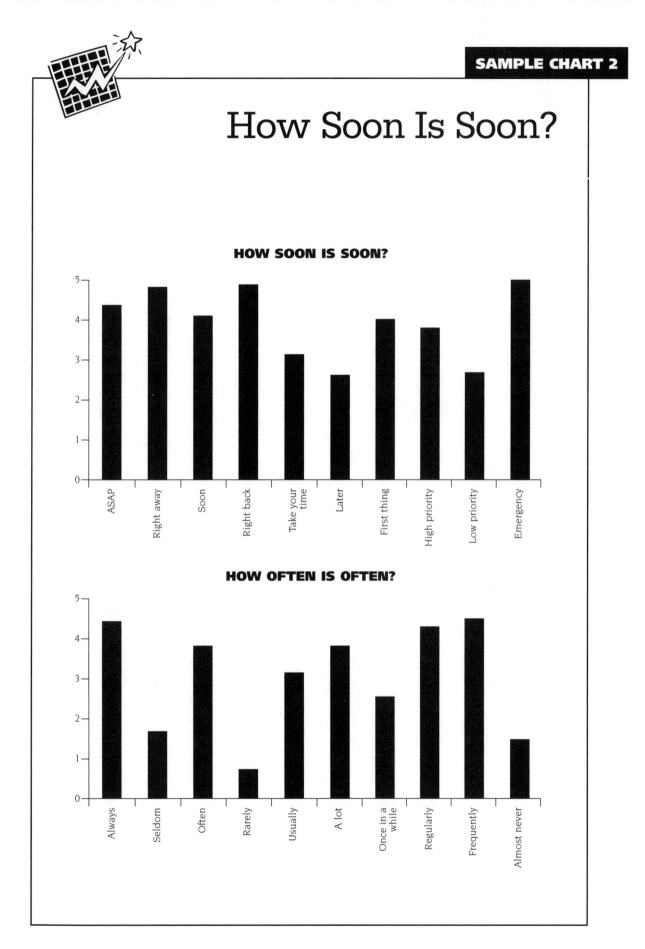

HOW SOON IS SOON?

ASAP | Right away | Soon | Right back | Take your time | Later | First thing | High priority | Low priority | Emergency

HOW OFTEN IS OFTEN?

Always | Seldom | Often | Rarely | Usually | A lot | Once in a while | Regularly | Frequently | Almost never

Three Blind Mice

Here's how it might look:

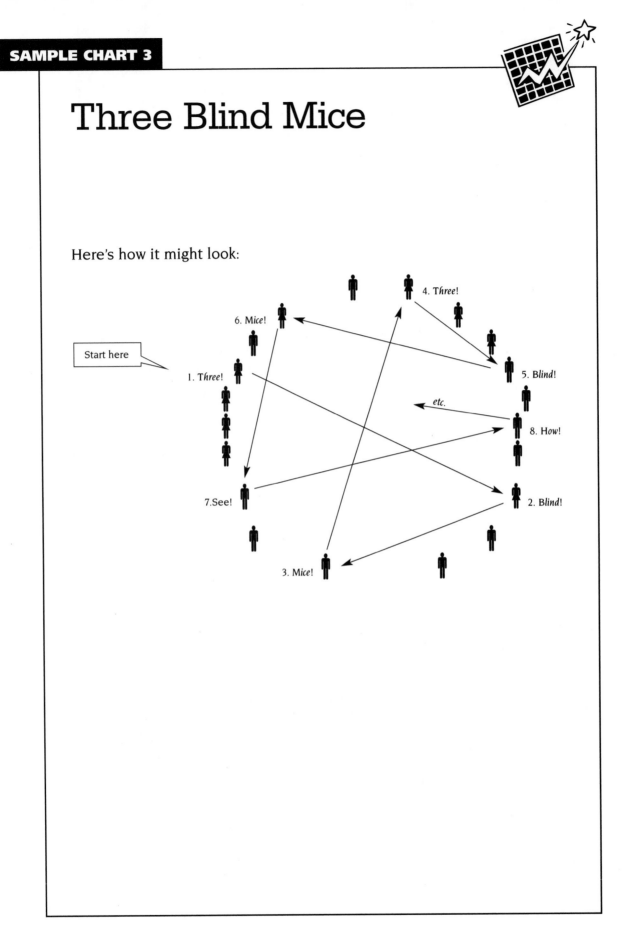

Timed Square Pattern

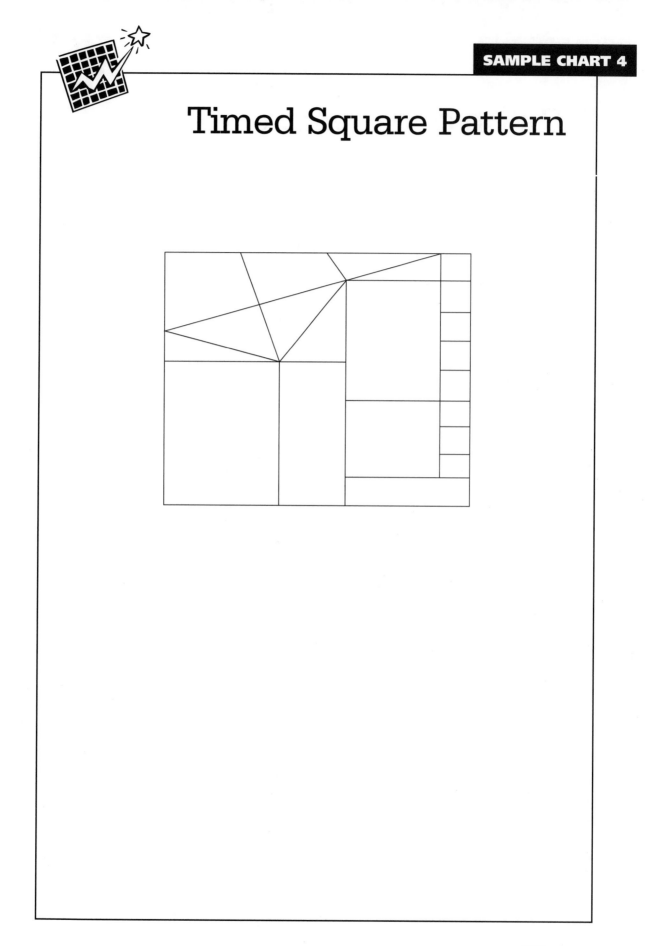

Ralph and Bianca

RALPH	**BIANCA**
1. Wants all of the office space for his group.	Ridiculous! B needs some of the space. Who does R think he is?
2. Not about who I am. About what I need. B go someplace else.	No reason for B to go someplace else. Why doesn't R go?
3. My group is more important.	Both are important. R being unreasonable.
4. I know what I need—don't care about what you need.	You better start caring. We're just going to move our stuff in.
5. Not if we beat you to it.	Don't be stupid.
6.	
7.	
8.	
9.	

Tips for Leading Group Activities

There are many fun ways to create teams of two or more in your workshops. Using these techniques not only makes the session more interesting, but also helps ensure that participants interact with different people during the class. Many times participants will tend to stay with the people they know, or with the same people at their table during a workshop. Breaking them into varied groups helps increase the learning by exposing them to new people with different types of experiences and thinking.

The following pages provide you with some techniques that you may want to try.

Fun Ways to Break into Groups

PURPOSE Use accelerated learning techniques in separating participants into small groups.

METHOD I: "STUCK ON STICKERS"

For creating teams of two or more

EQUIPMENT NEEDED Stickers that can be grouped either by type or by the exact number that you need to create your teams. For example, use different colored dots and break into teams according to the colors; get animal, floral, or another type of stickers and group teams according type; signs for tables (optional)

PREP Place one sticker at each setting in the room. Put them on seminar materials, on the backs of chairs, on nametags, under the seats; anywhere that participants can look at them when the activity is ready to begin.

TIME NEEDED 5–10 minutes, excluding prep time

EXERCISE OUTLINE

INTRODUCTION Introduce your main activity. Tell participants that you need to create groups of 2 to 5 people as the first step. Tell them that you have placed stickers at their seats and tell them where—on their workbook, nametag, etc. Ask them to locate their sticker and take a look at it.

FIND YOUR GROUP Have participants find others in the class that have the same sticker as theirs. Let them know what they are looking for. Tell them they are looking for people with same color dot, or for other people that have animal or flower stickers. Assign different parts of the room for the different groups.

SAY Now that you know what color star your have, you'll need to find the rest of your team. So everyone please move around the room and look for other people that have the same color star that you do. Once you find them, stay together. I would like to have all of the red stars here up front, all of the blue stars at the table in the back, and all of the green stars at the table over here.

Place each color/type of sticker on a small nametag or 3x5 card and put it on the tables where you want the groups to end up. Do this while people are looking for their groups.

BEGIN MAIN ACTIVITY   Once groups have been formed, begin the main activity.

METHOD II: "FIND A PARTNER, FORM A GROUP"

For creating teams of two or more

EQUIPMENT NEEDED   Signs for tables (optional)

PREP   None

TIME NEEDED   5–10 minutes

EXERCISE OUTLINE

INTRODUCTION   Introduce your main activity. Tell participants that you need to create groups of 2–5 people as the first step.

FIND YOUR GROUP   Tell participants to find a partner/people with whom they have not yet worked. Observe what everyone is doing. Make sure people are choosing others with whom they have not worked before. Tell them where in the room the groups should meet.

BEGIN ACTIVITY   Once groups have been formed, begin the main activity.

METHOD III: "PICK A CARD, PICK A TEAM"

For creating teams of two or more

EQUIPMENT NEEDED   3x5 cards, or deck of playing cards, old maid cards, or other card game with more than one type of card in the deck; Signs for tables—optional

PREP   Decide how many people you would like in a group. When using playing cards, create a new deck by choosing the number of cards you need from each suit to make the appropriately sized group. For example, to make 4 groups of 3, pick 3 Kings, 3 Jacks, 3 Queens, and 3 Aces. Shuffle the new deck.

When using 3×5 cards, create your own "deck" by writing the names of cars, states, candy bars, or anything you choose on the cards—one name to a card. For example, to make groups of 4 people, you can write the names of four cars, four candy bars, and four flowers on the 3×5 cards— one name to a card. Or to use a theme, make four cards with the word "Cadillac," four cards with the word "Jeep," and four cards with the word "Corvette" written on them. Then shuffle your deck.

TIME NEEDED   10–15 minutes, excluding prep time

EXERCISE OUTLINE

INTRODUCTION   Introduce your main activity. Tell participants that you need to create groups of 2–5 people as the first step.

FIND YOUR GROUP   Fan out your deck of cards facedown in your hand. Walk around the room, and ask each participant to pick a card from your hand. Tell them not to show their card to anyone else. Once everyone has a card, ask them to look at their cards. Then tell them to find other people/a person with the same card or card type. Instruct participants where to meet with their groups.

BEGIN MAIN ACTIVITY   Once groups have been formed, begin the main activity.

METHOD IV: "TWO HALVES MAKE A WHOLE"

For creating teams of two

EQUIPMENT NEEDED   Small, evenly cut pieces of paper; a jar, hat, basket, or other container, pen

PREP   During a break (or before the session if you have assigned seating), write the names of half the class on the small pieces of paper, one name to a piece of paper. Fold and place the pieces of paper into the jar, basket or hat.

TIME NEEDED   10–15 minutes, excluding prep time

EXERCISE OUTLINE

INTRODUCTION Introduce your main activity. Tell participants that you need to create groups of 2 as the first step. Tell them that you have placed the names of all the people on one side of the room on pieces of paper inside your jar. Then tell them that people on the other side of the room will pick the names. Explain that whomever they pick, is their partner for the next exercise. Let them know that only one side of the room will be picking from the jar.

FIND YOUR PARTNER Have each person on the side of room that will be picking from the jar, select a name. Once everyone has a name, ask participants to go to the other side of the room and find their partner. Let them decide where they will sit for the activity.

BEGIN MAIN ACTIVITY Once pairs have been formed, begin the main activity.

METHOD V: "SOUND OFF!"

For creating 3 or more groups

EQUIPMENT NEEDED Signs for tables (optional)

PREP Decide how many groups you want. The number of groups you want is the maximum number that you will have participants count to.

TIME NEEDED 5 minutes

EXERCISE OUTLINE

INTRODUCTION Introduce your main activity. Tell participants that you need to create 4 (or whatever number you need) groups. Ask participants to count aloud, as you point to them, from 1 to 4. They will continue to count, "1-2-3-4," "1-2-3-4," until each participant is assigned either a "1," a "2," a "3," or a "4."

FIND YOUR GROUP Tell participants where all the 1s should sit, where all the 2s should sit, all the 3s, and all the 4s. Then tell them to go to their team's table. Place a sign on each table that shows which number should be meeting there.

BEGIN MAIN ACTIVITY   Once groups have been formed, begin the main activity.

METHOD VI: "ICE CREAM & CAKE" OR "COFFEE & CREAM" OR "SHOES & SOCKS" OR "CHAMPAGNE & BEER," ETC.

For creating 2 large groups

EQUIPMENT NEEDED   2 sheets of flipchart paper and a marker

PREP   2 flipcharts placed on the walls where you would like the two large teams to work

TIME NEEDED   5 minutes

EXERCISE OUTLINE

INTRODUCTION   Introduce your main activity. Tell participants that you need to create 2 large groups. Ask participants to alternate saying either "ice cream" or "cake," as you point to them. They will continue to say "ice cream" and "cake" until each participant has spoken.

FIND YOUR GROUP   Tell participants that all the "ice cream" should meet in front of the flipchart that says "ice cream," and that all the "cake" can meet in front of the "cake" flipchart.

BEGIN MAIN ACTIVITY   Once groups have been formed, begin the main activity.

Additional Resources

This section will help you to dig more deeply into the topics we have covered in the book. Along with a list of books and Web sites, we have included the names, backgrounds, and contact information for some key people who have helped us in our work.

CENTERING

Richard Moon

Aiki Mastery by Richard Moon is the centering tape mentioned on page 77 in *Staying Cool in a Conflict*. The tape and a little book entitled *Aikido in Three Easy Lessons* by Richard can be ordered directly from: Richard Moon, 75 Los Piños, Nicasio, CA 94946, 415-662-6903.

Chris Thorsen

There was a time when people who did unexplainable things were called "magicians." Even in the twenty-first century, this thought must occur to people when they first see Chris Thorsen at work. Chris—by combining his knowledge of organizations and the practice of Aikido—helps us to integrate what happens in our minds with what happens in our bodies. Understanding that one continuously is changed by the other helps us to be open to the infinity of possibilities available to us in a conflict situation. In Chris' case, it helps him to dance on air while presenting a lecture.

Chris holds a black belt in Aikido, and uses the wonderful contradiction of this "peaceful martial art" to help people balance their dreams, needs, and fears with those of the world around them. As a consultant, Chris coaches executives and teams toward amazing breakthroughs. In his more than thirty years of service, Chris has helped groups in the United States, Europe, and Asia. Chris has also applied Aikido principles to his work as a peacemaker with Greek and Turkish factions on the Island of Cyprus.

Chris Thorsen is a professional poet, and has served over one hundred schools and organizations in the San Francisco Bay Area with workshops on haiku and creativity. He holds an M.A. in community organization and public service with a specialization in organizational development and has taught at The College of Marin, San Francisco State University, The University of San Francisco, and the California Institute of Integral Studies.

Chris lent us his patient expertise as we worked through several drafts of *Staying Cool in a Conflict* (page 77). *Centering under Pressure* (page 95), *Energy Jump* (page 46), and *I Lean* (page 105) are exercises from Chris' collection that even we nonmagicians can lead.

Chris is now offering a dynamic, interactive keynote presentation and seminar entitled "Leadership of the Spirit" that includes an exciting demonstration of Aikido. You can contact him by sending an e-mail to ct@quantumedge.org, or by telephone: 415-884-9446.

CONFLICT SKILLS

Jenny Beer

The Mediator's Handbook by Jennifer E. Beer with Eileen Stief (New Society Publishers, 1997) is a key resource for professional mediators and a popular textbook in schools and colleges. It is a valuable tool for anyone called on to help other people in conflict situations.

Jenny is a professional trainer, consultant, facilitator, and mediator. She has trained mediators for twenty years, and has mediated in community, nonprofit, human resource departments, and ombudsman's office and factory settings. Her anthropology background gives her particular skills in conflict assessment and in understanding the cultural and structural foundations of conflict. Jenny gave us the idea for *What You See Is What You Get* on page 73.

She earned a master's degree in International Administration from the School for International Training and an Anthropology Ph.D. from the University of California, Berkeley. Jenny's doctoral work focused on Japanese business, and she applies anthropological thinking and research methods to help her clients in a wide variety of organizations. She has taught courses on conflict, mediation, Japan, and communicating across cultures for American University and Bryn Mawr College, and teaches negotiation and dispute resolution at University of Pennsylvania's Wharton School. Jenny Beer's Web site—www.culture-at-work.com—is rich with information useful to anyone interested in training mediation, negotiation, and conflict resolution.

Kathy Hale

At our first planning meeting for this book, Bill said that one exercise we had to include is "Kathy Hale's leaf thing." Kathy was kind enough to share the notes, thoughts, and drawings for the exercise that we call *A New Leaf* (page 23).

Dr. Katherine Hale has over twenty years' university teaching experience in the areas of collaborative decision processes, leadership, organizational behavior and change, language of negotiation and cooperation, international negotiation and conflict resolution, intercultural communication, gender communication, mediation and conflict intervention, family communication, and research methods. With colleagues, she designed the curriculum for the Master of Arts degree in Antioch University McGregor's Conflict Resolution Program, where she is chair.

Kathy is currently working to establish the curriculum for a graduate certificate program at Antioch McGregor in the constructive engagement of environmental conflict in conjunction with the Bartos Institute of the United World College.

As a private consultant, Dr. Hale facilitates collaborative decision processes and provides conflict intervention and mediation, communication intervention and training, and board development. She has provided training for mediation programs, corporations, agencies, schools, and individuals.

To find out more about Kathy's work, visit www.mcgregor.edu and www.uwc-usa.org.

John McGlaughlin

John McGlaughlin's clients benefit from his unique combination of encyclopedic knowledge and down to earth approaches to the challenges facing groups and organizations. His ability to make theory accessible to his clients is shown in *Four Roads to Resolution* on page 81, our take on an exercise John created to help two warring departments in a large technology company.

A specialist in organizational design and development and the planning and facilitation of organizational change, John has worked both as an internal and an external consultant in manufacturing, transportation, technology, medical devices, travel management, financial services, and education settings. He holds a Ph.D. in psychoeducational processes from Temple University's School of Education. John is president and chief consultant with McGlaughlin and Associates, L.L.C. He may be contacted at jmcglaug@nothinbut.net.

Jay Rothman

Jay Rothman is president of the ARIA Group, Inc., a conflict resolution training and consulting company based in Yellow Springs, Ohio. He has kindly allowed us to use his ARIA and ROI models as the cornerstone of our *Write Your Own Case Study* exercise on page 173.

Jay's contributions as a conflict resolution theorist, teacher, and practitioner single him out as a true innovator and leader in the field. His books include *Resolving Identity-Based Conflict in Nations, Organizations and Communities* (Jossey-Bass, 1997). He has published more than two dozen articles on identity-based conflict, conflict resolution, and evaluation.

Jay has consulted, led workshops, and conducted interventions in more than a dozen countries, including Cyprus, Israel and Palestine, Northern Ireland, and Sri Lanka. In 2001, he was appointed by a federal judge to help bring about what is surely one of the most important resolutions of police-community relations issues ever in the United States.

Previously, Jay was scholar-in-residence at the McGregor School of Antioch University, where he directed the Action Evaluation Research Project and continues to teach in its conflict resolution program. He also was assistant professor at Haverford and Bryn Mawr Colleges, where he was the coordinator of the peace and conflict studies program. Jay was visiting professor at The Hebrew University from 1987 to 1991, where he was also director of the Jerusalem Peace Initiative.

One important mark of a true teacher is an eagerness to share new thinking. Jay Rothman gave us a great deal of time and support as we were finetuning the final drafts of *Write*

Your Own Case Study (page 173). His operating philosophy is to freely share his ideas with as many people as possible. Anyone interested in peace work in communities, nations, and/or organizations should regularly visit www.ariagroup.com for fresh insights into identity-based conflict, conflict resolution, and evaluation.

CULTURAL DIVERSITY

Catherine Mercer Bing

Cass Bing's *Missing the Meaning* exercise (page 113) is an accurate take on what it feels like to try to make your way in a new language. While most English-speaking North Americans only have this experience when on brief vacations, it is an everyday challenge for many of us.

Cass is vice president of human resources and new business development for the cross-cultural consulting and training firm ITAP International. She has served major corporations in the HR function both internally and as a consultant, and has done public relations work in both the for-profit and nonprofit sectors. Earlier in her career, Cass taught school in the United States and in Tehran, Iran.

At ITAP International, much of her focus is on the challenges facing global, virtual, and multicultural teams. She has recently, with Dr. John Bing and Dr. Lionel Laroche, co-authored "Beyond Translation: Globalization of Training." She wrote "Helping Global Teams Compete" with John Bing. Both articles appeared in *Training and Development*. OD *Practitioner Magazine* published "Communications Technologies for Virtual Teams" authored by Cass and Dr. Laroche in May 2002.

Cass Bing can be contacted through www.itapintl.com.

Paul Pedersen

As we were writing this book, Paul Pedersen dropped us a line about his latest book-in-progress, tentatively titled 110 *Multicultural Experiences to Teach and Train*. This seems like a suitably sweeping project for this masterful teacher.

Since we met Paul at a National Multicultural Institute workshop in 1996, he has been a very supportive correspondent—answering questions, sharing materials, making recommendations, and always finding time. *Hold Please* (page 163) is adapted from one of Paul's presentations at that workshop. The *Synthetic Culture Lab* (page 168) is reported here almost exactly as we learned it from him. Paul has written up the Synthetic Culture Lab with Allen Ivey in *Culture-Centered Counseling Skills* (Greenwood Publishing, 1993).

Paul is currently professor emeritus at Syracuse University and visiting professor in the University of Hawaii's psychology department. His primary interests include the effect of group difference on interpersonal and intrapersonal interaction between cultural and nationality identities in the educational setting, organizations, and communities.

Paul has held teaching positions in the United States, Malaysia, Indonesia, and Taiwan, where he was a senior Fullbright fellow. He speaks Danish, English, Mandarin Chinese, Indonesian, and Malay. He has authored or edited 39 books and 184 book chapters, articles, and monographs. If there is a continent with people on it, Paul has taught, consulted, or done research there. His bachelor's degree is in history and philosophy; he has three M.A.'s—in American studies, theology, and educational psychology; and he holds a doctorate in Asian studies.

As impressive as this life of study is, Paul Pedersen the teacher makes all of what he has learned available and easy to understand and apply. There is a wealth of information on his Web site, http://soeweb.syr.edu/chs/pedersen/index.html. Mediators, teachers, trainers, counselors, and therapists interested in the challenges of working across cultures should make it a point to seek out one of the ten or so workshops that Paul conducts each year.

BOOKS

Beyond Race and Gender: Unleashing the Power of Your Total Workforce by Managing Diversity

Chockful of case studies, Q & A's, strategy and other practical information. R. Roosevelt Thomas' *Beyond Race and Gender* (AMACOM, 1992) helps the reader take a look at how managing the various types of diversity people represent has become a corporate imperative for basic survival. Often, these types of issues are the catalysts for communication breakdowns and conflict. Understanding the dynamics of these interactions is the first step in resolving them.

Cultures and Organizations, Software of the Mind

Geerte Hofstede's book (McGraw-Hill, 1997) provides an in-depth look at social and cultural norms, beliefs, and behaviors. It gives the reader a framework from which to view the world. When used during everyday life, this information can improve communication as well as help diffuse conflict situations. The insight you'll gain from this book will strengthen your skills in resolving conflict and facilitating better communication processes.

Cultural Diversity in Organizations

Written by Taylor Cox, Jr., this book (Berret-Koehler, 1994) does more than point out the need and value of diversity. It is a book of solutions. You will get good working definitions, theories, and practical applications from this publication. The book focuses on managing diversity in organizations, conflict management, and orchestrating change. Everything you might need to know about these topics is covered in an in-depth way, along with tried and true methods for carrying out what is presented. This is a valuable resource for those who need to be able to demonstrate how to implement what is taught.

DIALOGUE

Dialogue is "good conversation over the 'back fences' of our lives," writes Judy Brown in *Learning Organizations: Developing Cultures for Tomorrow's Workplace* (Productivity Press, 1995). Judy

Brown's article in that book—"Dialogue: Capacities and Stories"—is a clear how-to for dialogue, and tells how changing people's points of view can change an entire organization. David Bohm's *On Dialogue* (Routledge, 1996) is considered The Bible by many who lead dialogue groups in business and communities. An easy to follow explanation of Bohm's approach can be found in Peter M. Senge's *The Fifth Discipline* (Doubleday, 1990). A deeper approach to dialogue that includes thinking about the changes that take place before, during, and after meaningful contact with other people is discussed in the works of Martin Buber, most famously *I and Thou* (Charles Scribners and Sons, 1970) and *Between Man and Man* (Routledge, 1947/2002). A new entry—and an instant favorite for us—is Margaret Wheatley's *Turning to One Another: Simple Conversations to Restore Hope in the Future* (Berrett-Koehler Publishers, 2002). In this important and profound little book, Wheatley reminds us that dialogue does not need to be a complicated thing and helps us see a simple, honest way to talk with one another so that we can work for the things we care about the most.

Sarita Chawla

We met Sarita Chawla nine years ago when she was editing *Learning Organizations: Developing Cultures for Tomorrow's Workplace* (Productivity Press, 1995). Bill was co-writing a chapter for the book, we were in California on business, and Sarita invited us to dinner.

As we settled in around the dinner table, Sarita turned to Keami and asked, "What kind of world would you like your children to grow up in?" In most cases, this would be a startling way to begin a dinner conversation, but Sarita has a nonthreatening way of asking important questions. She makes the difficult task of getting people to think about what is important to them look easy. A tool that she developed to help people in large groups have meaningful conversations is the *Diversity Dialogue* exercise (page 157).

Sarita's current work includes co-leading several yearlong Professional Coaching Courses for New Ventures West. She holds a key role in women's dialogues both within the US and internationally, and she is leading a three-year effort in designing and facilitating race dialogues in the San Francisco Bay Area.

Sarita has a masters degree in Anthropology from Delhi University. She is a Founding partner of Demeter Matrix Alliance, and has served as a member of the Advisory Board of the Elmwood Institute (founded by Fritjof Capra), and as a Council Member of the Society of Organizational Learning.

Sarita has co-authored *Emergence of Wise Women: A Learning Chronicle*. She is currently working on a documentary/video project: *BeComing: Women's Circles, Women's Lives*.

If you have questions for Sarita Chawla, you can contact her at Metalens@aol or by telephoning 415-892-3930.

Zachary Green

We met Dr. Zachary Green in 1996 at a National Multicultural Institute conference in Washington, D.C.

Green, along with his colleague, Angelo Lewis, facilitated a workshop at the conference called "Dialogue and Diversity" that included the Right Listening technique described on page 26. We have been using it ever since in diversity workshops and other seminars that focus on conflict and communications skills.

Green is currently an Executive Coach at World Bank, as well as the Executive Director of The Alexander Institute for Psychotherapy and Consultation in Washington, D.C. He specializes in diversity training, group dynamics, strategic organizational planning, leadership training, and crisis intervention. Green consults and conducts workshops and training sessions for numerous organizations, educational institutions, public advocacy groups, and government agencies, most recently for the National Multicultural Institute and the Kennedy School of Government at Harvard University.

Green has written and co-authored several publications, including the manual *Racial Reconciliation Dialogue*, which has been put to use by the Council of Churches of Greater Washington. He has won the American Psychological Association Minority Fellowship, the Albert V. Danielsen Clinical Fellowship, and the Excellence in Teaching Award (given by the Shaker Heights City School District). He has worked as a project consultant at the Center for Applied Research, as a Senior Scholar at the James MacGregor Burns Academy of Leadership at the University of Maryland, and as a lecturer at Catholic University and George Washington University. Green received his doctorate in clinical psychology from Boston University.

SYSTEMS THINKING

Systems thinking—recognizing the importance of relationships among events, patterns of behavior, and people's deeply held beliefs—came to the attention of business people with the 1990 publication Peter M. Senge's *The Fifth Discipline: The Art and Practice of The Learning Organization* (Doubleday). This is still the essential book for anyone working to help organizations and the people in them to learn. Paolo Freire, in *The Pedagogy of the Oppressed* (Continuum, 1999) and—more accessibly—John Paul Lederach, in *Preparing for Peace: Conflict Transformation Across Cultures* (Syracuse University Press, 1995), write about how when one understands the system and one's role in it, one can effect change. Lederach's book should be particularly helpful to anyone interested in helping people learn about themselves, the system they are a part of, and how to apply that knowledge to conflict situations.

When a Butterfly Sneezes

One of the pleasant discoveries we made while putting this book together is the work of Linda Booth Sweeney. When we were still just thinking about what kind of book to write, Sarita Chawla told us, "You have to read *When a Butterfly Sneezes* and *The Systems Thinking Playbook*."

Sarita was right, and if you are interested in learning by asking questions about the complexity of life, you should read them, too. *When a Butterfly Sneezes: A Guide for Helping Children Explore Interconnections in Our World Through Favorite Stories* (Pegasus Communications, 2001) is a fun and fascinating look at children's stories from a systems perspective. The wonderful teacher's guide includes systems diagrams of Dr. Seuss favorites including *The Lorax* and *The Butter Battle Book* and newer works such as *The Old Ladies Who Liked Cats*. The book is designed for people who teach children, but any trainer or adult educator will find plenty of ideas to help explain systems thinking. This work is a jolt of creativity—a valuable reminder that profound lessons live in everyday stories and events.

The Systems Thinking Playbook

Linda Booth Sweeney co-authored *The Systems Thinking Playbook: Volumes I–III* (Turning Point/ Pegasus Communications, 1995/1998/2001) with Dr. Dennis Meadows. *Telephone Tales* (page 121) is based on an idea from Dennis. The *Playbook* is a handy three-ring binder filled with interactive lessons that breathe life into systems theory. Like *When a Butterfly Sneezes*, it makes sometimes intimidating concepts accessible and can inspire course designers to strike off in their own creative directions.

If any part of your job includes helping people function in groups or organizations, you should keep *The System Thinking Playbook* and *When a Butterfly Sneezes* within easy reach.

MAKING TRAINING STICK

Moving from Training to Performance

Dana Gaines Robinson and James C. Robinson have edited a book full of sound practices for improving performance. Moving From Training to Performance (ASTD, 1998) will help you understand that improving behavior is a process, and shows how to get the results you are looking for after the training event is long gone. It is an excellent resource for program designers and internal consultants.

Index

Bill Withers has worked as a business manager, consultant, speaker, writer, and trainer during the past twenty years. His current practice focuses on developing conflict resolution processes in cross-cultural business settings. He is now the Organizational Development Manager for R&B, Inc., in Colmar, Pennsylvania, a leading distributor of aftermarket auto parts, and, in that position, he is responsible for cultural change, training, and alternative dispute resolution programs. His most recent book was *The Conflict Management Skills Workshop* (AMACOM Books, 2002). He lives in Collingswood, New Jersey.

Keami D. Lewis has worked as an HRD Consultant, Program Designer, Trainer, and Business Leader specializing in Performance Management, Organizational Development, Diversity Management, and Human Resource Management for more than twelve years. Key areas of expertise include maximizing performance, organizational communication, and improving overall individual and team effectiveness. She has held various positions at Rosenbluth International and Showboat Casino when it was voted the "Benchmark for the Coming Decade" for management practices, strategies, and customer service by *The Observer.* Ms. Lewis currently works for Agere Systems as Senior Manager of Organizational Development & HR Programs, as well as consults in the areas of Human Resources Development, Organizational Performance, and Communications. She lives in Lansdale, Pennsylvania.